In Our Own Words

In Our Own Words

Students' Perspectives on School

EDITED BY JEFFREY SHULTZ
AND ALISON COOK-SATHER

ROWMAN & LITTLEFIELD PUBLISHERS, INC.
Lanham • Boulder • New York • Oxford

ROWMAN & LITTLEFIELD PUBLISHERS, INC.

Published in the United States of America
by Rowman & Littlefield Publishers, Inc.
4720 Boston Way, Lanham, Maryland 20706
www.rowmanlittlefield.com

12 Hid's Copse Road
Cumnor Hill, Oxford OX2 9JJ, England

British Library Cataloguing in Publication Information Available

Library of Congress Cataloging-in-Publication Data

In our own words : students' perspectives on school / edited by Jeffrey Shultz and Alison Cook-
Sather.
    p. cm.
    Includes bibliographical references and index.
    ISBN 0-8476-9565-4 (alk. paper) — ISBN 0-8476-9566-2 (pbk. : alk. paper)
    1. Middle school students—United States—Attitudes. 2. High school students—United
States—Attitudes. 3. Educational surveys—United States. I. Shultz, Jeffrey J. II. Cook-Sather,
Alison, 1964–

LA222 .I5 2001
373.18'0973—dc21

                                                                    2001019601

Printed in the United States of America

♾™ The paper used in this publication meets the minimum requirements of American
National Standard for Information Sciences—Permanence of Paper for Printed Library
Materials, ANSI/NISO Z39.48-1992.

To all students who have spoken out about school
and to those students whose voices have yet to be heard

Contents

Acknowledgments   ix

Preface   xi

Introduction: Starting Where the Learner Is: Listening to Students   1
Alison Cook-Sather and Jeffrey Shultz

1   Our World   19
    Maribelis Alfaro, Lornaliz Letriz, Maritzabeth Santos,
    Mariela Villanueva, and Rebecca Freeman

2   Speaking Out Loud: Girls Seeking Selfhood   39
    Quentina Judon, Jessye Cohen-Dan, Tyeasha Leonard,
    Sharita Stinson, Tara Colston, Jody Cohen, and Diane Brown

3   What's Your Bias? Cuts on Diversity in a Suburban Public School   57
    Kristin Dunderdale, Sara Tourscher, R.J. Yoo, Ondrea Reisinger,
    and Alison Cook-Sather

4   Cutting Class: Perspectives of Urban High School Students   73
    Fredo Sanon, Maurice Baxter, Lydia Fortune, and Susan Opotow

5   An Education for What? Reflections of Two High School   93
    Seniors on School
    Steven Marzan, Amy Peterson, Ceci Lewis, Scott Christian,
    and Eva Gold

6   Caught in the Storm of Reform: Five Student Perspectives on the   105
    Implementation of the Interactive Mathematics Program
    Dorothy V. Holt, Emily Gann, Sonia Gordon-Walinsky, Elissa Klinger,
    Rachel Toliver, and Edward (Ned) Wolff

7   Reflections: Writing and Talking about Race in Middle School   127
    Darreisha Bates, Noah Chase, Chris Ignasiak, Yvette Johnson,
    Tina Zaza, Tricia Niesz, Patti Buck, and Katherine Schultz
8   Writing the Wrong: Making Schools Better for Girls   149
    Margo Strucker, Lenelle N. Moise, Vicki Magee, and Holly Kreider
9   Negotiating Worlds and Words: Writing about Students'   165
    Experiences of School
    Alison Cook-Sather and Jeffrey Shultz

Index   179

About the Authors   183

Acknowledgments

Putting together this book was an exciting enterprise, and working with young authors yielded both anticipated and unanticipated challenges and joys. We are particularly grateful to the students who inspired us to edit this book in the first place and to those who shared their words and thoughts with us for inclusion in this volume. The researchers/teachers/authors were not only instrumental in identifying the student authors, but also in negotiating between them and us as editors and facilitating the composing of the chapters. At Rowman & Littlefield, Jill Rothenberg and Dean Birkenkamp took a chance with this idea. Dean has been a wonderful friend and editor, guiding us through the process of completing this book. We would also like to thank John Calderone, our production editor, and Christine Gatliffe for their help in seeing this book through the editing stages. A number of friends and colleagues provided helpful criticism and careful readings of the manuscript at various stages of completion. In particular, we are grateful to Jody Cohen, Susan Florio-Ruane, Robyn Newkumet, Norah Peters-Davis, Dina Portnoy, and Elliott Shore. Ginny Blaisdell and her assistants, Adrienne Cureton and Patricia Marnien, provided much needed and appreciated logistical support. Jonathan Shaw's indexing and editing skills proved to be essential. In spite of all this help, all errors remain our responsibility. Finally, our most special thanks go to Janet Theophano and Scott Cook-Sather for their companionship and support as we completed this project.

Preface

Students tell us that too often adults speak for them. The title of this volume, *In Our Own Words,* captures our goal in compiling this collection: to provide a forum for middle and high school students to express in their own voices their perceptions, feelings, and insights about school. Here, each of us tells the story of how we came to compose this book and of why we think this enterprise is important.

Jeff's Story

As a high school senior, my daughter Julia wrote the following in her first college application essay:

> I try to envision a society in which, above all else, children are instilled with the value of thinking for themselves. I picture a world in which there are no commonly accepted "rights" and "wrongs," and all sorts of choices are celebrated for their individual merit. I have seen too many people trapped by listening to the voices in their heads that are not their own, reaching the miserable point when their own voices are lost for good amongst all the jumble. I refuse to turn out that way.
>
> High school has been a stifling experience for me. I have done too much busy work and had too many biased opinions drilled into my head as if they were fact. I have experienced entirely too many classes where students have been criticized for expressing different ideas than the ones printed in the teacher's edition of the textbook. I believe with my entire heart that the answers go far beyond what is given, so far beyond the realms that we have ever been taught to explore.

> Julia Shultz
> September 29, 1995

In these two paragraphs, Julia describes her perceptions of how the society in which she grew up does not value what children think and how her own high school experiences have been limiting and constraining. It is significant that this essay was written as she was preparing to leave high school. Her insights, as are students' perceptions of their experiences in school in general, were never elicited and even less often volunteered. What students think plays virtually no role in the ongoing debates about what schools are and what they should be.

Similar themes dominated the conversations I held with a group of eighth-grade students at a middle school in Philadelphia during the 1993–1994 academic year. We met every week for one hour and talked about what was good about school, what was wrong with it, and how it could be fixed. These twelve students—half male, half female, half African American, half of European descent, some academically talented, others labeled "special needs"—were mostly concerned about the lack of respect they felt from school personnel and the fact that their needs, concerns, and wants were not being elicited, much less listened to. During the spring semester of 1995, while on sabbatical in England, I held similar conversations with a group of eighth-year students at a secondary school in the London Borough of Greenwich. They, too, told similar stories.

After hearing the same essential concerns voiced by such diverse groups of middle and high school students on two continents, I decided to put together this book, one in which these silenced voices would be given a hearing. These young people have a great deal to tell us about what is happening in schools and also about how to make the schools better.

Alison's Story

I begin with the words of Anub, a high school student with whom I've worked:

> Sometimes I wish I could sit down with one of my teachers and just tell them what I exactly think about their class. It might be good, it might be bad, it's just that you don't have the opportunity to do it.
>
> —Anub Abraham, high school senior,
> presentation at Pennsylvania Association of
> Colleges and Teacher Educators, November 10, 1995

Roughly a year before Anub spoke these words at a conference for teacher educators, one of his teachers, Ondrea Reisinger, and I had made a decision: to create a forum for conversation between the high school students she taught and the prospective teachers I taught. Convinced that the students had a lot to teach the teachers, we decided to give them the chance to do it.

The project we created in the fall of 1995 is called Teaching and Learning Together, and Anub is one of forty-eight high school students who have participated the last five years. The project pairs preservice teachers enrolled in an undergraduate education course with students who attend a local public high school. Each week the pairs exchange letters in which they discuss their ideas about teaching and learning, and each week the high school students meet as a group at the high school to discuss these same issues—conversations that are audiotaped and shared with the preservice teachers. From 1995 through 1997, Ondrea facilitated those discussions at the high school, and since 1998 Jean McWilliams has facilitated them. Originally supported by outside funding from the Ford Foundation and the Arthur Vining Davis Foundation, this project is now an integral part of the preparation of teachers through the Bryn Mawr/Haverford Education Program I direct.

Ondrea and I created the project because we felt that student perspectives are generally ignored in teacher preparation, and we believe that students have valuable pedagogical insights that they should be invited to share. But inviting students to participate in conversations about teaching and learning is a complex endeavor. In discussions within teacher education courses, in presentations made at academic conferences, and in articles written for academic journals, we have had to work against skepticism about students' interest in sharing and their ability to articulate their perspectives on pedagogical issues. So when Jeff asked me to coedit a collection of chapters authored primarily by students, I was excited to think that we could create a forum in which students could write for and about themselves and that their insights might gain some credence among a wider audience.

Each of us in our own work has made spaces for middle and high school students to articulate their perspectives on school and schooling. Our interest in producing this book emerged from our desire to invite students not only to speak, but also to write about school, to share not only with us, but also with others, their perceptions and feelings, and to do so in their own voices. The critical and inspiring insights offered by the students we have worked with have convinced us that educators at all levels have a lot to learn from students. We hope that readers differently positioned in the educational realm will use this book in the way that best suits them, letting the different foci of the chapters—rather than the book's organization—guide their reading. As editors, we intervene as little as possible because we want both the authors' and the readers' choices to be minimally impeded.

Starting Where the Learner Is: Listening to Students

Alison Cook-Sather and Jeffrey Shultz

Reach me with more than words from textbooks—but words from the soul and the mind connected to the heart. What got you to teach me? Wasn't it to reach me? . . . Relate to me, debate with me, respect me. Stop neglecting me. I get nothing but tired empty wordswordswords . . . make them real.

—Lenelle N. Moise, student author, chapter 8, "Writing the Wrong"

At first I thought that this whole thing about telling our story would be about our school, the Julia de Burgos Bilingual Middle Magnet School. But as time went by we discovered that it wasn't just about a school, but about how we live, how we speak, and our experiences.

—Maribelis Alfaro, student author, chapter 1, "Our World"

There are different ways that people learn. Some people learn through book work, some from hearing it. Some people can learn from reading it. Some learn by experiencing it. . . . If there are students [who] learn differently, they should [be] given a chance to learn their way.

—Steven Marzan, student author, chapter 5, "An Education for What?"

When we think of schools, we think of cinderblock hallways, classrooms full of rows or rings of desks, regulated curricula and hardbound textbooks, days divided by buzzers and bells. When we asked students to write about school, they rarely discussed these traditional features. Rather, their focus was on their relationships with the people who share and shape their schooling. This was true for

1

all of the student contributors to this book, regardless of race and gender, status in school, and school context. More than twenty years ago, Jerome Bruner urged us to start "where the learner is" (1977, xi). Where the learner is, according to the twenty-nine students who coauthored the chapters in this volume, is in relationship to others.

We open this chapter with the words of three very different learners. Lenelle is a Haitian-American female who attended an urban, public high school. Maribelis, a Puerto Rican female, attended a bilingual, urban, public middle school. An Asian-American male, Steve attended a rural, public high school. Different as these learners are, they have a number of things in common. They are passionate, insightful, and articulate. They care about their learning and how that learning shapes their lives. Their words capture the theme that threads its way throughout the chapters in this collection—what students experience and expect in their relationships with others and how these experiences and expectations translate into how schools need to be changed.

Inviting Students to Share Their Perspectives on School

For many years, educational researchers have studied students and students' lives. This study has been conducted within researchers' and more recently teachers' frameworks for problems of practice. Only recently have we encouraged students to speak and to write about their experiences of school. Our goal in compiling this collection was not only to invite student perspectives into the ongoing conversation about schools and school reform but also to foreground their voices. We wanted to explore what students frame as problems of practice. We believe that it is crucial to listen to what students have to say because until we truly understand what students are experiencing— what and how education means, looks, and feels to them—our efforts at school reform will not go very far.

The voices that speak to us from these pages issue from suburban, urban, and rural as well as middle and high school contexts. The student authors who write from and about these contexts include twenty-two female and six male students, ten of European-American descent, eight African-American, four Puerto Rican, two Asian-American, one Hispanic, two Haitian-American, and one of Scandinavian, Eastern European, and Native American descent. While there is significant diversity among the contributors, the perspectives included are not meant to be exhaustive or representative. Rather, these perspectives are a sampling of twenty-nine unique middle and high school students' perceptions, feelings, and insights about school.

In the early stages of compiling the collection, we approached teachers and researchers who worked closely with middle and high school students or who felt, as we do, that students' perspectives and voices have been too long ignored. We contacted colleagues across the United States in an attempt to gain access to the perspectives of diverse students in a variety of school settings. The eight chapters in this volume are authored primarily by students with the support of researchers/teachers.[1] For the most part, the student authors selected the focuses of the chapters and the modes or genres in which the chapters were composed. If the chapter emerged out of researchers'/teachers' work already in progress, students decided for themselves how to present their perspectives within the context of those existing investigations. Students chose their own words and framed their own arguments.

The coauthors labored under a variety of less than ideal circumstances. Loathe to take students out of class to work on the chapters, some researcher/teacher coauthors met with students during free periods or after school. Other writing teams lived in different states and composed their chapters via e-mail. Writing and rewriting together, all coauthors had to negotiate this new task of focusing on student experiences and highlighting student voices. A more extensive discussion of the challenges and rewards of composing and editing can be found in the volume's concluding chapter, "Negotiating Worlds and Words: Writing About Students' Experiences of School."

Every voice in the following pages tells a different story, but every story conveys the same message. These students want to be treated as unique individuals who are also inextricably connected to other individuals. They want to be respected and supported as they pursue the kinds of education they know they need.

What Occupies Students' Minds about School and Schooling?

In this introduction, we do not wish to nor can we speak for the students; they speak eloquently for themselves in the chapters. However, as educators and teacher educators, we read these students' words with particular perspectives that draw our attention to certain issues. Different readers will no doubt focus on other points raised by the students. In the following discussion we identify the themes that struck us.

Within the overarching theme of students' relationships with others, we see three interrelated subthemes weaving their way through the eight student chapters included in this volume. The first is that students want to have more human and humane interactions in school. They are looking for care, respect, and support from their teachers, peers, and others who influence their educational experiences. The second theme we see is that students want to be their whole selves;

they do not want to be fragmented, categorized, compared to and judged against one another, treated differently or discriminated against. And finally, a third theme is that students want school to be engaging. Countering the stereotype of apathetic, disaffected, or otherwise recalcitrant teenagers, these student authors describe the ways that they want their teachers to make school interesting and relevant and to invite students to actively participate in their learning.

Addressing their desire for more human and humane interactions in school, student authors emphasize the ways in which they have felt such humanity missing in their interactions; they reflect on the exceptional occasion when it was present; and they suggest how teachers might make school more humane. For instance, McGee et al. (chapter 8) write: "[W]e have found that our individual voices have been disregarded in the classroom . . . each of us has felt intimidated and unheard when speaking . . . all four of us have felt lonely, misunderstood, and excluded as students." Less frequently, the student authors describe teachers who had a positive effect on them, as Quentina Judon does in chapter 2 when she writes about one teacher who "took me in and cared, not because it was her job, but because she genuinely cared. She took the time out of her day to talk to me. She taught me there was more to life than my fist and the pain it held. . . . She said I could do anything I wanted to do." Speaking directly to the teachers they hope to reach, students, including Maurice Baxter in chapter 4, offer advice about how to be a little more human: "Just acknowledge someone. Just know that they're there. When you walk by, give them a little nod or something."

The second theme that threads its way throughout the chapters is related to students' desires to be seen for who they are and not categorized, stereotyped, or fragmented. Their resistance to such categorization spans many dimensions of diversity. The following examples focus on racial identity. Asserting that she does not want to be reduced to a single aspect of her identity, student author Darreisha Bates in chapter 7 explains: "When teachers, strangers, students, or people in general stamp a label on me by just looking at me, is when I don't want to be seen as my skin color. I don't want what I look like to determine where I am to be placed or how I am stereotyped. It's my personality that makes me Darreisha!" As another student author, Kristin Dunderdale in chapter 3, explains, the stories she and her coauthors gathered for their chapter "show how uncomfortable students can get if teachers treat them different." Kristin's coauthor, Sara Tourscher, offers this advice to teachers: "Teachers should respect their students enough not to judge their race. Students will appreciate it, even if it means that some students will stop getting preferential treatment, because all students will be treated equally and fairly."

Finally, the third theme we discerned is that students want teachers to make learning more engaging. One student author, Fredo Sanon in chapter 4, explains why: "If students are not actively engaged they lose concentration." Fredo's coauthor, Maurice Baxter, adds: "Everybody wants to be involved, whether it's putting in their little two cents—being able to raise their hand." For these students, education isn't just about learning math, social studies, or science; it is also about being active partners in their own learning—contributing their ideas, being listened to, making choices in their studies. The student authors of chapter 6, who wrote about choosing to enroll in the alternative interactive mathematics program (IMP), argue that they were better able to understand the subject by engaging with it: Rachel Toliver explains that "knowing the reasoning behind the formulas, rather then simply memorizing, is vital to true learning." Dorothy Holt elaborates on this point: "For me, IMP wasn't just a math course, it taught me how to approach problems in every subject." Another coauthor, Emily Gann, felt the program "is far more capable of engaging students' interest and respecting their ability to learn by discovery."

Throughout the chapters collected in this volume students discuss the relationships that shape their experiences of school—relationships that either distance them from or help to connect them to what they are learning, to others, and to themselves. They write about what they need and want from those relationships—support, understanding, and challenges. And they explore the implications of these relationships for school reform. The themes we identify above weave their way across this volume. Each chapter provides a glimpse into students' particular experiences in school. With this book we add these students' perspectives to those of the teachers and researchers who have written about young people and schooling.

Who Has Written about Young People and Schooling and How?

Published materials that address young people's perspectives are scarce, and approaches to ascertaining and representing those perspectives vary. Nevertheless, we want to acknowledge those who have noted the relative absence of student perspectives as well as identify a variety of examples we have found of published writing about youth and schooling.

For almost ten years, the absence of students' perspectives on school and school reform has been noted by critics (Phelan, Davidson, and Yu 1998; Phelan, Davidson, and Cao 1992; Erickson and Shultz 1992; Kozol 1991). In his introduction to *Savage Inequalities*, Jonathan Kozol wrote: "[W]e have not been listening much to children in these recent years of 'summit conferences' on education, of severe reports, and ominous prescriptions. The voices of children, frankly, have been missing from the whole discussion" (1991, 5). Yet it is only within the last five or six years that researchers and policy makers have discussed the importance of attending to what students have to say (Connell 1994; Corbett and Wilson 1995; Nieto 1994). In response, researchers have conducted a range of studies from large-scale surveys of student opinions (Metropolitan Life 1996) to intensive, interpretive studies of smaller groups of students in specific schools (Cook-Sather, under review; Oldfather 1995). In addition, a few examples have emerged in both the research and the popular literature of texts that address young people's experiences, some focused specifically on school.

In the following discussion we characterize the examples we have found of literature addressing adolescents' lives. In doing so, we focus, in particular, on the authors' stated purpose for writing the piece and the relationship between the author and the subjects of the texts (that is, young people). We also examine texts in which young people are authors or coauthors and texts that include young people's voices to a significant extent. We do not intend this as a comprehensive review of the literature. Rather, we mention representative examples that illustrate the distinctions we see across the different ways of writing about and by young people.

In the research literature in education, there has been a great deal written about young people in school. Our interest, however, is on pieces that attempt to present students' perspectives. One such work is *Adolescent Worlds: Negotiating Family, Peers, and School.* In their introduction, Phelan, Davidson, and Yu state that they wrote this book to ascertain "how adolescents view and define what is significant in affecting their school experiences" (1998, 5). Phelan, Davidson, and Yu draw on representative case studies of adolescents to present a typology of ways in which young people deal with family, peers, and school. The authors hoped that by uncovering adolescents' views about school and the people they encounter in that context they would be able to "illuminate those aspects of students' behavior that teachers had defined as important, curious, or problematic." Like Phelan, Davidson, and Yu, we wanted to learn about and from student perspectives, but unlike them, we were interested not in what adults found "important, curious, or problematic" but rather in what the students wanted to focus on.

The publication we found that most closely addressed many of the issues raised in the chapters in the present collection was the spring 1995 issue of *Theory into Practice,* titled "Learning from Student Voices." While discussing student voices in general, the articles contained in this volume focused mostly on the ways in which teachers need to pay attention to student voices in their classrooms. For example, Lincoln (1995), Johnston and Nicholls (1995), and Commeyras (1995) comment on how constructivist approaches to teaching require that teachers listen to student voices. Dahl (1995) and Heshusius (1995) discuss the ways in which teachers can become better teachers by listening closely to what students have to say. "Learning from children's voices allows us to know at a deeper level who children are as learners and, because we have that knowledge, to expand and enrich our sense of what it means to teach" (Dahl, 130). In the same volume, however, O'Loughlin warns that teachers "must resist the temptation to glamorize student voices, and recognize that the multiple voices students bring to the classroom, while potentially possessing some elements of resistance and transformation, are likely to be deeply imbued with status quo values" (1995, 112).

In a departure from the other articles in the collection, Oldfather also discusses what students learn from being given a voice. She describes a student research team with whom she worked for five years, from the time they were in fifth and sixth grades. While she argues that this experience was beneficial for all involved, she describes the challenges that Sally Thomas (her research partner) and she faced: "In our writing, how can Sally and I represent the students in the fairest ways possible and, at the same time, avoid relinquishing our roles in interpreting findings?" (1995, 134) Thus, while they acknowledged the importance of including students as researchers, they retained control over the interpretation of what the research team uncovered.

The collection ends with an article cowritten by Sally Thomas and three of the students on their research team: Florencia Garcia, John Kilgore, and Paul Rodriguez. The piece presents an edited version of a conversation among the four authors that examines issues of student voice in school and what it means to students. In all of the research literature that we have examined, this is one of the few places where students' voices are heard clearly and distinctly. While the conversation was edited, "the students speak for themselves here, without intervening interpretation. In the interest of space, with student permission, about half the dialogue is presented, retaining the original sequence and topics addressed" (Garcia, Kilgore, Rodriguez, and Thomas 1995, 139).

Finally, a collection of essays titled *Beyond Silenced Voices: Class, Race, and Gender in United States Schools* (Weis and Fine 1993) presents contributing authors' critiques of the policies and practices that have led to the silencing of teachers, students, and others in public schools. These authors invite "the voices of children and adolescents who have been expelled from the centers of their schools and the centers of our culture [to] speak" (1993, 2). For example, Jody Cohen, in her chapter titled "Constructing Race at an Urban High School: In Their Minds, Their Mouths, Their Hearts," talked with African American students about how they negotiated their school context. Using extensive quotes from students, Cohen explores themes of identity, difference, and racism in these students' lives.

In another chapter, "Sexuality, Schooling, and Adolescent Females: The Missing Discourse of Desire," Michelle Fine explores the prevailing discourses about female sexuality in public schools, which she identifies as "sexuality as violence";

"sexuality as victimization"; and "sexuality as individual morality." Missing, she suggests, is what she calls a "discourse of desire" (1993, 76–81). Drawing on interviews with and observations of students, Fine argues that adolescents are entitled to a discussion and exploration of the meaning of desire rather than antisex rhetoric that renders girls as passive objects (1993, 98).

A third example drawn from *Beyond Silenced Voices* is Richard Friend's chapter, "Choices, Not Closets: Heterosexism and Homophobia in Schools." Friend identifies categories for ways that heterosexism and homophobia are perpetuated in schools, including assumptions of heterosexuality, systematic exclusion, and systematic inclusion of homosexuality as pathology. As do Cohen and Fine, he quotes students throughout his discussion.

In all of the research literature about youth in schools that we have encountered, it is our impression that the perspectives and voices of the youth are used to advance and support the authors' positions, arguments, and theories. In other words, while the young people's perspectives are included, it is the authors who provide the interpretive frameworks and, in some cases, the focus of discussion that the students address. Oldfather (1995), in the quote cited above, raises this issue explicitly.

Like the academic literature about young people we refer to above, there are examples from popular writing that integrate students' perspectives and voices into their descriptions of life in schools. Jonathan Kozol's (1991) *Savage Inequalities* aims to raise public awareness of race and class inequities that permeate schools. Kozol visited city schools and, in the course of discussions with students, teachers, and administrators in these schools, he realized that all three groups shared the same concerns but that the children were, by and large, not listened to. Kozol's goal was "wherever possible, to let [children's] voices and their judgments and their longings find a place within this book—and maybe too within the nation's dialogue about their destinies" (1991, 5–6).

A more recent piece appeared in *Time* magazine on October 25, 1999: "A Week in the Life of a High School." In this article, Nancy Gibbs aims to give an insider's perspective on what teachers, students, and administrators experience during a typical week in their high school. Like Kozol, Gibbs gives equal weight to the voices and perspectives of students as she gives to those of the adults she interviews.

Texts that address the experiences of adolescents, although not necessarily in reference to school, are among the only other examples we could find in which student perspectives and voices were included. In *A Totally Alien Life-Form*, Sidney Lewis interviewed teenagers to learn something about "the weight and texture of these lives, their experiences of being young in this country now, as we near the end of the millennium" (1996, 13). Intent to gather as evocative a group as possible, Lewis interviewed young people differing widely in age and geographic and social backgrounds. Similarly, with the aim of gathering and presenting adolescent girls' own experiences in their own words, Sara Shandler wrote *Ophelia Speaks* with the goal of helping adults understand adolescents and letting adolescent girls hear their own voices. Shandler wanted to create a forum within which young people, in her case adolescent girls, could speak for themselves rather than be spoken for by adults (1999, xiii).

In our attempt to understand the role of adolescents' voices in print media, we also examined books written by young people about others. For instance, *Minds Stayed on Freedom* (1991) was written by the Youth of the Rural Organizing and Cultural Center in Holmes Country, Mississippi. As part of a summer education program, students interviewed residents who had lived through the Civil Rights movement in the 1960s, providing an oral history of that era. Specifically, the students wanted to tell people's stories from their own perspectives and in their own voices. Similarly, the Foxfire series was compiled by students who studied the folklore and folklife of people in the Appalachian Mountains in West Virginia. (See, for example, Wigginton, 1972.) While we hear the young people's voices in these texts, they are not writing about themselves, but rather about others whom they have researched.

Thus we have found a variety of ways in which young people have been represented and have written themselves in published texts. These range from reports of studies conducted by university-based researchers to popular accounts of adolescent life. Even though the perspectives of adolescents are represented in the texts, in all of these examples the adult authors of the texts provide the analytical framework and interpretations. In the other examples of texts we include, adolescents write about others, but not themselves. Our goal in this collection is to combine these approaches, to present students' perspectives on school in their own voices.

Overview of the Chapters

The chapters in this volume offer eight very different glimpses into students' experiences in school. Each chapter emerged out of a different existing or new relationship between the student authors and the researcher/teacher authors. In every case, the student authors knew prior to beginning work on the chapters the researcher/teacher authors with whom they collaborated, but the nature and extent of the relationships varied considerably. We offer for each chapter a few words of background and a general overview.

Chapter 1, "Our World," coauthored by students Maribelis Alfaro, Lornaliz Letriz, Maritzabeth Santos, and Mariela Villanueva and researcher Rebecca Freeman, evokes the world of an urban bilingual middle school as seen through the eyes of four Puerto Rican students who attend it. Prior to coauthoring this chapter, Rebecca had been working since the spring of 1997 on an ethnographic research project at the middle school, where she met the students.

The first part of "Our World" focuses on the girls' and their families' struggles with issues of migration. Describing school as a place where they can learn what they need to know to succeed in this society, these students advocate bilingual education because, as Maribelis explains, "it works both ways . . . Before we went to Spanish class, we all could speak both languages but we couldn't read or write in Spanish. So thanks to bilingual education, we can now read and write Spanish and we can help our family members with translation." These young women offer a perspective on bilingual education in marked contrast to assertions made by critics such as Richard Rodriguez, who has argued that one must abandon one's home culture and language to succeed in the English-speaking world (Rodriguez 1981). Being bilingual is important to these students because, they argue, it keeps them connected to their families and helps them to succeed in school.

Chapter 2, "Speaking Out Loud: Girls Seeking Selfhood," is coauthored by students Quentina Judon, Jessye Cohen-Dan, Tyeasha Leonard, Sharita Stinson, and Tara Colson and researcher authors Jody Cohen and Diane Brown. The student authors had various relationships to the researcher authors of this chapter. Jody and Diane had been working with four of the students, Quentina, Tyeasha, Sharita, and Tara, through STAR (Sisters Together in Action Research), an urban middle school girls' leadership program. Jessye's contributions emerged from conversations she and Jody, her mother, were already having and writing sessions she shared with Quentina.

The student authors of "Speaking Out Loud" explain both directly and through illustrative stories that they want to be recognized as "whole beings." These girls' learning and growth take place within many contexts: middle and high school classrooms, schools, and the communities of the urban and suburban environments in which they live. The girls explain that they want the people with whom they interact to support them and take them seriously. As Quentina Judon puts it: "People say 'you're only affected if you make yourself be affected.' I don't agree with any of this. I am very affected by what's going on."

Chapter 3, "What's Your Bias?: Cuts on Diversity in a Suburban Public School," coauthored by students Kristin Dunderdale, Sara Tourscher, and R.J. Yoo and researcher/teacher authors Ondrea Reisinger and Alison Cook-Sather, offers high school students' perspectives, gathered by the three students, on how the assumptions and biases of teachers can result in differential treatment of students. Kristin, Sara, and R.J. had all participated in a project Ondrea and Alison designed called Teaching and Learning Together, an approach to teacher education that integrates high school students into the preparation of undergraduate, preservice teachers (see Cook-Sather 2001; Cook-Sather under review; and Cook-Sather and Reisinger 2001). The focus of the chapter—teacher bias in relation to student diversity—was selected by the students and was thus new, but the students were accustomed to being asked to articulate their perspectives on school and schooling through having maintained a weekly written exchange of letters with preservice teachers and having participated in weekly conversations, facilitated by Ondrea, about issues of teaching and learning.

The students articulate their concerns in "What's Your Bias?" about differential treatment by teachers in general, specifically teachers' perceptions of students' abilities, their assumptions about students based on race, and their differential treatment of students based on gender. The stories the student authors have gathered and retold to illustrate instances of differential treatment by teachers reflect how attentive students are to the subtle (and not so subtle) assumptions and behaviors of teachers. They pay attention not only to what is being taught but to the array of messages that teachers send to students based on their conscious and unconscious biases. Kristin articulates clearly the main message students want to send with this chapter: "Teachers should treat people equally. That's it."

Chapter 4, "Cutting Class: Perspectives of Urban High School Students," is coauthored by students Fredo Sanon and Maurice Baxter, graduate student–researcher Lydia Fortune (who graduated during the project but remained involved), and professor–researcher Susan Opotow. Fredo and Maurice worked with Lydia and Susan for four years researching the question: Why do students cut class? (Opotow 1999).

Composed primarily of a dialogue between Fredo and Maurice and drawing on recorded discussions they had with other students in their own and other urban high schools, this chapter offers a variety of explanations for why students cut class. Many of these are related to their relationships with teachers and peers. For example, they suggest that teachers don't respect students, they experience pressure from their peers, and they feel too monitored and restrained in school. The solutions that Fredo and Maurice propose for these problems are that students need to be involved, recognized, connected, and respected. In addition, students need to believe that what they're doing is meaningful.

Chapter 5, "An Education for What?' Reflections of Two High School Seniors on School," is coauthored by students Steven Marzan and Amy Peterson, who attend a rural high school, teacher Ceci Lewis, and researchers Scott Christian and Eva Gold. This chapter emerged out of a project with quite a different focus: Eva and Scott had been working with Ceci, a teacher at the student authors' high school, as part of the Bread Loaf Rural Teacher Network (BLRTN). Eva and Scott were documenting the reform initiatives of BLRTN, which include the use of telecommunications to stimulate and support student writing.

In this chapter, Steve and Amy focus on how school is not preparing them for life. In particular, Amy discusses the absence of social interaction in academic classes at her school and how this limits her preparation to function in the real world, and Steve describes his experience of being a visual and hands-on learner in a school system that privileges more abstract approaches to learning. Amy explains: "My classroom education has fallen short of giving me the most vital skills needed to survive in the world today. It has failed to teach me that effort ought to be rewarded, regardless of the overall product, it has failed to teach me how to communicate with others, in short it has failed to teach me any type of social skills." She emphasizes that school should better prepare her to relate to others. Steve's focus, as expressed in the quote at the beginning of this chapter, is on how teachers should take into consideration his and other students' different learning styles.

Chapter 6, "Caught in the Storm of Reform: Five Student Perspectives on the Implementation of the Interactive Mathematics Program," is coauthored by students Dorothy Holt, Emily Gann, Sonia Gordon-Walinsky, Elissa Klinger, and Rachel Toliver and researcher/teacher Ned Wolff. All of the student authors of this chapter had attended an urban magnet high school at which they enrolled in an innovative math program facilitated by Ned. Although they had a history as students and teacher, this was the first time the authors had worked together to write about their experience.

In "Caught in the Storm of Reform," the student authors write about their previous experiences with math education, their interest in this alternative approach, some of the tensions they experienced, the differential treatment and negative attitudes of peers and teachers toward this alternative program, and how it prepared them for college math. This is an example of an attempted reform in a particular curricular area that highlights the challenges that any alternative approach to education faces, including resistance from more traditional teachers, skepticism from students for whom traditional approaches work and in which they believe, and the transition from an alternative approach back into more traditional educational contexts.

Chapter 7, "Reflections: Writing and Talk about Race in Middle School," is coauthored by students Darreisha Bates, Noah Chase, Chris Ignasiak, Yvette Johnson, and Tina Zaza and university-based researchers Tricia Niesz, Patti Buck, and Katherine Schultz. Since 1996, Katherine has been conducting focus groups with students at Skyline Middle School to elicit their perspectives on race relations in a post-desegregation school setting. Tricia and Patti have been working with Katherine for the last two years doing ethnographic research at the school on this project.

This chapter focuses on how students perceive and write about racial identity and interracial relations at their desegregated middle school. Drawing from life experiences, writing group discussions and popular culture, the chapter presents three different "takes" on students' perceptions of race and race relations. Students used the format of a play to write about issues that often were silenced at school. After finishing the play, they discussed why and how they chose to write a play to represent race relations. And, as part of the ongoing process of composing their thoughts about this issue, the students wrote informally about race. Altogether, these three "takes" reflect these middle school students' perceptions of race and race relations.

Chapter 8, "Writing the Wrong: Making Schools Better for Girls," is coauthored by students Margo Strucker and Lenelle N. Moise, and graduate students Vicki Lynn Magee, and Holly Kreider. The authors engaged in freewriting activities to reflect on their experiences of school. As the authors explain, "Freewriting is a writing exercise that often involves a set period of time and the use of a prompt; for instance words, phrases, photographs, objects, or music." Lenelle and Margo were high school seniors when they began working on this chapter.

"Writing the Wrong" is about how this group of women believed there was no place for them to explore what they were thinking about while they were in school. They describe their use of freewrites to capture their "school experiences, good and bad, that centered on relationships with teachers and students whom we saw every day at school." For the most part, these women felt their teachers remained "faceless and inhuman" and their peers "often offered nothing but criticism and animosity." To "write the wrongs" for girls in schools, the authors suggest that girls' voices be invited and included in discussions of educational reform, and that the use of collaborative freewriting has both academic and personal benefits for girls. The authors call for making real connections, communicating, and relevance in what students experience in school.

The Challenges and Rewards of Listening to Students

These chapters were composed through the cooperation of a wide range of researcher/teachers and students. Diversity was important to us, but most important was that we find teams of students and researcher/teachers who were committed to having the students be the primary authors of the chapters. In explaining the intention of the project to prospective contributors, we emphasized that we wanted students to offer their own perspectives in their own words and that we wanted minimal editing of the student voices on the part of the researcher/teachers.

There was extensive and ongoing negotiation among the authors of the chapters and between the authors and us as editors as we worked to achieve a balance between inviting unedited student perspectives and framing those for public presentation. As we discuss in the final chapter of this collection, "Negotiating Worlds and Words: Writing about Students' Experiences of School," the invitation from us as editors—who work primarily within the worlds of higher education, academic conferences, and publishing—to students—who live in the worlds of the urban, suburban, and rural middle and high schools they attend—required the mediation of researchers and teachers who have a foot in each of these worlds. In spite of the ongoing negotiation of logistical challenges and issues of authority, this process proved to be fulfilling to all involved.

What the students in this volume have to say reinforces what progressive educators have been advocating for close to 100 years—that classrooms need to be places that engage learners in deep and meaningful ways. The particular insights that the student authors offer in these pages emphasize that meaningful engagement to them means being respected enough to be taken seriously as learners, to be acknowledged as whole and complex human beings, and to be given more of a say in what happens in their everyday lives in school.

We hope this book will reach teachers, teacher educators, parents, and policy makers and inspire each of them to create forums in which to listen to students. Teacher educators, legislators, and bureaucrats, as well as constituencies with a wide variety of interests in education, need to be mindful of these student concerns as they design and implement educational programs and policies. These conversations with students need to be ongoing so that as student perspectives and concerns change students continue to be part of the discussions about educational reform.

A Note on Format

In an attempt to create uniformity of style across chapters, we have used the following conventions. Each chapter opens with an introduction that highlights the focus of the chapter, identifies the coauthors, and describes their writing process. With the exception of chapter 8, the opening segment of every chapter is written by the researcher/teacher author(s), as indicated by their names appended to the subheading "Introduction." Chapter 8 is the exception because that chapter was written entirely collaboratively.

In the body of the chapters, different sections are written by different authors and are always identified. Again excepting chapter 8, the body of the chapters is written entirely by students with researcher/teacher support. We have used italics for the interchapter transitions and clarifications about frame, background, and context. In chapters 1, 2, 4, 5, and 7, these segments were written by researcher/teacher authors, and in chapters 3, 6, and 8, they were written by student authors.

In all but two chapters real names are used for both people and schools. In chapters 3 and 7, the student and/or researcher/teacher authors felt it was important to preserve the anonymity of the people and schools and thus used pseudonyms to mask their identities.

Note

1. We use the term "researcher/teacher" to refer to the authors of the chapters who fulfilled one or both of these roles in relation to the student authors. Thus, some of these individuals were the teachers of the student authors, others were researchers who were doing research on and/or with the student authors, and a small minority were both teachers and researchers of the student authors. The term should not be confused with "teacher-researcher" used by Cochran-Smith and Lytle (1993) and others.

References

Bruner, J. 1977. *The Process of Education.* Cambridge, Mass.: Harvard University Press.

Cochran-Smith, M., and S. Lytle. 1993. *Inside/Outside: Teacher Research and Knowledge.* New York City: Teachers College Press.

Cohen, J. 1993. "Constructing Race at an Urban High School: In Their Minds, Their Mouths, Their Hearts." In *Beyond Silenced Voices: Class, Race, and Gender in United States Schools,* edited by L. Weis and M. Fine. Albany: State University of New York Press.

Commeyras, M. 1995. "What Can We Learn from Students' Questions?" *Theory into Practice* 43(2): 101–6.

Connell, R. W. 1994. "Poverty and Education." *Harvard Educational Review* 64(2): 125–49.

Cook-Sather, A. 2001. "Translating Themselves: Becoming a Teacher through Text and Talk." In *Talking Shop: Authentic Conversation and Teacher Learning,* edited by Christopher M. Clark. New York City: Teachers College Press, 2001.

Cook-Sather, A. "Re(in)forming the Conversations: Including High School Teachers and Students in Pre-Service Teacher Education." Under review at *Teachers College Record.*

Cook-Sather, A., and O. Reisinger. 2001. "Seeing the Students behind the Stereotypes: The Perspectives of Five Pre-Service Teachers." *The Teacher Educator* 37:2.

Corbett, D., and B. Wilson. 1995. "Make a Difference with, Not for, Students: A Plea for Researchers and Reformers." *Educational Researcher* 24(5): 12–17.

Dahl, K. 1995. "Challenges in Understanding the Learner's Perspective." *Theory into Practice* 43(2): 124–30.

Erickson, F., and J. Shultz. 1992. "Students' Experience of Curriculum." In *Handbook of Research on Curriculum,* edited by Philip W. Jackson. New York City: Macmillan.

Fine, M. 1993. "Sexuality, Schooling, and Adolescent Females: The Missing Discourse of Desire." In *Beyond Silenced Voices: Class, Race, and Gender in United States Schools*, edited by L. Weis and M. Fine. Albany: State University of New York Press.

Friend, R. 1993. "Choices Not Closets: Heterosexism and Homophobia in Schools." In *Beyond Silenced Voices: Class, Race, and Gender in United States Schools*, edited by L. Weis and M. Fine. Albany: State University of New York Press.

Garcia, F., J. Kilgore, P. Rodriquez, and S. Thomas. 1995. "'It's Like Having a Metal Detector at the Door': A Conversation with Students about Voice." *Theory into Practice* 43(2): 138–44.

Gibbs, N. 1999. "A Week in the Life of a High School." *Time,* October 25.

Heshusius, L. 1995. "Listening to Children: 'What Could We Possibly Have in Common?' From Concerns with Self to Participatory Consciousness." *Theory into Practice* 43(2): 117–23.

Jenlink, P. M., K. Kinnucan-Welsch, and S. J. Odell. 1996. "Designing Professional Development Learning Communities." In *Preparing Tomorrow's Teachers: The Field Experience—Teacher Education Yearbook IV,* edited by D. John McIntyre and David M. Byrd. Thousand Oaks, Calif.: Corwin Press.

Johnston, P., and J. Nicholls. 1995. "Voices We Want to Hear and Voices We Don't." *Theory into Practice* 43(2): 94–100.

Kozol, J. 1991. *Savage Inequalities: Children in America's Schools.* New York City: Harper Perennial.

Lewis, S. 1996. *A Totally Alien Life-Form.* New York City: New Press.

Lincoln, Y. 1995. "In Search of Students' Voices." *Theory into Practice* 43(2): 88–93.

Metropolitan Life Insurance Company. 1996. The Metropolitan Life Survey of the American Teacher, 1996: Students Voice Their Opinions on: Their Education, Teachers and Schools. Part II. Conducted for Metropolitan Life Insurance Company by Louis Harris and Associates, Inc.

Minds Stayed on Freedom. 1991. Compiled by the Youth of the Rural Organizing and Cultural Center in Holmes Country, Mississippi. Boulder, Colo.: Westview Press.

Nieto, S. 1994. "Lessons from Students on Creating a Chance to Dream." *Harvard Educational Review* 64(4): 392–426.

Oldfather, P., ed. 1995. "Learning from Student Voices." *Theory into Practice* 43(2).

Oldfather, P. 1995. "Songs 'Come Back Most to Them': Students' Experiences as Researchers." *Theory into Practice* 43(2): 131–37.

O'Loughlin, M. 1995. "Daring the Imagination: Unlocking Voices of Dissent and Possibility in Teaching." *Theory into Practice* 43(2): 107–16.

Opotow, S. 1999. "Trickle-Up Service and Outreach: Collaborative Research on Class Cutting with High School Students." *Journal of Public Service and Outreach,* fall.

Phelan, P., A. L. Davidson, and H. T. Cao. 1992. "Speaking Up: Students' Perspectives on School." *Phi Delta Kappan* 73(9): 695–704.

Phelan, P., A. L. Davidson, and H. C. Yu. 1998. *Adolescents' Worlds: Negotiating Family, Peers, and School.* New York City: Teachers College Press.

Rodriguez, R. 1981. *The Hunger of Memory. The Education of Richard Rodriguez: An Autobiography.* Boston: D. R. Godine.

Shandler, S. 1999. *Ophelia Speaks: Adolescent Girls Write about Their Search for Self.* New York City: HarperCollins.

Weis, L., and M. Fine, eds. 1993. *Beyond Silenced Voices: Class, Race, and Gender in United States Schools.* Albany: State University of New York Press.

Weston, N. 1997. "Distant Voices, Shared Lives: Students Creating the Global Learning Community." *Educational Horizons* 75(4): 165–71.

Wigginton, E. 1972. *The Foxfire Book: Hog Dressing; Log Cabin Building; Mountain Crafts and Foods; Planting by the Signs; Snake Lore, Hunting Tales, Faith Healing; Moonshining; and Other Affairs of Plain Living.* Garden City, N.Y.: Doubleday.

CHAPTER 1

Our World

Student Authors: Maribelis Alfaro, Lornaliz Letriz,
Maritzabeth Santos, and Mariela Villanueva
Researcher/Teacher Author: Rebecca Freeman

Introduction

Rebecca Freeman

Working on this project with Maribelis, Lornaliz, Maritzabeth, and Mariela has been one of the most educational experiences I've had since I began my ethnographic research at Julia de Burgos Bilingual Middle Magnet School in the predominantly Puerto Rican community in North Philadelphia about three years ago. When I first imagined this piece, I assumed that I would write an introduction that highlights the historical, political, and economic context of the school. However, after Maribelis, Maritzabeth, Mariela, and Lornaliz wrote their life stories, I realized that their words provided a much richer picture of how migration influences bilingualism and education for Puerto Ricans at school in North Philadelphia than I could ever write. So instead I'll use this introduction to briefly describe the writing process. Because we worked together in many different ways in order to produce this chapter, I'm going to describe our collaborative process in some detail.

The majority of this piece was written by Maribelis Alfaro, whom I met in the summer of 1997 when I was working on a collaborative ethnographic research project with ten teachers and sixty students from Julia de Burgos. One day Maribelis told me that she wanted to be a writer, and that she generally wrote about four hours a day. Later, when Jeff Shultz asked me if I wanted to work with students from Julia de Burgos for this collection, Maribelis immediately came to mind.

Maribelis began her contribution in the spring of 1997 by working with a graduate assistant from the Graduate School of Education at the University of

Pennsylvania. Maribelis wanted to know about the history of the school, so she worked with the graduate assistant to brainstorm interview questions. By the end of the semester, she had written a short piece (about one page handwritten) titled "Julia de Burgos: Then and Now," based on her interviews with several of her family members who had graduated from Julia de Burgos.

Throughout the fall of 1998, Maribelis worked with me to build on what she had written. This was very challenging at first because of the limited time and space we had. For example, we generally worked together either at lunchtime in the cafeteria or after school in the library. I gave Maribelis a spiral notebook, and we would talk about issues at school. Either she or I would write a question or a series of questions in her notebook that had come out of our conversation, and she would take the notebook home, write about the issue, and bring it back to me another day at school. We would talk more about what she had written and think of more questions for her to explore. I would take home the pages from the spiral notebook and put what she had written on the computer. By the end of the fall semester, we had a series of short pieces on disk about various aspects of life at school. Both of us wondered if this would ever turn into a complete chapter.

We had a real turning point in February 1999. I was invited to Maribelis's house to meet her family and to work with her at home. This was the first time that we had longer than forty-five minutes to work together, and I brought my laptop. We looked through all of the pieces she had written and put them in what she decided was a logical order on disk. She wrote transitions between sections and we talked about areas that were missing. Sometimes Maribelis would dictate an idea to me that I would write on the computer, and sometimes she would compose silently at the computer while I talked to her other family members. Since the computer seemed to really help the process, I decided to leave it with her for the weekend. Since she and her other family members had shared so many fascinating stories with me about themselves, I asked Maribelis to write her life story. The following Monday when I met Maribelis at school, she had produced a beautiful piece, titled "My Life." For the first time, both of us knew that this project had really moved from being a series of short essays about the school to a moving piece about relationships between her life at home and school.

Julia de Burgos Bilingual Middle Magnet School has two very different social worlds: one that is educated through English and the other that is educated through Spanish and English. Because Maribelis is educated primarily through English, I decided to ask students from the bilingual program to contribute their perspectives on their experiences at the school also. Maritzabeth and Mariela joined the project in the fall of 1998. To encourage them to write, I gave them each cameras and asked them to document a day in their life at school and then to write about their experiences using the photographs as a foundation. While we began to get some good photographs, this approach didn't really generate much writing. After the turning point in Maribelis's writing that I described above, I decided to share her writing with Maritzabeth and Mariela. First they read Maribelis's life story, and then they each wrote their life story at the computer after school. When they had finished this part, I read Maribelis's description of "Julia de Burgos: Then and Now" out loud, and Maritzabeth and Mariela collaborated in their written response at the computer. I have indicated which parts Maritzabeth and Mariela added so that it is clear who wrote what throughout the chapter.

Although Maritzabeth and Mariela are perfectly comfortable in Spanish and English, several of the students on the bilingual program are just beginning to learn English. In the spring of 1999, I decided to ask Lornaliz, an English-language learner, to join the project. I showed her the evolving chapter and briefly described the sections to her in Spanish. I asked her to tell me her life story (in Spanish), which she then wrote down on paper. A few days later, Maritzabeth, Mariela, Lornaliz, and I were working together in Maritzabeth's living room. Maritzabeth translated Lornaliz's life story to English, and Mariela and Maritzabeth took turns reading the entire chapter out loud and translating orally to Spanish so that Lornaliz could understand and contribute.

I'm sorry to say that although Lornaliz was able to understand what the others had written, she didn't choose to add anything else—I don't know if it was because Lornaliz really believed that the text was fine as it was or whether the fact that it was all written first in English prevented her from really contributing. Despite this problem, I want to emphasize how much this bilingual writing process revealed about the students' diverse abilities in spoken and written Spanish and English, diversity that reflects their varied migration and education histories.

Throughout the spring semester, I generally worked with Maribelis at her house, or with Maritzabeth, Mariela, and Lornaliz at Maritzabeth's house. As Maribelis read what the others were writing about their experiences at Julia de Burgos, she began to really think about how different their lives were. As Maribelis and I talked about bilingual education in all of their lives, I realized that she wasn't aware that bilingual education is such a controversial issue in the United States today. That day on the front page of the *Philadelphia Inquirer* was an article about California's Proposition 227, which eliminated bilingual education from California's educational policy in September 1998. Maribelis and I read the article and discussed the controversy. Maribelis then wrote the conclusion to this chapter, which presents her perspective on bilingual education.

By working with the students at their homes, I was able to learn a great deal about their bilingual literacy practices. For example, after Mariela and Maritzabeth translated Lornaliz's life story to English, they each decided that they wanted to translate their life stories to Spanish. I realized that Maritzabeth has outstanding translation skills, which she has really developed by helping her monolingual, Spanish-speaking mother and stepfather interact with mainstream institutions in the United States. Maritzabeth was going to work with the other students to translate the entire chapter to Spanish. By this time, however, our deadline was quickly approaching. Maritzabeth and Mariela decided that it was important to include their life stories in Spanish and English, which reflects the importance of bilingualism in their lives. If we had had more time, we all would have really preferred to have presented this chapter entirely in Spanish and English, because the students' world is really a bilingual world.

Our World

Every morning everyone on Earth wakes up to go somewhere, to see someone, or to have things to do. We all get dressed, brush our teeth, and eat breakfast, and then we all leave. That is something that everyone shares no matter if we are poor or rich because we all do that. But we don't all have the same day.

In the city of brotherly love live four teenage girls who don't even really know each other that well, and they all see life in Philly in their own way. Although they see things differently from each other, they all have one thing in common. They all go to the same middle school called Julia de Burgos Bilingual Middle Magnet School. One girl is in the eighth grade and the other three are in the seventh grade.

In our story we write about what it's like in our side of the city. At first I thought that this whole thing about telling our story would be about our school, the Julia de Burgos Bilingual Middle Magnet School. But as time went by we discovered that it wasn't just about a school, but about how we live, how we speak, and our experiences. In the beginning of our story we present you with many interesting stories about us, the writers.

Maribelis Alfaro

My name is Maribelis Alfaro, I'm fourteen years old and I'm in the eighth grade. I have two sisters and one brother, and we have never lived anywhere outside of Philadelphia. Both of my parents were born in Puerto Rico (PR) and they were both brought to the United States (US) as teenagers.

My mother was born in Guayama. My grandparents brought my mother and their other children to the US because my grandpa had accepted a job here as a construction worker. He made a good decision to move his family to the US because it's not easy to find work in PR. My grandpa dropped out of school when he was in the fifth grade because his family was very poor and they couldn't pay his way to continue his studies. Since my grandpa couldn't attend school anymore, he worked in the fields with his father and he learned how to grow crops. As my grandpa got older he learned how to build houses out of concrete, he learned how to repair electric wires and he learned other things. But the payment for good work like my grandpa's wasn't enough to support a wife and ten kids. Until one day he was lucky and someone in the US wanted to hire him. He thought that raising his kids in the land of opportunity would be the best place for them. That's why he accepted the job in the US.

My father is from Utuado, PR. My grandma brought my father to the US because my grandpa had died. She was left alone to take care of her children so she used my grandpa's insurance money to bring the family to the US because she had other married children living there. She thought that it would be a good decision to live in the US because her older sons and daughters could help her take care of their brothers and sisters.

My mom was sixteen years old when she was brought to the US and my dad was thirteen years old when he was brought to the US. My dad was brought to the US at a younger age than my mother so he is able to speak English well. But at first when he was brought to the US he didn't know English at all. As a teenager, my dad was a fighter so he didn't learn English at school all the time. He would learn it by watching TV in English, listening to English music, and to how people spoke. By the time he went to Edison High School he spoke proper English but he was still a fighter, a fighter who is real good with math, speech, and technology. My mom was sixteen when she was flown in from PR, so she went to Kensington High School. She learned English in school, but at that time there were a lot of PR teenagers so she didn't worry about learning English fast to make friends because she was put in a bilingual classroom. She did learn to understand English but her writing, reading, and speech weren't so good.

My parents got married in their twenties and they had three daughters. My dad wanted the three of us to learn English as our first language because he didn't want us to go through what he went through when he first came here. My mother wanted the three of us to learn Spanish because Spanish was her family language. The three of us are a big deal to my mom's side of the family because we're my grandparent's first grandchildren. And my grandparents can only speak Spanish.

So my parents made an agreement—the three of us were taught English as our first language and then when we had finally made English as our first language we would begin to learn Spanish. Our English was really good because when we would go to school the three of us would learn as much as we could about the alphabet, the sound a letter makes, and the English rules of writing because when we got home my dad would take any book and teach us how to read.

Then five years later my parents had my little brother. At that time my dad had to work two jobs to support four kids and a wife. So when my sisters and I came home my dad couldn't teach us how to read English or help us with our homework because he wasn't home. My mom couldn't teach us English because we felt so uncomfortable being taught by her. And most of the time she didn't understand what we were saying. So while my dad was working, my brother would sleep in his crib, my little sister would play with her dolls while my twin sister and I would watch TV. Whenever my dad wasn't around to teach us or talk to us we would just sit on the rocking chair and watch the Thunder Cats cartoon, the Ninja Turtles or some other cartoon. We used to watch TV a lot so we learned English a lot faster that way because we would repeat every word that was mentioned in the cartoon and we would watch how they used the words to express their emotion.

We spoke English very well but our Spanish wasn't yet taught to us. In our family every Sunday after church the whole family would meet at my grandparents' house. Everyone would be so happy to see us but sometimes we weren't happy to see them because they all spoke Spanish and we didn't. At first it didn't bother us because all we did at my grandparents' house was watch TV. But when we got a little bit older and a little wiser we felt out of place because everyone else could speak a whole different language and we couldn't.

It was hard and embarrassing to be a part of a family that a person can't even talk to because that person can't speak their family language. I never wanted Sunday to come because every time we went to visit the family they would laugh at me, tease me, or just ask me the question that I never liked, "What are you—an American or a Puerto Rican?" Of course it was hard for me because what do I know, I was just a kid. What was I going to tell them? But imagine how my mom felt. Everyone used to tease her because sometimes when we talked to her she didn't understand a word we said. It must be sad to have kids and not be able to understand what they're saying.

All those negative things that both sides of the family gave us we put to good use. Every weekend my mom would sit us down in the kitchen table and teach us the alphabet in Spanish. We never liked it because not only that we took a lot of time learning but on the weekends our favorite cartoons would be on and we could never watch them. The more and more practice we had and the better we got to understanding it. But my mom thought that we needed to learn some words so she noticed that we learned more when we were watching TV. So every night from 7 P.M. to 9 P.M. we would all go up to my mom's room and watch the "novelas" (soap operas).

My Spanish was getting better but it wasn't enough to talk to my family correctly because we would mix the two languages together and they used to won-

der "which language are you speaking—English or Spanish?" Years later we
moved out of our second home into our third home. My mom arranged it so
that my sisters, brother, and I would go to school at Potter Thomas Elementary.
She understood that in that elementary school it had a Spanish class so my mom
wanted us to go there.

To get in the Spanish class a woman had to test me to judge the Spanish that
I already knew. My sisters and I passed the test and were put in the class. We
studied Spanish in that class for four years and it turned out to be good for me.
The more and more we studied and the more that we watched TV, the better we
made Spanish our second language. But our only problem was that we have an
accent when we speak Spanish. Yet all is well. We learned both languages and we
are the smartest teenagers in our family because we are the only ones that can
speak, read, write, and understand both languages.

Lornaliz Letriz

Mi nombre es Lornaliz Letriz. Tengo trece años y estoy en grado siete. Yo nací en
septiembre 24 del 1985. Yo nací en Aguadilla, Puerto Rico. Yo le puedo contar
varias de mis experiencias.

Cuando yo viví en Aguadilla, mi padrastro trataba mal a mi mamá y él la
amenazó con matarla. Pues mi mamá tuvo que irse de Aguadilla para Caguas. En
Caguas no pasamos mucho tiempo viviendo. De Caguas nos fuimos para
Barceloneta. Yo estudié y pasé de grado seis pero nos tuvimos que ir de nuevo
porque un carro muy estraño nos seguía. De Barceloneta nos fuimos para
Corozal y me pusieron de nuevo en la escuela en grado seis y pasé de grado seis
de nuevo. Pues en verano nos fuimos para Aguada para ver a mi abuela. Pues mi
mamá se enteró que le habían robado y por eso nos tuvimos que ir para Aguada.
Estuvimos mucho tiempo viviendo en casa de mi tío. Mi mamá lo ayudaba con
los biles y con la renta. De Aguada nos fuimos para Nueva York a vivir. Estuvimos como diez meses viviendo en Nueva York. Estuve en la escuela en grado siete, pero no pasé de grado. Nos tuvimos que ir de nuevo y nos fuimos para
Filadelfia. Ahora estudio en la escuela Julia de Burgos.

Nosotros vivimos con mi mamá y mis hermanos aquí en Filadelfia. Mi
mamá nos puede mantener porque a mis hermanos les manda seguro social y
a mi mamá también. Pues de mi hermana y yo recibimos cupones y chavos.
Mi mamá ha trabajado en la fábrica de ventanas y la de calendarios y ahora
está buscando trabajo.

Yo no hablo inglés todavía pero estoy aprendiendolo en la escuela ahora. Yo
estoy cogiendo clases con la maestra Mrs. Rodriquez. Ella me recoge en la clase
y nos lleva a un salón para enseñarme inglés. Yo pienso que el inglés y el español
se tiene que aprender porque si uno sale al cualquier lado en los Estados Unidos

y no sabe inglés, no puede hablar y no puede entender lo que te dicen. Y si yo vuelvo para Puerto Rico y no sé español, me bajan de grado.

My name is Lornaliz Letriz. I am thirteen years old and I'm in seventh grade. I was born on September 24, 1985. I was born in Aguadilla, PR. I can tell you some of my experiences.

When I lived in Aguadilla, my stepfather used to treat my mother wrong, and he threatened to kill her. Well, my mom needed to move from Aguadilla to Caguas, PR. We didn't spend much time in Caguas. From Caguas, we moved to Barceloneta. I studied there and passed sixth grade, but we needed to move because a strange car always followed us. From Barceloneta, we moved to Corozal and they put me in a new school in sixth grade and I passed sixth grade again. In the summer we went to Aguada to see my grandmother. So my mother found out that they had robbed her, and that's why we had to move to Aguada. We spent a lot of time living in my uncle's house. My mother helped him to pay the bills and the rent. From Aguada, PR, we moved to New York to live. We lived in New York about ten months. I was in school, but I didn't finish the seventh grade. We had to leave New York and we came to Philadelphia. Now I study at Julia de Burgos.

Now I live with my mother and my brothers here in Philadelphia. My mother can support us because they send my brothers and my mother social security. My sister and I receive food stamps and money. My mother has worked in the window and calendar factories, and now she is looking for work.

I don't speak English, but I'm learning at school. I am taking classes with Mrs. Rodriguez. She picks me up at class and takes us to a room where she teaches us English. I think that everyone has to learn English and Spanish because if you don't know English in the US, you can't speak and you can't understand what they say to you. And if I return to PR and I don't know Spanish, they will fail me.

—Translated by Maritzabeth Santos

Maritzabeth Santos

My name is Maritzabeth Santos. I'm twelve years old and I'm in the seventh grade at Julia de Burgos Bilingual School. My mom, Margarita Robles, and my dad, Marcelino Santos, were born in Coamo, Puerto Rico, and they had two children in Puerto Rico.

My mother and my father came to the United States to start a new life with their family. When they first came to the US, they lived in Perth Amboy, New Jersey, where they had two more children. Then they moved to New Haven, Connecticut, where they had me. After I was born, my mom, my dad, my brothers, and I moved to Puerto Rico and lived there for a year. After Puerto Rico we moved to Perth Amboy, New Jersey. One of my brothers moved to Connecticut to live with my aunt, and three of my brothers, my mom, and my dad, and I moved to Philadelphia, where I have lived for ten years. I have moved four times since I've been in Philadelphia because of housing problems.

My brother who lived in Connecticut died of a drug overdose in November 1992, and my father died in June 1996 in a car accident. I feel sad right now because I can't talk to my father about my problems, and I feel sad about my brother because he's not here to have happy times together.

Now I live with my mom and my stepfather. My stepfather is really nice to me and he buys me everything I need. Two of my brothers live in Puerto Rico, and the other one lives here in Philadelphia. My mom works taking care of kids (baby-sitter). My stepfather works in a wire factory and he has to use gloves.

I usually speak Spanish at home because my mom and my stepfather don't know English. With my brothers, I talk in English because they don't speak Spanish very well. With my mom they talk Spanish, but not that well because they get messed up. With my friends I talk in Spanish and English.

I have been in two different schools. I went to Potter Thomas Elementary School and now I go to Julia de Burgos Middle School. Since I speak Spanish and English at home, I've always gone to bilingual schools. I prefer to have classes in both languages and if I could learn another language I'd be really proud.

Mi nombre es Maritzabeth Santos. Tengo doce años y estoy en séptimo grado en la escuela Julia de Burgos. Mi madre, Margarita Robles, y mi padre, Marcelino Santos, nacieron en Coamo, Puerto Rico, y tuvieron dos hijos en Puerto Rico.

Mi madre y mi padre se mudaron para los Estados Unidos para empezar una nueva vida con su familia. Cuando llegaron a los Estados Unidos, vivieron en Perth Amboy, NJ, donde tuvieron dos hijos más. Luego se mudaron para New Haven, Connecticut, donde me tuvieron a mí. Después que yo nací, mi madre, mi padre, mis hermanos, y yo nos mudamos para Puerto Rico donde vivimos por un año. Después de Puerto Rico, nosotros nos mudamos para Perth Amboy, NJ. Uno de mis hermanos se mudó para Connecticut para vivir con mi tía, y tres de mis hermanos, mi madre, mi padre, y yo nos mudamos para Filadelfia donde hemos estado viviendo por diez años. Yo me he mudado cuatro veces desde que vivo en Filadelfia por problemas de casa.

Mi hermano que vivió en Connecticut se murió de una sobredosis de droga en noviembre de 1992, y mi padre murió en junio de 1996 en un accidente de carro. Yo me siento triste ahora porque no le puedo hablar a mi padre sobre mis problemas, y me siento triste por mi hermano porque él no está aquí para pasarlo bien juntos.

Ahora vivo con mi madre y mi padrasto. Mi padrasto es muy bueno conmigo y me compra todo lo que me hace falta. Dos de mis hermanos viven en Puerto Rico, y uno vive aquí en Filadelfia. Mi madre trabaja cuidando niños. Mi padrasto trabaja en una fábrica de cables y tiene que usar guantes.

Yo hablo español en mi casa porque mi madre y mi padrasto no saben inglés. Con mis hermanos hablo inglés porque ellos no saben tanto español. Con mi madre ellos hablan español pero no hablan muy bien porque se turban. Con mis amigas/os hablo inglés y español.

Yo he estado en dos escuelas diferentes. Yo he estudiado en la escuela Potter Thomas y ahora voy a la escuela Julia de Burgos. A causa que hablo español y inglés, siempre he estudiado en escuelas bilingües. Yo prefiero tener clases en los dos idiomas y si pudiera aprender otro idioma estaría muy orgullosa.

—Translated by Maritzabeth Santos

Mariela Villanueva

My name is Mariela Villanueva. I was born in Aguadilla, Puerto Rico. My mom was born in Philadelphia, and when she was eighteen she went to PR where she met my father. They had three children, me, my sister, and my brother. My mom has two more kids from another person.

My mom moved us to Philadelphia because of her job. In Philadelphia, she has worked as a hotel manager, an accounts manager, and as a bookkeeper. My father came to be a mechanic and to learn English. He found a job in Norristown, PA. A couple of months later he had an accident where his leg was really hurt. Since his accident he couldn't work or walk properly. My mom was by herself struggling to get us what we want and so she had to get two jobs. Since then our life has been hard to get and buy the stuff we need. Then my father started in his family's garage, and now he can walk and work without problems. Now he works in his brother's garage in North Philadelphia.

I was three years old when we moved to Philadelphia. Then I didn't know English. I went to Potter Thomas Elementary School where I graduated in the fifth grade, and I learned in Spanish and English. Now I speak both languages. My family uses both English and Spanish in our home. My dad can't speak good English, but his Spanish is great. To my father I speak Spanish, but to my mom I speak English because she knows more English than Spanish. My mom's Spanish is not perfect but she is trying. To my brothers and sister I speak English because they speak English as their first language. I speak English with my friends. I think it's good because I can read, write, and speak in both languages.

Mi nombre es Mariela Villanueva. Nací en Aguadilla, Puerto Rico. Mi mamá nació en Filadelfia, y cuando tenía dieciocho años ella fue para Puerto Rico donde ella conoció a mi papá. Ellos tenían tres niños, yo, mi hermana, y mi hermano. Mi mamá tenía dos otros niños de otra persona.

Mi mamá se mudó a Filadelfia por su trabajo. En Filadelfia ella ha trabajado como gerente de hoteles, gerente de cuentos, y "bookkeeper." Mi papá venía a Filadelfia para ser un mecánico y para aprender inglés. Encontró un trabajo en Norristown, PA. Unos meses después tenía un accidente donde se lastimó su pierna. Después del accidente él no podía trabajar o caminar bien. Mi mamá estaba sola trabajando dura para encontrar lo que queríamos. Ella tenía que encontrar dos trabajos. Después de todo esto, nuestra vida ha sido difícil y ha sido difícil comprar lo que necesitamos. Mi papá empezó a trabajar en el garaje de la familia y ahora él puede caminar y trabajar sin problemas. Ahora él trabaja en el garaje de su hermano en Filadelfia.

Yo tenía tres años cuando me mudé para Filadelfia. Yo no sabía inglés. Fui a Potter Thomas Elementary School donde me gradué de quinto grado y aprendí en español e inglés. Ahora hablo los dos idiomas. Mi familia usa los dos idiomas en casa. Mi papá no sabe inglés, pero su español es perfecto. Con mi papá hablo español, pero a mi mamá hablo inglés porque ella sabe más inglés que español. El español de mi mamá no es perfecto pero está aprendiéndolo. Con mi hermano y hermana hablo inglés porque es su primer lenguaje. Con mis amigas hablo inglés y español. Yo creo que esto es bueno porque yo puedo escribir, leer, y hablar perfecto los dos idiomas.

—Translated by Mariela Villanueva

Julia de Burgos: Then and Now

Julia de Burgos Bilingual Middle Magnet School is a building that is always changing. What I mean by that is the building hasn't changed but the people who attend there have changed. At first I (Maribelis) wanted to know what the school was like before it became Julia de Burgos Bilingual Middle School. I talked to my aunt and my dad because they used to go to the school when it was Thomas Edison High School. They told me some of the history that I'm going to write about here.

In reality, the school is very old. It's probably one of the oldest buildings standing in the neighborhood. When you first see the school building, you'll think it was a castle because the building is built out of stone. It has stone gargoyles on the top and there are many windows all around the building. But every window has bars on it. The outside of the building looks old and scary.

The school used to be called Northeast, and it was a school for boys. But as time went by, the community changed and so did the school. The school became a school for boys and girls and it was called Thomas Edison High School. I talked to some of the original Thomas Edison students. They told me that back in their day there were a lot of whites, few blacks, and very few Hispanics in the neighborhood. Now the neighborhoods are full with Hispanics and blacks. Each year the whites kept on leaving and the Hispanics and blacks kept on coming.

My aunt, Milagros Ramos, talked about how difficult it was to go to school at Edison. Some of the reasons were: there were no new history books, new desks or tables, typewriters, or fields. My dad, Tigere Blanco, mentioned the principal, Fierra. Principal Fierra fought for the Edison students so that they would have a brand new school, which Fierra successfully achieved.

In time the school couldn't be named Thomas Edison High School because the kids who lived in the school's area were Hispanic preteenagers in the age of twelve, thirteen, fourteen, or fifteen, and because Edison High School had a new building. So they had to change it from a high school to a middle school. They also had to change the name because most of the students that went to the school were Hispanic or half-Hispanic. So they decided to name the school after a great Hispanic poet named Julia de Burgos.

During my research about Julia de Burgos I noticed that all the white people are gone. I really don't know why the whites left. Maybe it was because they wanted a change, maybe the streets weren't safe anymore, or maybe it was because some of them left so others decided to leave too. Today there aren't any white people in this part of Philadelphia. Is it because they think they're better than us? Is it because they are afraid of us? Or is it because they just don't want to be here? I know that I sound like I'm angry and they might have an opinion about blacks and Hispanics that I would take insulting. That's not it. I just find it very curious that a race of people used to live in a place and then they leave one by one.

Although this did happen, I'm not saying that it was a big loss. I mean my neighborhood is great. Everyone knows each other, everyone comes outside with food, music, games, kids, and babies. We keep our neighborhood clean and everyone tries to look out for one another. To be honest, I wouldn't change my neighborhood for anything. There are some neighborhoods that no one knows their neighbors, it's too dangerous to be outside, or something else. In my neighborhood everyone comes outside happily and ready to talk to somebody—it doesn't matter who it is as long as it's a person. Other neighborhoods, you see drug dealers, gunfights, and that kind of stuff. But on my block we try to put that part of our lives aside so that we can live smoothly without worries.

I would say live quietly but I'd be lying to you because when Hispanics and blacks live together, we're not quiet. We like to show how happy we are. We will put on loud music and laugh hard, just to show how happy we are.

While Mariela and Maritzabeth agreed with Maribelis's description of the neighborhood, they also thought it was important to mention some of the problems around the school because these problems influence their experiences at school. Here's what they added:

I (Mariela) think some things in this neighborhood are a bad influence because some people don't care. Yesterday after school there was a fire, because somebody tried to burn the school. Last month there was a bomb threat. It's hard being in a neighborhood with drug dealing and crimes. For example, there are some drug corners around Julia de Burgos. They should stop the drug corners because students can learn something bad and won't do something with their lives in the future. And four or five years ago they raped a girl in the stairwell outside of the school at 6 in the morning. It was horrible because an innocent person was accused. After this happened, the school put up a gate so that nobody else could go down and do something bad. I think there should be police officers around to protect us.

Maribelis continues by talking about some of the physical problems with the school building:

In my opinion, the school is a wreck. The school is so old that rain enters the classrooms through leaky roofs. The paint is peeling off the walls and you could get sick from that because it could be poisonous. The floor makes a weird noise and some of our tables have a lot of holes. At the outside of the building there's graffiti, but there's not a lot. The people who study and work there are what makes the school, which is good. But the building is just not working. We need a new school fast.

Our principals, parents, and students have asked the board of education to build us a new school for eleven years and they still haven't given us one. We've given them like a hundred reasons why we need one. For example, sometimes the heater doesn't work and we have to spend at least a week in a school with no heat. Sometimes the electricity goes out and we have to spend at least two days without school. This year it happened in November. When I got to school I found out that the electricity went out, so they asked us if we wanted to stay at school or to go home. I went home but other kids stayed. I don't know why because every kid would love to get two days off from school. Also, the ceilings have cracks in them and sometimes dust just falls right out from them onto us in class. We have to call the repairman to fix it, but the repair doesn't last very long. We don't understand why they have wasted time on us and not built our school when they have gone off and built the new Roberto Clemente Middle School and the new Edison High School in the neighborhood. And we are still just waiting for them to give us land so that we can start building.

Maritzabeth and Mariela add:

Recently we heard that they are planning to build a new school in front of Fairhill Square Park, which is located on Fourth and Lehigh, about four blocks away. They haven't told us when they are planning to build the new school, or when they think it will be open.

I (Mariela) don't think they are really going to build a new school because they said this before and it never happened. They're just trying to get us excited. But I believe that they should build another building like they are proposing and I think that kids should have a recreation center there with a basketball court and programs for kids and summer jobs for kids to help them accomplish their dreams.

I (Maritzabeth) believe they are going to build the new school because our principal is really fighting for a new school now.

Maribelis continues with her description of the school by turning her attention from the physical building to the programs and the people who make the school special:

But looks can be deceiving. Although the school looks really bad, there are a lot of great educational programs. In the de Burgos Middle School we have teams. Since I've been there the teams have changed a little. The first floor has always been the PED team, Program of Economic Development. The second floor used to be the multiple intelligence team and the communications team, but now it's just the communications team. The third floor has had different teams, like the ecology team, the architecture team, and the health team.

In some cases students get to decide which team they want to be on. For example, when I was in fifth grade, a couple of days before graduation two representatives from Julia de Burgos came to Potter Thomas Elementary School and passed out sheets of paper describing the teams in their school. So we read the paper, and they gave us another piece of paper to check off which teams we want to go to for the first year, the second year, and the third year. I chose the multiple intelligence team because the name really caught my eye and at that point they had a Spanish class and I had to catch up on my Spanish. My second choice was the PED team because they talked about business and if I stayed on that team I could go downtown and work in a bank. My third choice was the ecology team. Although I had the opportunity to decide which team I wanted to be on, my little sister wasn't given the opportunity to decide. The school decided that she would be on the communications team for her first year, and on the architecture team the second year. I don't know why some students get to choose and others don't. Maybe the school society changed during the year and they had to make different decisions.

My first year I got to go to the multiple intelligence team. To me it's called the multiple intelligence team because it's not only a team of one language but of two. What I like about the multiple intelligence team is that everyone can speak either English or Spanish, because a lot of teachers understand what you're saying either way. In the multiple intelligence team we had the mentally gifted class, homework help, the best computer class, and they have the best Spanish class.

During my years on the multiple intelligence team, I improved a whole lot. How well I did got all the way up to Mr. Kaplan, who was the head of the PED team. He heard how well I did and he decided to talk to me and to test my math skills and my other learning ability in the stock market game and he decided that I should go to the PED team for eighth grade.

In the PED team what we do is study the wonderful world of business. We take all of our main classes, which are math, English, science, social studies, and reading. In each of our classes we are being trained to be good entrepreneurs. For example, my science teacher explains to us the art of observation. Observation is an art because when you are dealing with money, situations change. If we don't observe very closely what we're doing, the smallest mistake can make work look ugly. My social studies teacher shows us that in a business sometimes you have to take a risk. In our history books we learn that there were explorers sailing out in the ocean trying to find a new world. These people took a risk, they left their homes and their families just to prove that there were other worlds. The same thing is found in a business. Sometimes we put all of our money on the line just to prove that an idea works. This method is used everyday. It's called choice. My reading teacher explains to us the importance of understanding. If we don't understand what we are reading or what a person is saying, we are not the right people to run a business. My math teacher shows us that in a business it's one big word problem. It involves percentages, math procedures like addition, subtraction, division, and multiplication. It also involves the use of words. Like I said before, business is one big word problem. We have to know the procedure and work closely to solve it. Now my English teacher tells us the importance of speaking perfect English. She mentions that to us so much because it's important that we speak clearly so that other people can understand what we're saying. That to me is "good presentation." If we speak good English without being shy or acting silly, then that shows that you're serious and that you have everyone's attention.

In the economics team, the students run a store. Our store is called the Commodities Corner Cafe. We sell sodas, chips, cookies, and pretzels. We also make the decisions on what we should sell, when we should sell it, are there going to be specials, etc. But all of the students on the PED team don't make those decisions. Each class on the PED team chooses two representatives to join the board of directors. The board of directors are one big group of students from each class. They are the students who make the business decisions.

I like being a part of the PED team because we get to visit other businesses. For example, we are scheduled to visit a business in New York in March or in May. I also like working at the store, counting the money, paying the bills, and preparing to sell. The one thing that is so exciting about the PED team is that at the end of the year all of the students on the team get paid real money. The best part is that everything is completely legal. We really don't know how much. But what we do know is that everyone gets a fair share.

When I was on the multiple intelligence team, it was like any other classes that you can go to. Everyone spoke English and everyone went to their normal classes together. However, we were separated for Spanish class, and there were three different levels. One was the advanced Spanish class, one was the very low Spanish class, and one was the middle. Advanced means you know a whole lot of Spanish and you try to learn even more to make it better. The middle Spanish class was for students who know a little bit and try to improve in their speaking. The low Spanish class was for students who don't know Spanish at all. I was in the advanced class. There were only these three Spanish classes.

Now the school has changed and we have more Spanish-speaking students than we did last year. Not all of our teachers can speak good Spanish, which means we can't spread all of the Spanish-speaking students around the school. So we have to keep them all on one floor. So this year, there is no multiple intelligence team, and the communications team is bigger and takes up the whole second floor and all of the Spanish speakers are on that team. Some of the teachers on the second floor are Puerto Rican, some are black, and some are white, but they can all speak Spanish. What changed on the second floor, instead of teaching them in English, they teach their main subjects like science and math in Spanish.

Now, the rest of the students in the school know the second floor as the "hick" floor. Last year, the second floor had blacks and Spanish and it wasn't a hick floor. There were hick classes but mostly all of the kids on the second floor talked English and not Spanish. Now everyone considers the second floor as the hick floor, and considers the Spanish-speaking students as *jíbaros,* which means people that live in the countryside of Puerto Rico. They don't understand a word we say because they all speak Spanish. And when they speak English it sounds funny.

What makes the hick floor different from the other floors is the way the students conduct themselves. They speak loud, they're always making a joke of things, and the way they dress makes a big difference in our school. I mean, have you ever seen an American guy wearing a shirt with flowers on it? Some were born in America but they are being taught Spanish a whole lot and English would be their second language.

The rest of us call them *jíbaros* no matter where they come from because they have a strong accent, they conduct themselves like *jíbaros,* they dress like *jíbaros.* Some of them are born in the United States and some of them were born in Puerto Rico. It's how you look and how you talk that makes you a *jíbaro* or not. Sometimes I talk to the students on the second floor in Spanish but it's hard to communicate with them because they speak Spanish so well and I don't and it makes it difficult to continue a conversation.

Mariela and Maritzabeth respond:

The people on the first floor and the third floor call the people on the second floor "hicks" because we know more Spanish and we speak both languages. They think that we speak only Spanish. I don't think they should call us hicks because I think that they should be proud that we know both languages, both Spanish and English. In the world, we'll have more opportunities because we know both languages and we probably could learn more languages if we wanted to study them. Like Mr. Trautner, who was our sixth-grade teacher, he taught us French. He knows a lot of languages and has visited a lot of places.

Not all of the people on the second floor are *jíbaros*. I (Mariela) am not a *jíbara* even though I was born in Puerto Rico. I consider myself both Puerto Rican and American because in Puerto Rico they taught me Spanish and in Philadelphia they taught me English. I'm from both worlds.

I (Maritzabeth) don't consider myself *jíbara*. I don't get embarrassed when students call me *jíbara* because I'm proud of my culture.

In the two-way bilingual TV/communications team we study all of our subjects (math, science, social studies, literature, visual communications) in Spanish and English. In visual communications we use the video cameras to make shows. For example, we made a show about racism on the second floor that was supposed to help students from different cultures resolve conflicts and get along with each other. We also make the news with Ms. Soto.

This year I (Maritzabeth) came out in the "Noticiero de Burgos," which is the bilingual news broadcast (on video) for the whole school. We produce the news about what is happening on each of the teams. We also make commercials and talk shows.

Last year we did a novela where I (Mariela) played the part of Ana. We are learning how to use the video cameras, how to write scripts, and how to produce different kinds of shows in both Spanish and English.

In Ms. Fernandez's class we're talking about the conditions of Fairhill Square Park, which is across the street from where the new school is supposed to be located. We've been working with Jorge Arauz, a community leader, and other members of the community, and we are planting new trees, cleaning the park, and we're trying to see if we can build a new playground and take away the old Moon Theater. The plan is to knock down the theater because there is a lot of crime around it. But because the Moon Theater is beautiful, we plan to leave the artwork.

While we are at the park, we take pictures of the bad things we find and also of our good work cleaning up. One thing we do with the pictures is we put them in the bilingual newspaper with articles that we write about the work that we are doing. We deliver the newspaper, which is called *Lluvia de Ideas* (*Rainfall of Ideas*) to the community to let them know about our work.

After the students had finished writing about their experiences at school, I asked Maribelis to read through this section and write a conclusion to the section "Julia de Burgos: Then and Now." She writes:

In the beginning of our writing we mentioned all of these bad things that were going on about our school like—how wrecked the building is, the bomb threats, the disrespectful kids, the police searching through our stuff, and the fires that we have, but then we mentioned all of these good things that's been happening like on the Program of Economic Development and on the communications team. Our school is getting better in a lot of ways. For example, Temple University wants to help our school by offering a couple of students the opportunity to study with them during the summer, we have summer school for the students who are failing, we're really getting the new school that we talked about, and now the school is going to hire teachers who are ready to give all of their attention to their students.

I (Maribelis) am happy that our school is getting everything that they worked for because our school has gone through a lot to achieve what it has today. But to be honest you could say that I'm selfish because I'm sorry that the school is getting all of these wonderful things and I won't be there to enjoy it all because I'm going to high school.

Mariela, Maritzabeth, and Lornaliz will still attend the school and enjoy everything that it has to offer. And you know what? All of this change that has happened to our school and to the students probably is for the best. Things never stay the same, and in time everyone and everything has to go somewhere. So now I'm leaving to high school and the other girls are going to the eighth grade and everyone is moving on. I think that's mainly what we're talking about: moving on and change. In my opinion, I THINK THAT'S COOL.

Because bilingual education is such a controversial issue in the United States today, and because Maribelis, Lornaliz, Maritzabeth, and Mariela all believe that being bilingual and going to a bilingual school are very positive parts of their lives, I decided to ask Maribelis to address the bilingual education controversy directly. When I realized that she wasn't aware that there was anything controversial about bilingual education, I showed her an article that appeared on the front page of the Philadelphia Inquirer about California's Proposition 227. We talked about the controversy, and Maribelis wrote the following as a conclusion to this chapter.

MY OPINION ABOUT BILINGUAL EDUCATION

The question that I (Maribelis) was asked was, "What do you think of bilingual education?" I think that bilingual education is very useful. Whoever wants to learn Spanish or English can learn these languages properly using bilingual education. If states like California end bilingual education, that means that kids with families like mine will have a hard time communicating with their own families because they may only speak Spanish while their children can only speak English. And no one knows how hard it is to have a family or live in a community with people that can speak one way while you speak another. So I believe that whoever thinks that ending bilingual education is right, then that person is selfish and thoughtless because the decisions people make affect everyone that they're responsible for.

There's a lot of reasons to keep bilingual education. For example, students that don't know any English, like my mom and dad, didn't expect to learn English on their own. They thought that they would have a bilingual teacher to make their time here easier. But it didn't happen that way. People want to teach Spanish speakers how to speak English by putting them in an all-English class with teachers who speak English all the time. They mean well in doing this, but they are going about it the wrong way. I mean, how is a student who only speaks Spanish going to learn English, or learn math or any other subject in English, if they don't even know the language to begin with and can't understand what anybody is talking about? Now students like Lornaliz have bilingual teachers to help them learn their English and to explain how to do their other school work in Spanish.

I also think that Puerto Ricans and other Spanish speakers should be able to keep their language. If people try to stop Puerto Ricans from learning our language, it's like ordering us to stop breathing because our language is a part of us. People may not act like they want to take away the Spanish language, but they show it a whole lot. Like one time I went to New Jersey, to Wildwood, and I saw this shirt that said, "You're in America—now speak English." Anybody who sees that is kind of insulted. Our country should learn to love and take care of our language for the simple reason that we live here too. This country is known as the country of freedom and the land of opportunity. If people make it possible to end bilingual education, or take away our language, then this country doesn't deserve its name.

My last good reason to keep bilingual education is that it works both ways. Students who don't speak any Spanish who want to learn Spanish can learn to speak it properly in bilingual schools. For example, in my advisory everyone that I know can speak English and a little Spanish. Half of my classmates are Spanish descendents and the other half were born in Puerto Rico but raised in

America. Before we went to Spanish class, we all could speak both languages but we couldn't read or write in Spanish. So thanks to bilingual education we can now read and write Spanish and we can help our family members with translation. We can also communicate with Dominicans, Mexicans, and with the other Spanish speakers in school because we know how to communicate with them in their language. People don't have to feel like they have enemies or that they're alone in North Philly because we all can communicate with each other. The bilingual education program brings English and Spanish cultures together so that we can live together as one unit and not as different groups of people.

CHAPTER 2

Speaking Out Loud: Girls Seeking Selfhood

Student Authors: Quentina Judon, Jessye Cohen-Dan, Tyeasha Leonard, Sharita Stinson, and Tara Colston

Researcher/Teacher Authors: Jody Cohen and Diane Brown

When I went to school, they taught us algebra, and how to do experiments in the lab, and how to read adult books, but they didn't teach us how to be human. They didn't teach us how to relate to other people.

—Jewel, singer and pop star

People say, "Well, this doesn't concern you," they say, "You are only affected if you make yourself be affected." I don't agree with any of this. I am very affected by what is going on.

—Quentina

This (chapter) is not an explanation of who we are, but rather, a sharing of our battle to find that person. And this is about school because student is part of who we are, learning is part of what we do, and school is where who we are and want to be collides with who everyone else is, where we attempt to learn who we are and begin to understand how to be who we want to be.

—Jessye

Introduction

Jody Cohen

We live in a society that divides emotion from intellect as if people were fractions. It is no surprise then that our schools should follow suit, dividing feeling from thinking, experiential and affective from academic learning, so that

39

by logical extension we are teaching students to be fractured rather than whole. The girl writers of this chapter challenge these divisions, this miseducation. In this chapter, the girl authors reflect on their relationships with a variety of people in their lives—teachers, parents, principals, and peers. They describe a range of situations, from interactions in classrooms and encounters in hallways to collisions with school policies and representations in the media. As they suggest both implicitly and explicitly in the excerpts of their writing, Quentina, Sharita, Tyeasha, Jessye, and Tara seek to bring their whole selves to bear on the possibilities and dilemmas of their everyday lives.

When we began this chapter, the shootings in Littleton, Colorado, had not yet occurred. We did not set out to address the devastating implications of this tragedy—for ourselves or for our schools. Instead, we meandered into this writing singly and in pairs, at home and in school, on and off over many months, and with the goal of describing in students' own words their experiences as young women in middle and high school. To this end, the students wrote about what seemed important at the time: the challenges of figuring out who they are, often in relation to others; the dilemmas facing them and their friends, schools, and communities; and how school does and doesn't support their efforts to understand, make choices, take actions. It was later, as I looked back through these writings while also suffering, along with so many others, over what we needed to be giving our teenagers, that I began to hear the girls' stories and reflections as a quest for and demonstration of wholeness as opposed to fragmentation, integration as opposed to disintegration, both within the self and between people.

As Jessye says, "There are lots of times in girls' lives when things don't make sense and you feel different than your friends." In this chapter we listen to girls explore such gaps and conflicts as they seek to understand themselves and others, to assess their commonalities and differences, to handle outrage and act with compassion. They tell us about adults in their lives who hinder and those who support the girl writers' endeavors to develop whole selves from which to interact with the world; likewise, they describe institutional structures that stymie as well as those that scaffold their efforts. Within these contexts, the girls struggle to develop and maintain their integrity.

The Writing Process

In late spring of 1998 I (Jody) planned out the book chapter. I was excited: This would give me—a white Jewish woman, an educator who has conducted research with urban, mostly African-American students, and especially girls—an opportunity to let students speak and write for themselves. I would work with Quentina, a high school student and girl leader whom I'd come to know as a middle schooler, and she would help me handpick a writing group from STAR (Sisters Together in Action Research), an urban middle school girls' leadership program. We would collaborate on a piece about girls, school, and the STAR program. However, the writing took another path.

Later that summer, in the final weeks before the school year began, my daughter Jessye and I bicycled through deserted streets, only blocks from the city but undeniably in the suburbs. We talked about school: her worries and hopes, seventh and eighth grade, the supposed "diversity" of her middle school. As we sat side by side on our porch swing, careful not to touch in the heat, Jessye began to write. And in the next weeks we kept talking and she kept writing. In this way, she became the first student writer of this chapter. Her initial writing foreshadowed a direction that all of the girls' early pieces would take, as each girl set out to describe who she was in the context of her life in school.

When Quentina came to visit on a Saturday, she brought a draft of her college essay. We talked, she wrote. It was October. My colleague, Diane Brown, had begun meeting with this year's middle school STAR girls. She arranged a lunch with Sharita and Tyeasha in the school library. Again, we talked and wrote; we taped the talk, listened, and the girls wrote some more. In this fashion the chapter took shape. While I composed words on the page to stitch together the girls' writings, Diane's words and thoughts—expressed in our ongoing conversations about their writings—were woven throughout. Meanwhile, in a separate and parallel process, Sharita, Tyeasha, and Tara designed and wrote about an "action" that they took as STAR girls to influence a school policy, and in this way Tara became the last author of this chapter.

Identities and Challenges

In this opening section, the girls locate themselves in their schools. Each girl explores dimensions of her developing identity in the context of possibilities and challenges posed by her school setting. Across settings the girls share the struggle to become and to be themselves in school. As Tyeasha says, "What we do is who we will become."

Jessye Cohen-Dan

Last year my social studies teacher raised the issue of diversity in the cafeteria. She asked us to see if there was a racial mix in who sat with whom. I looked and I saw what I had always seen. In our junior high lunchroom, people sat with their friends. And as it happens, friends coincided with race. This year, at the onset of eighth grade, my social studies teacher again raised the cafeteria issue. But this year, many white students (social studies was mostly white) raised their hands and talked about sitting with their friends. A few even brought up spending their early school years in an all-white school. Hearing more teachers talk about this makes me feel like they really don't know what goes on.

Our school is split up, a lot by race or by religion. A lot of people are friends with people because of going to the same schools, growing up in the same neighborhood, or being family friends. Something else a Puerto Rican friend keeps bringing up: there are a miniscule number of Hispanics out of almost 900 students. People who do not fit in, racially, are forced to fit in wherever they can. But adults here talk as if racial diversity means having an equal number of blacks and whites. Even if we're all still largely segregated from each other.

To some people, cool means having an entourage. But to a lot of people, cool means being in an "in" group and being "known." Some people can come and naturally become leaders of a group, but I have never been entirely sure of where I fit into this dynamic. There is a guy in my school who was convinced I was Native American or Iraqi. It freaked me out a little but it was strangely refreshing. Sometimes the people in other groups accept easily. Sometimes, they don't. To me, though, it makes a difference to be able to understand different kinds of people.

When people say you're white it's like saying you don't have the black or Hispanic or Asian heritage. And more than that, it's a stereotype of middle–upper-class preppiness, a stereotype that I see is, sadly, true as often as not. I have friends in different races and religions, but I'll never be like the people who create these groups of different races, because I'm sure enough of who I am to not only hang out with people like me, or . . . maybe I'm not sure enough.

In my seventh grade social studies class, my teacher created an atmosphere where however different we were outside, inside her classroom we were all the same, and the differences we still had just added to what we could learn. We talked about intolerance and racism, we had discussions, but in the end it was each other we still looked to for acceptance, for the go-ahead. Outside in the halls we were ourselves again, and nothing had changed, and in the end we all had to walk out into the hallway eventually. In school, we discussed things, and we opened up issues, but nothing changed. School was for talking, but not for change. Maybe because no one cared enough, or maybe because they were all afraid. I say "they" because I don't mean everyone, and because I don't know if I even mean myself. I've always felt unafraid to connect with people not like me, but more and more, I realize that some of my fears and discomforts are truly there, just buried below the surface.

Although now a junior in high school, Quentina too describes eighth grade as a pivotal time in her life and particularly in her relationship to school.

Quentina Judon

Who am I? What do I represent? For these questions I have no exact answer, but what I can say is that I'm a leader. I have always been looked up to by younger children, but a lot of the time I just didn't know it or know why I was looked up to. They saw something in me that I didn't see.

In the seventh grade I felt as if the whole world was against me. I had no real friends. I didn't want to go to school so I was cutting. And at this time my family was really going through a tough time that I just couldn't get a hold to. My sister ran away from home and nobody knew why. She was always the one with the straight A's. Everybody had such high expectations for her, I guess she didn't want to disappoint anyone. My sister had ran away and taken my mother's heart with her. I knew that my mother loved me, she just hurt so bad she wasn't showing it very well. So the only thing I knew to do was rebel.

I didn't know how bad I really was hurting. The hurt was hid behind my fist. This was the only way I could live without total destruction. But I had one teacher who wouldn't leave me alone. I remember her so well. She taught at my elementary school. Then when I graduated and went to Gillespie Middle School, she came there to teach. Her name was Jean Sanders. I really didn't pay any of her speeches any mind.

Jean was always there for me. When I got into trouble (little stuff), she was right there to counsel me. Whenever I needed to talk, she was there to lend a helping hand. But even though I didn't see it at the time, my mother was there for me more than anybody. Sometimes you need to hear things from other people than your parents. For me, Jean was that person.

Jean took me in and cared, not because it was her job, but because she genuinely cared. She took the time out of her day to talk to me. She taught me there was more to life than my fist and the pain it held. She told me I didn't have to be like my sister. She said I could do anything I wanted to do.

When I made it to eighth grade, all this finally sunk in. I did my best and, for the first time since sixth grade, I made the honor roll with straight A's. But meanwhile my sister had managed to get herself pregnant. She left the baby with my family and then took off again, so I was baby-sitting every day after school. Once again my sister bows us with a strike of her mighty ax.

I began involving myself more in schoolwork, and because of my effort I was recognized for it. I was asked to be on the School Leadership Team. An organization called AAUW (American Association of University Women) was doing a documentary on girls in middle school. And I was asked to be in the research and the video because of my dramatic turnaround.

Through this organization I had the chance to travel and speak to different people, like teachers and the press. I was so scared of speaking to people, especially a large group of people. But after a while I became used to it, and actually looked forward to doing it again. This opened up many doors for me.

Sharita and Tyeasha, like Jessye, are eighth graders. They are also members of the STAR program for girls at Gillespie Middle School, where Quentina has returned to become a mentor. STAR, a school-based extracurricular program directed by chapter coauthor Diane Brown, provides a bridge for middle school girls between the narrowly defined academic world of school and the more complexly interwoven demands of life. STAR girls practice such skills as focused looking, listening, and speaking and are coached to develop empathetic awareness and the capacity to make decisions and take effective actions.

Sharita Stinson

My sixth-, seventh-, and eighth-grade years at Gillespie Middle School I've been faced with peer pressure to do drugs and cut school with my friends, and I pushed it away. A majority of the girls and boys that do that type of stuff just want to get attention, or they want to feel good, or they have low self-esteem.

Sometimes I feel uncomfortable in my school because of the boys and girls here. In my class some boys and girls feel intimidated by my intelligence and by me standing strong and proud for being the girl I am. I ignore what they say but it gets me inside. Boys in that school think I'm just another girl in that school and I'm conceited by my intelligence. Well, I'm not conceited and I am not like every girl in this school. I am my own person, I'm Sharita and I always will be.

I understand that being a girl is hard, in school, at home, and in the community. In my school we are made another statistic because of being black and young. Some girls that I know are out doing drugs, having sex, and having babies. The majority of adults think that if you do bad things such as drugs, having sex, and not attending school, you're a bad person, but sometimes that's not the case when you're an adolescent girl. I feel as though it is unfair and inhuman of a person to think that way about another person, especially if you don't even know them. Maybe that girl had too much pressure on her that she had to do these things. Then again maybe it's just being rebellious against her parents. Therefore if the girl is rebelling her parents should talk to her and let her know how things work in the world, and what's good and bad.

For the last two years of my middle school life I joined a program called STAR. STAR is a program for girls who want to find guidance in themselves and to research the answers to their questions. Not to sugarcoat anything, but STAR has been a wonderful experience for me.

The past two years of STAR I interacted with other girls in different schools and girls in my school. I learned new things and the meaning of the phrase "girl power." STAR has made me more of what I think I am in my mind, and it has also made a big impact on my life. I'm only thirteen and I feel as though I can do whatever I want to do in this male-dominated world. It has helped me to have self-motivation, self-confidence, and respect for myself. Other girls in STAR have also changed, maturity-wise, from my perspective. My mentors are the administrators of the STAR program. I admire them because they are hard workers and they try their best to keep STAR together. STAR has given me opportunities that I thought I could never get in my lifetime. When I leave middle school I want the STAR legacy to live on forever.

Tyeasha Leonard

Being a girl in Gillespie Middle School is hard. Every woman for herself. I have to worry about being called a lot of things and names every day. Most girls are more worried about other girls. You have to watch yourself and watch what you say because it can come back on you. A girl that I interviewed said, "Every time you turn around someone wants to fight you or is jealous of you, and they're talking about you and always want to start trouble."

When you walk around school you see how different girls carry themselves in many different ways. The way you act is what everyone looks at. If you talk a certain way people are going to notice. Everything you do and say is being recorded, because somebody somewhere is watching. You also are being watched more as a girl because we have more rumors said about us. A boy can do a lot of bad things and be called nothing, but a girl can just cough and be called the worst of names.

That's why self-esteem is such a great matter in being a girl. If you think a bad way about yourself, so will other people. If you carry yourself a certain way, that's what other people are going to think about you. I think this statement that teachers say every day is true. You have to respect yourself to respect others. And if you don't have respect, what do you have? How you carry yourself is a part of respect and esteem toward you and others.

Every girl wants something for themselves, no one wants to share. But we all have at least one thing in common, and that is that we are all girls and we have to stick together.

What advice do I give girls that are coming up?

The advice that I will give girls is in one word: respect.
The common key to life.
Everywhere you go you have to give it to receive it.

That's what gets you through a lot of things in life,
as well as Life itself.
Even when you want a job
you have to show respect,
when you're in school
you have to show respect.
You always have to have this as a proper manner that should be automatically
given.
Respect also includes the way you think talk and walk.
You always have respect for yourself before you respect anyone else.
So that will be my advice for girls coming up in the world today and in the
future.

I also look at respect as a big word I have used as a stand out:

Reality
Economy
Self
Proper
Enteract
Common lifestyles
Teach one another

How Girls Meet the Challenges: Decisions, Dialogues, and Deeds

In the first section of this chapter, each girl identified herself in the context of challenges in her school setting. In the second section, the girls use their knowledge of themselves and others to "read" key dynamics in their social settings and respond to these dynamics through what they decide, what they say, and what they do. Here they discuss the choices they make in their struggle to speak and act with integrity in their classrooms, schools, and communities.

MEETING CHALLENGES IN THE CLASSROOM

Jessye Cohen-Dan

To most people I probably seem quiet. Most teachers might think I have nothing to say, which, of course, isn't true, as my family and friends know, I'm sure.

I have strong feelings and opinions about everything, although my camp voted me "Most Easygoing." A lot of times I'm just thinking really hard, and people think I'm shy. In class I mostly don't say much, except in my favorite classes or in a class where we're talking about something important to me, like the dynamics of how things work in our school or issues in the world, not like the French Revolution or grammar. [A teacher] probably thinks I'm the type of student who's gonna try to just sail by. In classes like Latin, though, where I try my absolute best, I do well and so the teacher notices me because I ask questions and make improvements. I think most teachers don't look past how someone acts in the classroom.

I think though that as a person, I'm just myself, and I don't think I judge myself by the same standards that other people do. I have a set of standards that I use to think about my friends—things like smart, outgoing, funny, pretty—but I don't look at myself that way. When we look in the mirror, we try to see ourselves as transcending those labels, and as being special enough to succeed in that.

I think for most people, it's probably easier to not try, really, in school. And I felt that way for a while. While we lived in Germantown [a neighborhood in Philadelphia], it never occurred to me to do less than what I was told to in school. Then we moved and in fifth grade, I wrote my paper on the atmosphere and got an F. That's when I learned I could do badly and the entire universe wouldn't spontaneously combust. So for a couple of years I did like half good, half bad, but in eighth grade I don't know, I just sort of decided, not really trying wasn't working out that great, so maybe I should try to do real good. It's not like I'm even sure this will last past the second quarter. But I'm getting older and even if I'm not who I want to be, or where I want to be, I'm not helping anyone by merely existing.

But the weirdest part is that when I do bad, I feel like I failed everyone but not myself. I feel like I have something different to put out that is more special than what others want me to put out. And I started to want to show that I have more important things to say than an F paper because I wrote it during math class, or a D in English because I wasn't listening when the work was assigned. But whenever I start doing good, I feel like there's only this little part of me that's really getting her life together. The other part, the real me, is just sort of standing in the shadows, the me that thinks real thoughts and feels real things. While the other one is out there, with her friends and family and schoolwork, but just barely hangin' on, doing what she has to do. And I have a feeling that one of these days the two me's will collide and one of the me's will get lost in the hustle. Maybe one already has.

During the summer before eighth grade I realized that I wanted something. Funny as that sounds, I hadn't really desired anything specific for a long time. I think you begin to realize at that time that you're about to go to high school. High school. Which is a whole different story. You have so many choices and decisions in high school that you've never had before. If you decide to fail, no one's going to stop you, no one's going to save you or protect you. No one's going to make sure you're okay and that you have everything you want. So you start to want real things, things you can get for yourself. And I did. I wanted to be able to go to Central [a magnet high school in the city]. And I began to understand that no one could get that for me. I had to get it for myself. There's a time in everyone's life when they realize that there's something they want that only they themselves can get. I guess that I was lucky that my time came in eighth grade, because by the time that the time comes for some people, it's too late.

MEETING CHALLENGES IN SCHOOL

Like Jessye, Quentina tried out different versions of herself and in the eighth grade reached a decision about who she would become. Since that time she has contributed as well as learned from her position as a leader and mentor with middle school girls in her community.

Quentina Judon

Ever since 1995 I have gone to girl talk groups in different middle schools. I wanted to share my experience of life and its many disappointments but also the up side of life where there are people who care. My input and opinions were always asked. At Gillespie Middle School, I serve as a mentor in a girl talk group called STAR. I would tell the girls there about right and wrong, about not fighting (fighting was a sport in the school). But I still had this big problem with solving every problem with my fist. I really don't understand till this day what it all meant, but I do know that the girls' talk group really helped me to see that fighting wasn't the answer.

One day at Gillespie I was about to fight a girl because she wouldn't leave me alone. This girl didn't like me because she said I thought I was "all that." She thought I thought I was better than everyone else, and here I thought everyone was better than me. So she came up to me and starting talking about all the things she was going to do to me. I could have ignored that, which I did, but then she started calling me every name in the book. I went off, I was ready to "punch her lights out." Then one of the girls in STAR came up to me and said, "How can you tell us not to fight and you are about to fight?" I felt so bad, I just turned and walked away. The next day I apologized to the group for not handling myself better in that situation. At that moment they seemed to look up to me more. I guess I fixed the wrong and made it right.

Being a leader with younger girls helped me deal with a lot of things that even at this point I hadn't dealt with. I saw people were looking up to me and not down. They believed that I was something, instead of that I would never be anything. I needed this. They just do not know that helping them with their feelings and their problems I was also working out my own.

The girls [in STAR] asked me about going to college. At first my response was, "It's just more school." Later I came to realize that they wanted more than that, they wanted to know where I'm going to be and the whole nine yards. So I told them. In going to college I hope to gain more leadership qualities and maybe share with others the qualities I possess. I wish to gain the needed education to become someone who will make a difference. I believe college can give that to me.

MEETING THE CHALLENGE IN THE SCHOOL COMMUNITY

As a high school student, Quentina has also confronted the challenge of understanding a complex and volatile situation in her school community and speaking out with integrity in this context. In December, the Philadelphia Inquirer *ran a front-page article about "racial tension" being played out at one of the city's magnet high schools. The newspaper coverage featured adults' perspectives—an angry letter written by the Home and School president, the response of the principal, and comments from several teachers at the school and administrators downtown. Knowing that this was Quentina's school, I solicited her account of what was happening.*

Quentina Judon

I go to George Washington Carver High School of Engineering and Science. It is a magnet school, which means that you have to have good grades to get in. I came from middle school to Carver with seven A's and two B's on my eighth-grade final report card.

Carver is like a big diversity family. Some choose not to be a part of this family and that is totally their choice. But others enjoy the feeling of having people there for them, to help them along the way when times are hard. No matter what race or religion you are, you are a part of the Carver family.

Lately, though, George Washington Carver has been in an uproar. Myself, being a senior, I feel very affected by all that is happening. Our Home and School [local parent-teacher organization] president wrote a six-page letter to our school's principal. In this letter, according to the newspapers, were accusations that our teachers are racist. This letter was written in January and is now coming out in November. Why?

Some say it is a conspiracy. Some say it is an attempt to push our principal out of office. As for me I am not sure of its purpose but what I am sure of is that it is completely unfounded and not true.

The newspaper article about the letter the Home and School president wrote said, "The white/Jewish teachers are not providing an adequate education for the children of Carver." But then he says, "I am honored to have my son being taught under [the principal], an African-American woman." He accuses our teachers of being racist but then he himself makes a racist comment.

The fact that our principal is black should mean nothing at all. How well she does her job is what should matter. Just the fact that he would make a statement like that shows that he has no foundation for his accusations. Being Jewish should not be considered as a factor in how well you teach. Instead, it should be the method or style by which you get students to learn. What good is teaching if nobody is learning?

Furthermore, there are laws which say people are allowed to choose what religion they would like to be. A person's religion is not what makes the person, it's that person's attitude and personality that makes them who they are.

Being a senior I can say that I know the teachers here very well, better than ninth, tenth, and eleventh graders. I have had these "white/Jewish teachers" and they are nothing like the Home and School president says they are. Most of my teachers have been "white/Jewish" and they were in no way racist. They cared about getting us to learn. They did care if we didn't understand, and they would take the extra time to help us understand. He says they don't care for us, but yet they take the extra time to tutor or have activities for us. He says they are not good teachers, yet we have 100 percent college acceptance.

People say, "Well this doesn't concern you," they say, "You are only affected if you make yourself be affected." I don't agree with any of this. I am very affected by what is going on. I feel that the teachers are getting a bad rap for something they had nothing to do with. I think that the Home and School president is only making these accusations because his son is failing. If his son had good grades, what would he be saying then?

Morally, I don't see how he could stay in office feeling like this toward our teachers. How can he serve our school needs to his fullest ability if he doesn't "like" our teachers and is accusing them of being racist?

If he had a problem with some teachers, he should have asked for a conference. If he had a problem with certain teachers then he should not have made such a broad statement about "white/Jewish teachers." What he has done affects so much more than the teachers he has a conflict with. Writing such a negative letter was not the adult way of handling the situation. The Home and School president should serve as a model for the students of Carver. These are not the marks of a good leader.

MEETING THE CHALLENGE IN PROGRAM AND POLICY

While Quentina responded as an individual to what was going on in her school, as STAR girls Tyeasha, Sharita, and Tara were encouraged to martial their resources and respond collectively to an issue in their school community.

This year the STAR program has focused on the development of critical literacy (that is, using reading, writing, listening, and speaking skills to investigate and take action on relevant issues) as well as interpersonal and intrapersonal literacy (using attention to self and others to inform choices). Tyeasha connects writing and reading with her own developing identity and sense of empowerment.

Tyeasha Leonard

How I became a writer: I always had a lot of thoughts during my life. But I first discovered that I had my talent in the sixth grade when we were told to write a poem about your race and color and how do you feel about the way you are. I really reacted to this topic. When I first wrote this poem the title really caught my interest and I liked the feeling that I got when I performed it. When I got up there and performed everyone cheered and clapped, and that felt so great to me that it opened my door to really write and read educational things in my life. That was the first time when I was writing and reading about a lot of famous poets. That's always been my inspiration, and to this day I have that first poem that I wrote.

As part of the focus on literacy, STAR girls decided that as a group they wanted to read and discuss Flyy Girl, *a book about African-American girls in North Philadelphia who are dealing with many of the challenges and choices that confront the STAR girls in their daily lives. Talking about this text would enable them to have conversations in an intergenerational women's group about such "hot" topics as sexuality and sexual pressure, drugs and alcohol, and family issues. However, the school administration decided that the book was too controversial and thus inappropriate for use in a school-based program. Tara Colston, a Gillespie eighth grader and STAR girl, joined Sharita and Tyeasha to do something about the situation. In consultation with STAR adults, the three girls took action.*

Sharita Stinson

The eighth-grade girls of STAR wanted to read the book *Flyy Girl*. We had a hard time trying to get the book so we can read it. The adult leaders of STAR tried to get the book for us. When we found out that we couldn't read the book, this was a time for myself, Tara, and Tyeasha to step up to the plate.

The three of us had chose to be on a certain committee to map out a plan to read *Flyy Girl*. This plan was our first "action" plan. We started this plan Monday after school. Ms. Rhonda [an adult facilitator], myself, Tara, and Tyeasha stayed after school for about twenty minutes collaborating on ideas and coming up with specific themes that we felt comfortable to talk about [with the principal]. I worked on the parental issues, which talked about all of the concerns parents may have, and on what Mrs. Dawson's [the principal's] concerns may be. I also had an idea, which was brought to my attention by Tara, and I backed up with some other research and information I found out about other students and teachers.

Tyeasha's theme was about how the book makes us feel, what the book means to the girls, and how we can relate to the book. She also came up with how the book can save us from bad experiences, because this book deals with controversial issues like sex and drugs.

Tara was given the job of the introduction and the conclusion of our action plan. What she did was basically reassure Mrs. Dawson the plans will go into effect as agreed on. When we all were done Mrs. Dawson was ecstatic at what a good job we did by having an organized plan that was put together diligently. We took our time, and we also gave her some promises that we kept. Our promises were that we [STAR girls] would keep the book to ourselves, we would show her the progress that we made with the permission slips, and our permission slips would get signed by parents.

Mrs. Dawson's answer was yes, and Tara, Tyeasha, and myself were very ecstatic as Mrs. Dawson was. Ms. Rhonda burst into tears because of the great job we had done. I was very happy because of the work, time, and effort I put in, and Tara and Tyeasha as well. I was fortunate to work with such a dedicated team. Tara, Tyeasha, and I worked on this for long periods of time, prepared it just right so we could present it to Mrs. Dawson. I think that our presentation was great and it gave me the encouragement to do further presentations like this one.

Tyeasha Leonard

I volunteered to be part of the committee to do the action on *Flyy Girl* because this is one of the best books out there for teens, and I felt that the only way other teenagers like STAR girls would get the book's message was if we were able to read this book and talk about it. The theme that I chose for our action was why we wanted to read the book and what it meant to us. I chose this theme because the book really touched me in a special way.

I think *Flyy Girl* is such a great book because there are a lot of issues that teens around my age can relate to. Everything is centered around the area

[Philadelphia] that we live in today. This is more than just a book to me, it's more like a person I know and how they were telling a story about their life. The author wrote some good points that most girls should try to recognize about the life that we live in today. I don't think the principal would include this book for us to read in school because it's already here, this is our life.

I felt very nervous and scared when we had to present to Mrs. Dawson, even though I was relaxed with my thoughts and how I felt about the book. But overall, the discussion was great. We got what we wanted and what we expected. Mrs. Dawson told us that when the [STAR] adults came to her she did not budge, but when Tara, Sharita, and I went to her in such a professional way she said that we could read the book, we just have to give out the permission slips and then everyone will receive the book. I am proud of all of us who have achieved our goal.

Tara Colston

My feelings about the action that Tyeasha, Sharita, and myself worked on were good. I think it was a good experience for me. It made me feel as if I could do anything I put my mind to, as long as I worked hard for it. The project made me feel more self-confident. I think Sharita and Tyeasha liked the experience as much as I did.

When we all got together and started thinking of ideas we did pretty well. I thought of the idea where we make up permission slips for the STAR girls to give to their parents to sign. Sharita thought that it would be good for us to share an excerpt from the book with the parents, which led into the discussion of parental issues. That was basically about what we felt the parents might ask questions about. Pertaining to that, we drew up a list of questions that Mrs. Dawson and the parents might have, and answered them as best we could. That theory helped a lot because the questions we brainstormed happened to be the actual questions. Tyeasha thought that we should explain to Mrs. Dawson about how the book *Flyy Girl* related to us and how it touched us in a special way.

So after we presented to Mrs. Dawson we received an answer: The answer yes! She said that if we were successful with the permission slips we could do it. Mrs. Dawson was pleased with our hard-earned achievement and efforts, as were we.

Once again it proves my point of if you put your mind to something nothing can stop you. I think you should always shoot for high goals.

Below are several artifacts that track the girls' follow-through: their letter to the principal confirming their agreement and expressing their appreciation; a permission slip for parents of STAR girl participants; and a contract for STAR girls themselves that lays out the terms.

2-11-99
Dear Mrs. Dawson,

We the girls of STAR, Tyeasha Leonard, Tara Colston, and Sharita Stinson, would like to thank you for the time that you have given us to propose our actions. It was a pleasure meeting you women to women discussing women-to-women issues as adults. We really appreciate the time you took out of your business schedule to listen to our opinions. It shows that you deeply care about the students in Gillespie Middle School, and the students really need a principal like you. Once again we really want to thank you for your support.

STAR

Dear Parent or Guardian,

Your child _____ will be given the book *Flyy Girl*, which is about an inner city girl growing up in Philadelphia. Tracey, the character the book is based on, is going from a child into an adolescent girl. This book is a very wonderful book and it has controversial issues. It is wonderful because it adds life to literature, grabs the reader's attention, and girls can relate to Tracey's experience. It is controversial because it has themes of drugs and sex. The benefits we feel in reading the book in our STAR club is that we learn not to make the wrong decision in our lives, and we will talk about its controversial issues with our STAR adult leaders. If you have any questions or concerns, you may contact Ms. Rhonda, Ms. Diane, and Ms. Pat.

Dear STAR girl,

We would like for you to sign a contract promising not to let anyone read your STAR book. The action committee made a promise to Mrs. Dawson that the material will not be released to anyone under any circumstances. We trust that you will live up to your promise and commit to STAR.

I _____ promise to not share my *Flyy Girl* with any of our peers.

X _____.

Concluding Reflections

Jody Cohen

This year the STAR girls created a quilt. Each girl used fabrics and other materials to compose a square that was a statement of herself and also of the collective. One girl made tiny representations of her family members, another included a briefcase to signal professional intentions, a third created a beautiful collage of fabrics to suggest her own beauty and the beauty of STAR. A quilter is currently working to stitch these varied squares into a work of harmony in diversity.

Likewise, this chapter presents the stories of five girls, distinct both within and among, stitched together with words that seek to illuminate each while also weaving together the whole. Like each girl and each story, "the whole" is neither singular nor inevitable but is about many things. We have chosen to weave together the squares using as stitching the girls' efforts to become, to voice, and to enact their whole selves; we use these threads both because tracings of this process are in evidence across the girls' writings and because events in the world have made abundantly clear the need for schools to help young people to develop and honor these very capacities. Quentina's response to the situation at her high school is just one instance that suggests how much adults have to learn from young people—about how to look and listen, about how to learn from and live with others who are different from ourselves, about the link between leadership and respect. Looking beyond racist stereotypes, Quentina asks us to know and appreciate people for who they are, for their ethics and commitments.

In the writings for this chapter, these girls demonstrate their striving to look and listen, to pay ongoing attention to their own and others' struggles, and to make thoughtful choices about what they say and do—often without the benefit of schools' recognizing, legitimating, and teaching these skills. They seek to create and act from whole selves, with integrity, both individually and in concert with others. What if schools acknowledged and coached young people in developing such crucial capacities as self-knowledge, relationality, and internal strength, so that students became fluid and fluent in their awareness of themselves, in listening to and really hearing the concerns of diverse others, in negotiating relationships and institutions? Some schools have begun to recognize the importance of this work and are trying out programs that "[make] emotions and social life themselves topics, rather than treating these most compelling facets of a child's day as irrelevant intrusions" or cause for disciplinary measures (Goleman 1995, 263). We suggest that schools could play a critical role in supporting young people's development as whole human beings—responsible for who they are and are becoming, deeply connected with others, capable of difference and even conflict infused with respect.

As we talked and wrote last winter, well before I had begun to think of the chapter in these terms, Tyeasha foreshadowed this theme in her excited description of a classroom where young people would investigate the very questions and dilemmas of their "so-called outside life." As she reflects later, "I'm basically talking about a class where kids can take care of their outside life and learn how can you deal with the things you do every day."

Tyeasha Leonard

I want to be a teacher, I think I have a lot to teach. I want to make up a new class called social life—everything that's happening out of school and how people feel about it. This would be a good class because everything that happens in the so-called outside life of school most kids bring in school, like their feelings, behavior, and speech, and if we were to give a class on this issue maybe more kids would act better toward their education and look toward coming to school and maybe be a better student. We'd talk about questions like, How do you feel about your way of life, your life, yourself? It would be a great class, every boy and girl would have straight A's in that class.

Reference

Goleman, D. 1995. *Emotional Intelligence: Why It Can Matter More Than IQ.* New York: Bantam Books.

CHAPTER 3

What's Your Bias? Cuts on Diversity in a Suburban Public School

Student Authors: Kristin Dunderdale, Sara Tourscher, and R.J. Yoo

Researcher/Teacher Authors: Ondrea Reisinger and Alison Cook-Sather

Introduction

Ondrea Reisinger and Alison Cook-Sather

R.J. was generally the first to arrive at the coffee shop where we met to work, with Ondrea, Alison, and Kristin next. Sara almost always came late, rushing in breathless with a bag of bagels to share with the group. Soon the two tables we pulled together were covered with notebooks and napkins, cups of tea and coffee, and a variety of bagels. After the quick check-ins about schoolwork, cheerleading, band, and other life activities, we reminded one another of what we had discussed the last time we met and what we hoped to accomplish at this meeting. Then R.J., Kristin, and Sara would begin to share the stories they had written about different kinds of biased treatment by teachers the three students had experienced, witnessed, or gathered from their peers.

Sara usually led the discussion, drawing on the multiple pages she had written, talking and gesticulating rapidly and with little hesitation. R.J. preferred to read directly from the pieces he had written, which were crafted and polished into animated narratives. Kristin often chose to share her pieces last, and her contributions were carefully researched, drawing on the perspectives of friends and of students with whom she had not previously interacted. As each student author shared his or her story, the other two offered questions and made connections to their own stories. Alison and Ondrea listened, sometimes laughed, sometimes shared their surprise or dismay.

After every story had been shared, Ondrea or Alison asked everyone to step back and think about what sense they could make out of the stories and what the most important points they wanted to be sure to emphasize in the chapter might be. Based on the students' analyses, Alison or Ondrea suggested a next step—what we should all do in preparation for the next time we were to meet.

What we describe above was a typical work-session, each of which lasted about an hour and which we convened approximately once a month during the fall of 1998. At these meetings we developed a fairly comfortable and effective dynamic, but they were not without moments of tension, uncertainty, and hesitation. Who should lead and who should follow? How much did Ondrea's and Alison's identities and presence as teachers influence what Kristin, R.J., and Sara wrote and said? How honest should the students be? How directive should the researcher/teachers be? These questions remind us that teachers and students sharing and coconstructing their understanding about issues of teaching and learning is a complex and challenging process.

This chapter emerges out of an ongoing project[1] that has at its center a vision of teachers and students engaging in dialogue with one another about teaching and learning. R.J.'s, Kristin's, and Sara's different styles of participation in the working sessions for this chapter illustrate that students have different approaches to sharing and analyzing ideas. As teachers, our (Alison and Ondrea) hesitations and our attempts to offer guidance reflect the challenge we felt of finding a balance between listening to and leading students. The animated interactions we had as a group suggest that teachers and students can work together toward better understandings of students' experiences in school if the process is one of ongoing sharing and negotiating.

This chapter offered us a unique opportunity to invite high school students to think and write about some of the issues they feel teachers should consider. When we chose the student participants, we did not have any preconceived notions about what the topic of the chapter would be. Because we were already engaged in an ongoing project that elicited student perspectives, we felt comfortable from the beginning leaving the choice of topic to the student authors. What we did feel committed to was not simply eliciting student stories as a starting point for recasting them as another kind of prose. Rather, we wanted the student authors to tell their stories in the way they felt most comfortable and analyze them using their own categories of analysis.

After an initial brainstorming session in which a number of possible topics were proposed, the student authors chose to focus on diversity, and they wrote and gathered stories in response to the following question we generated as a group: What experiences (good or bad) have you had, witnessed, or heard about where differences or diversity of some kind affected a situation in school? The stories they gathered focused most often on race, ability, and gender. Drawing on the stories Kristin, R.J., and Sara told, as a group we discerned categories that they would use to frame and analyze the stories. The categories reflect what the student authors felt that teachers and prospective teachers should keep in mind—lessons from the field from the perspective of students. The categories we agreed on were:

1. How teacher bias leads to differential treatment based on labels, stereotypes, and teachers' perceptions of students' abilities.
2. How teacher bias leads to differential treatment based on race.
3. How teacher bias leads to differential treatment based on gender.

To help Kristin, R.J., and Sara approach the analytical portion of this chapter, we asked them to address four questions for each of the categories of stories:

1. What messages about what and who matters are these stories sending to the students in the stories?
2. What assumptions are teachers in the stories making about students?
3. What insights/lessons should future and practicing teachers take away from these stories?
4. Anything else you want to say about this set of stories?

What emerged out of this process are the stories and analyses that follow. These are only three students' perspectives, and they are not meant to be inclusive or exhaustive. They are stories that the student authors felt were important to tell so that teachers who read them might begin to reflect on the ways that their teaching affects students. The student authors emphasized in our discussions that even well-intentioned teachers can cause conflict and discomfort and perpetuate stereotypes.

Because the focus the student authors selected was diversity, let us introduce ourselves in terms of the dimensions of diversity explored in this chapter. As we mentioned earlier, all of us have participated in an ongoing project that brings teachers and students into dialogue with one another about pedagogical issues.

• Kristin is a Caucasian female student who participated in the project in 1996 when she was a sophomore enrolled in regular education classes and identified as a learning support student at Stonybrook High School.[2]
• Sara is a Caucasian woman who participated in the dialogue project in 1997 when she was a senior enrolled in both honors and regular-level courses at Stonybrook High School.
• R.J. is a Korean-American male who participated in the project in 1997 when he was a junior enrolled in all AP- (advanced placement-) level courses at Stonybrook.
• During the first three years of the project, Ondrea, a Caucasian woman in her thirties, was an English teacher at Stonybrook High School (she has since changed schools). She has been teaching high school English for eight years.

- Alison, also a Caucasian woman in her thirties, is a former high school English teacher and currently is an assistant professor of education and director of the bicollege, undergraduate education program at Bryn Mawr and Haverford Colleges.

This chapter is divided into three parts, each focused on a different dimension of diversity identified by the student authors as significant at Stonybrook High School and each of which includes stories of teachers' treatment of students based, in the students' assessment, on that dimension of diversity. Each section includes stories gathered by all the student authors, and each section is framed and concluded by one of the student authors, drawing on the analyses of the stories all three students wrote. The heading of each section reflects the guiding question the student authors used in gathering their stories.

How Teacher Bias Leads to Differential Treatment Based on Labels, Stereotypes, and Teachers' Perceptions of Students' Abilities

INTRODUCTION

R.J. Yoo

These specific stories were ones that were about differential treatment based on students' abilities. From reading these stories, the reader can pick out many problems and perhaps think of some solutions to these problems.

Sara, Kristin, and I all believed that in these stories the teachers were assuming too much. The teachers assumed that each child could be on the same level of learning, or that students would feel great about themselves by hearing how much "smarter" they are than someone else. The teachers also assumed that they know who the "smart students" are and this leads to favoritism.

The message I saw that these stories were sending out to students was that teachers think that by complimenting and comparing the students, the students will feel better and like the teachers more. In fact, that kind of complimenting and comparing does the exact opposite by shocking and embarrassing the students. Sara and Kristin thought that another message from these stories is that the teachers seem to have a certain standard that they expect students to strive for. In these particular examples, the teachers' standards seem set by the AP classes. By setting such standards, the teacher creates an uncomfortable and negative learning environment by comparing all students to AP standards. Teachers put pressure on students who try their hardest, yet students may be unable to attain such a high standard.

SO INTELLIGENT THAT GRADING ISN'T EVEN NEEDED

This story was related by the character known as Kerrie in the story. Kerrie is a Caucasian female who is at the top of her class in twelfth grade.

Kerrie and Elizabeth were chatting one day after English class. They were both excellent writers and in the AP English class. They had just gotten back their papers that day. "What'd you get on your paper?" Kerrie inquired of Elizabeth.

"Another hundred," replied Elizabeth nonchalantly. "How'd you do?"

"Oh, I got a hundred, too," remarked Kerrie. "This class seems so much easier than last year's. Don't you think?"

"Yeah, it does," replied Elizabeth. "You know what Mr. Parsons told me? He said that sometimes he doesn't even bother reading carefully with my papers. He knows that I'm a good writer, so he doesn't expect anything less."

Kerrie hid her emotions with a shrug. She could not believe that Mr. Parsons would do such a thing. To learn that a teacher would have so much favoritism as to lessen the severity of a grading system was disturbing. She couldn't complain because she was getting good grades, too.

The two split off to go to their next classes, each holding their papers in hand.

THE MIXED OUTCOMES OF TEAM TESTING

The student who told this story is a Caucasian, tenth-grade female in the regular track.

I was on my way to my third period algebra class, when I remembered that today was team test day. The teacher was going to match us up with another student in the classroom and we would take the math test together. The team pairing was based somewhat on grades. Mr. Flynn, our teacher, tried to match up the students who seemed to be understanding the concepts easily with the students who seemed to be struggling.

When Mr. Flynn first told the class about this testing procedure some people worried about their grades and their partners. He assured us that the grades of the students who normally did well on the tests would not suffer just because the students had to take the test with someone else. The motive behind the team test was to help the students who were struggling with the material get a better grade and understand what we were learning more thoroughly.

I was one of the students in the class who studied hard for the test and algebra was one of my strengths, so I figured that I would get paired up with someone who needed more help. I got paired up with someone who was a friend of mine, and it was also helpful for me to take the test with another person.

Even though this system of testing can be beneficial for some people, there can be some bad points to the system. There were students in the class who were struggling with math who got paired up with "smarter" students and the struggling students ended up not feeling good about themselves.

NON-AP PROJECTS ARE AWFULLY PATHETIC

R.J. uses the personal "I" in this story to reflect that he personally witnessed and was involved in this situation. R.J. is a Korean male in the gifted track as an eleventh grader.

Jason and I were very nervous. Today was the day we were to give an oral presentation of an historical era. "Well, Jason, today's the day," I said.

"It's our first AP project," replied Jason. "How do you think we'll do?"

"I have no idea," I returned. "All we can do is pray that our presentation takes ninety minutes." Fists clenched, we started our presentation. Feeling nervous at first, our voices were shaky and we stuttered a lot. As the clock ticked away, the two of us became more comfortable and the words flowed more easily. When the bell rang, Mr. Smithe called Jason and me over to his desk. "Absolutely marvelous presentation you two!" exclaimed Mr. Smithe.

"Really?" Jason and I questioned.

"Really," replied Mr. Smithe. "You had a lot of information, a wonderful presentation. The movie clips you added were a nice touch, too. You two looked like you had complete control and knew everything that was going on." Jason and I looked at each other and let out sighs of relief.

"You did much better than the students that had the same topic as you in my second-period class," Mr. Smithe stated. "They were so unprepared and sloppy. I should have you two come into my second-period class and give them your presentation, so you can show them what a good presentation looks like."

"Thanks very much, Mr. Smithe," we replied with startled looks on our faces. We walked out of the classroom and headed toward our next classes.

"That was so unfair that he compared our project to his second period's," I said.

"I know," replied Jason. "We're an AP class, and they were the regular class. It's stupid that he would compare the two different levels like that. I hope he doesn't grade the second period's really bad just because we did well." We came to an intersection where we separated to go to our different classes. As I walked alone to my next class my mind dwelled on the comments that Mr. Smithe had made. His comments sounded as if he would grade the second period's projects on the same scale as my AP class's. I thought that it was wrong that he would do that, but what can I do?

WHEN COMPLIMENTS FEEL LIKE NEGATIVE COMPARISONS

The student who told this story is a Caucasian, eleventh-grade female in the AP/ honors track.

I have seen firsthand how teachers judge their students based on their abilities. I was in an AP American government class my junior year. Although there were problems with the class, we had some excellent discussion. At times, however, Mr. Hayes made remarks about the discussions they had. He didn't hold back about the kinds of discussions he had in the other classes. For instance, he would say: "See, I could never have that conversation with my retard classes." This kind of comment ruined all of the positive energy coming from the discussion. It was quite possible that he was trying to make us feel good about ourselves, but he only created an environment that put students in a difficult situation.

EDUCATION BELONGS ONLY TO THE GIFTED

The student who relayed the information used for this story is represented by the character named Henry. Henry is an Indian male in the gifted track and is in twelfth grade.

It was yet another boring day in Mr. Harding's class. Henry looked around at his classmates who, like himself, were nodding off to sleep. Mr. Harding's class would get boring rather quickly, and Henry would find himself looking at the clock often. Henry came to attention when one of his classmates had answered a question correctly.

"Excellent," Mr. Harding exclaimed. "This is why I enjoy teaching the AP course so much. You're all bright students, full of excellent questions and answers. You guys understand everything so quickly. I wouldn't even begin to teach this to my second-period class." Henry could not believe what he was hearing. To learn the fact that a teacher would blatantly not teach information to a class just because they were not AP was disturbing. He could see that the second-period class was being discriminated against, and he felt totally hopeless. He was one student, how could he make a difference?

SPAZZING ABOUT GRADES ISN'T EVERYTHING

The student who told this story is a Caucasian, eleventh-grade female in the AP/ honors track.

In high school I was not much of a spaz[3] for grades. I didn't let wanting to ace everything overcome me. To me, learning was more important than grades. Nevertheless, in some cases I was really upset by grades. In all of my classes, there were people (mainly girls) who cared so much about their grades that they would spaz out before a test, outline the chapter word for word, spend the entire weekend on a four-page paper, which they could have written in half the time just as well. These people let their spazness show to their teachers and it doesn't take long for the teachers to pick out which students will be getting the A's, and which ones the teacher will have to read. I have seen it happen where two people could work equally long and hard on a paper and the A student will get the A and the other student with an almost equal paper will get a B. Some students work hard as the spazzes, even though they don't put on such a display.

CONCLUSION

R.J. Yoo

Sara, Kristin, and I all feel that teachers can take away many lessons from these stories. They should not compare students, whether according to who gets better grades, or who is in what class/level. By comparing, they show favoritism for the "smarter" students. They should realize that each class must have a different grading standard based on ability. The teachers should also take an equal amount of time grading each student's work. They should not assume that an "A" student will always get A's. By doing this, it shows that the "A" students can turn in lesser quality work and still receive a good grade. If the teacher can just assume that the "A" students will always get A's, then why not assume that "C" students will always get C's? Perhaps a "C" student had wonderful ideas and worked very diligently preparing a marvelous paper, and it is returned to him with a C. This destroys the student's self-esteem as well as his will power to do any work. Therefore, you can see our point as to why teachers should look at each student's work with equal time and effort.

How Teacher Bias Leads to Differential Treatment Based on Race

INTRODUCTION

Sara Tourscher

In many of the following accounts teachers assume that students will not be affected by what teachers say and do. These assumptions take a number of different forms. For example, in some instances, a teacher assumes that if no one in the class is of a particular race, no one will take offense at a comment made about that race. In other stories, we see that teachers/administrators make an assumption that because of a student's race she knows about that race's culture. In yet others, the teachers feel it is their job to entertain the students and they don't realize that their racial jokes or conversations are offending anybody. The bottom line is that these assumptions send a message that students can be treated differently because of their race.

TOO CLOSE FOR COMFORT

The student who related this story is Caucasian female in the regular track in her junior year.

When my friend was a freshman in high school, this girl that he knew and lived near was going out with a black man and she was white. One of her neighbors found out about this and he went from door to door along with his wife and told all the neighbors what was going on. He felt it was his job to tell everyone, so they could all show how they were not going to let this happen in their neighborhood. The worst part is that the man was a teacher at the local high school! So every day when those two students went to school they had to face this teacher who got her whole neighborhood against them.

LET THE PUNISHMENT FIT THE CRIME, NOT THE COLOR

The student who related this story is an African-American male in the regular track in his senior year.

One of my friends had this teacher who favored blacks over whites and was very open about it. One day these two kids got in trouble for doing the same thing and when they approached her desk she gave the white student hell and said nothing to the black student. In the end she gave the white student a detention and told the black student not to do it again.

Another thing that she did was that in class she would try to embarrass and give a hard time to the white students while she would go easy on the black students. She would also give the third degree to a white student who made excuses about homework and not question the black student. I know students who get her in class and try to change classes because they do not feel like going through that discrimination. They would rather get a teacher who is much harder academically than sit in this teacher's class.

YOU'RE INDIAN, SO WHAT DO YOU THINK?

The student who told this story is a Caucasian, eleventh-grade female in the AP/honors track.

I used to love American history; the subject was interesting. I decided to take Advanced Placement American history. I learned a lot in the class about the subject, but history is not all I learned in this class. My teacher, Mr. Griffin, did not mean to be insensitive to his students; he just was. I've seen this characteristic in many teachers so I am led to the conclusion that this example is not isolated. In class one day we were discussing different cultures. Mr. Griffin called on the only non-Caucasian in the class: "Nitu, you are Indian, why don't you tell us about your culture." Taken off guard by this question, my friend didn't know whether to be hurt or appalled or both. A better way to handle this situation would be to ask if anyone wants to add anything rather than assume that a student of the said culture had something to add.

Assuming is a big mistake. Teachers should not assume that students want to talk about their ethnic or racial backgrounds. Teachers shouldn't even assume that students know about their cultures or practice their cultural traditions.

It's important not to single students out because of what you think they have to say. And, Caucasians have heritage, too.

DO AS I SAY?

The student who told this story is a Caucasian, twelfth-grade female in the AP/honors track.

Advice from teachers can be very helpful for many students. I had one teacher my senior year who loved to tell our Advanced Placement American government about his views on everything. He always followed his comments up with: "Now this is only my view, which you are free to disagree with me. . . ." The typical "what you are supposed to say to not get in trouble." It helps if you mean what you say, though.

Mr. Phylle, my teacher, spent many class periods talking about things happening in the news, issues pertinent to our lives, etc. However, his views held sway in the conversation. One day we were talking about China and he made a comment, which the majority of the class found extremely humorous. He said, "My generation is safe, but you guys better watch out because those people in China are not going to be sitting on their rice patties forever." He continued by explaining to us how one day they are going to use their numbers and take over the world.

I was shocked and angry to hear my teacher, someone who is supposed to be a role model and mentor, make such an inappropriate comment. I was also ashamed to be part of a school community that would find that comment entertaining.

Mr. Phylle's comment illustrates that teachers need to be careful what they say to students. Comments like the one made by Mr. Phylle not only insult students; they also make possible the idea that students can make racial slurs and they won't be punished. The teacher, whether or not he or she knows it, sets the example for the class.

Teachers need to set a good example for their classrooms. They can do that by watching what they say, recognizing their prejudices, acknowledging them, and keeping them in check.

WE'RE ALL LISTENING

The student who told this story is a Caucasian, twelfth-grade female in the AP/ honors track.

I have found that teachers take cues from the students based on who makes up the class. In one of my classes we only had one non-Caucasian student, and he was rarely in class. I guess Mr. Peabody figured that because no one in our class was African American, he was free to say things that he might not have said had there been African Americans in the class. For instance, in a discussion about welfare, indirectly the conversation was mostly directed toward African Americans. A lot of generalizations were made about how people on welfare think about education, occupation, etc. I was upset that my teacher was generalizing saying, "They don't care . . ." I asked him how he knew what "these people" thought; had he ever spoken to any one of them?

I love class discussions but I need to feel secure in the topic. I feel very uncomfortable when I sit out of the conversation, when I don't want to participate because I get so angry by what people, including my teacher, say. Teachers should try to keep the class in check.

AN EXTRA PUSH

The information from this story was gathered from a male of Italian heritage in the gifted track in the tenth grade who is called Frank in the story.

Frank stood in the band room along with many of his friends. They would always socialize in the band room before heading their separate ways. That day's topic was one of great interest to Frank. One of his friends, Kaitlin, was talking about her schedule. Frank looked at her schedule and noticed that major cultures was missing. This would be a problem for Kaitlin, since the class was needed to graduate. "Did you notice that you don't have major cultures?" Frank inquired. "You should get that fixed."

"Oh, I talked to Mr. Barrett about that already," replied Kaitlin. "I felt that I didn't need to take major cultures, because I already know a lot about different cultures, and since I'm Indian, I have a background of a different culture."

Frank felt a little angry. He felt as if he had been cheated out of an opportunity. He was from another background, so why should he be any different from Kaitlin? But he knew that he would be turned down if he went to ask of the same favor from Mr. Barrett. After all, Kaitlin was ranked number one in their class, and was also in many more challenging courses than he was. Angry and frustrated, Frank departed for his class as the bell rang.

CONCLUSION

Sara Tourscher

All of these stories deal with students being treated differently, either directly or indirectly, because of their race. Teachers should respect their students enough not to judge their race. Students will appreciate it, even if it means that some students will stop getting preferential treatment, because all students will be treated equally and fairly.

Teachers shouldn't make assumptions about how their students will react; I don't want teachers to assume that I will let racial jokes slide because I am white. Furthermore, teacher comments may insult someone even if she is not in the room.

Education is not only for a certain race, it is for all. Everyone has their prejudices; teachers need to be aware of their prejudices. By knowing themselves they can be attentive to the choices they make.

How Teacher Bias Leads to Differential Treatment Based on Gender

INTRODUCTION

Kristin Dunderdale

The three stories about gender bias all focus on teachers being biased against boys. Although there was no example of boys receiving better treatment, I am sure that there are teachers that will give the females a rougher time and absolutely adore their male students. But even when the girls get supposedly better treatment, it doesn't make them feel better because it sends the wrong message.

For instance, these stories send the message that if you're a girl, wearing short skirts gets you better grades than working hard. But female students don't want teachers to try to make things easier for them because they are women.

These stories seem to show that it can be easier for one sex than the other to be able to succeed. In the first story the message is that girls need help to win a game that they shouldn't. The second story is sending the message that if you dress sexy you will get a better grade no matter how much better your presentation is. The third story is about harassment.

A LUCKY WIN?

The story was shared by the character represented as Michelle. Michelle is a Caucasian female in the gifted track and in the ninth grade.

Michelle sat looking bored in the classroom. The teacher said, "All right class, now it's time to play a review game! It will be the boys versus the girls." Michelle smiled at the thought of this battle of the sexes. As the game commenced, she realized that the girls would lose. She watched as the teacher asked a member of her team a question.

"What is the tallest mountain in the world?" the teacher inquired.

"Mount Olympus?" the girl replied.

The game went on like this, and Michelle became worried because it seemed hopeless. The point difference was too great for the girls to come back. But then the teacher turned to the girls' team and said, "All right. I'll give you one chance to win. Here's a fifty-point question. Who was the third president of the United States?"

"Thomas Jefferson," Michelle replied immediately. The boys were outraged at this. Michelle looked at the situation in her mind and thought, *This really is unfair.* There was no way that the girls should have come back. That last question was really stupid, too.

"Okay, now we'll split into groups and do group work," said the teacher. "Oh, and girls, make sure the guys do some of the work, okay?" Michelle sat in shock at this apparent favoritism toward the girls in her class. She felt that something should be done, but what?

IT'S HOW YOU LOOK, NOT WHAT YOU SAY AND DO

This story was told by a Caucasian female in the regular track of her junior year.

There is this rumor that goes around our school that a certain male teacher gives a female student higher grades on a project if she wears a skirt or dress on the day of her presentation. Now I do not listen to rumors, but I had this certain teacher and I wanted to see if it was true. One week each student was given a topic but the teacher did not have enough topics so some topics were given to two people to do. The students could not work together because he wanted to see how each student did his or her own work.

On the day of presentations two girls presented the same topic. The one girl had on a skirt and a sweater and the other one had on a baggy sweater and jeans. I really listened to both reports and thought that their reports were really quite the same. They had close to the same facts and their visuals were both really good. I personally thought that the girl with the baggy clothes on did a little bit better on her presentation and the way she explained everything. But the next day when I asked both girls what they got, the girl with the baggy clothes got a B and the other girl with the skirt got an A.

A (TOO?) STRONG COMPLIMENT

This story was provided by the character known as Leslie. Leslie is a Caucasian female who is in the regular track and in the eleventh grade.

Leslie walked through the corridors that led toward her next classroom. She liked to dress nicely for school, rather than follow the crowd and wear the common jeans and T-shirt combo. She was dressed in a skirt, buttoned-down shirt, a black coat, and heels. She thought about her next class: "I hate going to this class. It seems like Mr. Smithe is flirting with me all the time. I heard so many things about him from kids that had him last year, too."

While continuing her walk, she was stopped by a tap on the shoulder. There stood Mr. Smithe. He stood there smiling at her. "I'm sorry Leslie. I thought you were a teacher for a second there, because you look so mature from behind."

Leslie just smiled and played along with him. She continued walking and thought, "He's my teacher. This is wrong, but what can I do? He might hate me and it might affect my grade."

CONCLUSION

Kristin Dunderdale

These stories show how uncomfortable students can get if teachers treat them different based on their gender. Teachers should stop and observe themselves to see if they have any favoritisms. They should realize that the classroom should be an environment of equal opportunity for each and every individual. In particular, teachers should not treat genders different. They should be honest and fair. Each gender has to be challenged! Teachers should treat people equally. That's it.

Final Thoughts

Ondrea Reisinger and Alison Cook-Sather

For the last five years, we, the researcher/teachers, have been learning from students—constructing dialogues between high school students and preservice teachers and listening to what they have to say. And yet we are continually amazed and inspired by how much students think about their own education and how their attention demands ours. The all-too-prevalent image of students as apathetic, disaffected, or disengaged was proven false by Sara, R.J., and Kristin, as it is every time we invite students to offer their perspectives on school and schooling. In working on this chapter, we learned again that students think deeply about educational issues, they have striking insights into them, and they have a great deal to say about them.

In listening to, reading, and discussing the stories with Kristin, R.J., and Sara, we were reminded of how much students attend to and discern teacher biases, whether or not those biases are intentional. It was striking, both at the outset and throughout our work together, how quickly the student authors could recall a significant number of experiences and stories of biased treatment of students, and it was equally striking how powerful these experiences and stories are. Students pay attention to a great deal more than the content of what they are being taught. They remind us that everything we say and do as teachers—tone of voice, gestures, side comments, references, kinds of questions and responses to student work, unintentional comparisons—sends an array of messages to students that they absorb perhaps even in greater quantities and with greater consequences than the content to which they are exposed. R.J., Kristin, and Sara did recount positive stories as well as the negative examples included here; however, they decided that their point would be better made with examples of what not to do in the classroom. At our final meeting, the student coauthors emphasized that teachers who are aware of their biases can be positive role models for their students. Thus, Sara, R.J., and Kristin offer us a reminder to check ourselves for our own conscious and unconscious biases. They remind us to attend to each student as an individual worthy of respect.

Students are not only interested in their own experiences. As the above stories and commentary illustrate, students recognize inequities and injustices that affect others, and they recognize some of the ways in which they are unfairly privileged and are bothered by that as well. Their stories illustrate that what progressive, critical educational research tells us schools should be like are the same things that the students want. But they are also telling us that we are not there yet. One way to help us move toward those ideals is to keep asking students for their perspectives and listening to what they have to say.

Notes

1. Our vision of teachers and students learning together took its first form in 1995 with a project we designed with the support of the Ford Foundation. We maintained this project the subsequent year without grant support, and we then received a three-year grant from the Arthur Vining Davis Foundations to continue the project. Sara, R.J., and Kristin are three of the forty-eight high school students who have participated in this project during the past four years. Based in the curriculum and pedagogy seminar Alison teaches at Bryn Mawr College—the methods course preservice teachers take prior to their student teaching semester—the project offers a forum within which preservice teachers and high school students can explore together pedagogical issues raised in the course and in their own experiences. Students who participate in the project range in ability levels and experiences (special education through gifted) and grade levels (tenth through twelfth) and are of different racial and cultural identities. The project includes weekly meetings between Ondrea and the high school students at the high school; weekly meetings of the preservice teachers and Alison in the curriculum and pedagogy seminar at the college; a weekly exchange of letters between the high school students and their college partners; and a final analysis paper, drawing on all of these sources, written by each of the college students.

2. Stonybrook High School is a pseudonym for the suburban public high school that the student authors attend or attended.

3. Spazzing means being hypersensitive to and somewhat out of control in one's attitude and behavior toward something—in this case, grades.

CHAPTER 4

Cutting Class: Perspectives of Urban High School Students

Student Authors: Fredo Sanon and Maurice Baxter

Researcher/Teacher Authors: Lydia Fortune and Susan Opotow

Introduction

Susan Opotow

During the past two decades, class cutting by high school students has increased dramatically. Cutting occurs when a student comes to school, is officially marked present, but selectively misses, skips, or "cuts" one or more classes during the school day. In some urban public high schools, more than half the students cut one or more classes a day on a regular basis (Opotow 1994; Opotow, Fortune, Baxter, and Sanon 1998). Cutting only one class can be an innocuous decision, but cuts add up quickly.

With even a few cuts, continuity is lost, classes become difficult to follow, homework becomes difficult to complete, and tests become harder to pass. Then test days are cut. Grades suffer, and students fail class. As progress toward graduation slows, students become discouraged. Because this process is difficult to reverse, cutting becomes the process of dropping out in slow motion—a series of seemingly insignificant decisions made class by class in students' everyday lives. Not only does cutting lead to negative outcomes for students, but it also has negative outcomes for schools as funds and professional energy are siphoned into security rather than educational initiatives.

Antidotes depend on a better understanding of cutting. When schools seek solutions, however, they often occur as administrative directives with students' voices and perspectives missing. To understand why students cut class and what can be done about it, this research turned to those in the best position to understand, explain, and advise what to do: high school students.

Two years before work on this chapter began, several high school students, a graduate student, and a social psychologist began meeting at a Boston high school to analyze a set of qualitative data on cutting. These data, which had been collected over the past few years by high school students in New York City in open-ended interviews with peers, explored what class cutting meant to students. To analyze these interviews, the social psychologist sought out high school students as expert informants who could interpret data from the students' perspective. The group met weekly during the class period of a cooperating teacher. Their data analysis strategy depended on reading, thinking, and talking together to understand the data and identify relevant themes. Discussions were audio-taped, transcribed, and themselves became data that tracked the process of analysis.

During the two years of analytic work together, the composition of our group changed. Several students left the school, but two, Fredo Sanon and Maurice Baxter, remained. Both students displayed a considerable talent for data analysis. They initiated additional data collection to test their ideas and ground their analysis in the experiences and thoughts of their peers. They conducted focus groups in classes and at a youth conference to hear what other students had to say about class cutting. They also designed and administered a survey to learn about the prevalence and rationale for cutting among students. They analyzed these data and presented their findings to teachers, parents, and administrators. As the third year of our work began, Jeff Shultz and Alison Cook-Sather invited us to contribute a chapter to their edited volume. Their vision of the book challenged us to consolidate what we knew about cutting and to find accessible ways to explain it. This chapter integrates more than twelve hours of discussions about the content and organization of the chapter that occurred in ten meetings during one academic year.

Fredo Sanon and Maurice Baxter began our work by selecting four transcripts from the previous year to review. They chose transcripts that included many students' voices: one was a workshop on cutting they led at a conference for middle school and high school students in the greater Boston area; two were focus groups conducted in classrooms; and the fourth was a video in which they discussed cutting with two other students. These four transcripts prompted further discussions that fleshed out ideas we saw in the transcripts. Our analytical discussions continued to revisit these ideas and elaborate on them. This process of elaboration permitted us to consider ideas in depth and from multiple perspectives.

After three meetings, the students asked Lydia Fortune to distill our discussions (which had been transcribed) into a working chapter draft. She did this by searching for "threads of conversation" describing Maurice and Fredo's understanding of the process of cutting. She selected and connected the text on topics such as boredom, teacher-student relationships, and substitutes, which surfaced and resurfaced in our discussions and that Maurice and Fredo identified as important. Her initial chapter draft, like the five drafts that followed it, prompted further discussion that clarified our thinking and refined the chapter.

The chapter text, while based on our transcripts, is not itself a literal transcript. It is instead a synthesis of transcript-based discussions. It translates spoken into written language, the result of Fredo and Maurice's request that we "clean it up" so that it reads well. "Gonna," for example, is translated into "going to." The chapter includes several talking points by unidentified students from the original four transcripts that prompted discussion on our part. We structured the chapter with headings. Because many causes of cutting are interconnected, however, there is some overlap among our subtopics. The student–researchers felt that this permitted the rich interplay among these topics to remain evident.

Why Do Students Cut Class?

SCHOOL IS STRESSFUL

STUDENT IN FOCUS GROUP [transcript]: The reason why kids cut class is because school is boring. Teachers should worry more about teaching than talking to each student in class. Shorten the class day to save time. More field trips for students and activities for school.

FREDO: This is the sort of thing that kids feel. School is stressful. I mean you should learn but also enjoy it at the same time. You can go on a field trip and make it something you can learn from. It doesn't have to be Water Country [an amusement park]. It can be the museum of science. Something like that.

STUDENT IN FOCUS GROUP: Students don't like class when it's boring. When the teacher doesn't make the work interesting kids don't want to do it. And they probably have more fun outside of class.

FREDO: Kids want to get out of school because they think it's more fun out of school and because school is so stressful. Teachers need to make students want to come to school and enjoy being there. When you are in class and you lose concentration, you are tempted to just leave. That's the boredom thing again. If students are not actively engaged they lose concentration. Some people don't, but some people do. They just get stressed out. Some people think that if you don't have that motivation you are a bad kid or a bad student and you don't want to learn. That's not true.

STUDENT IN FOCUS GROUP: You can't make school not boring. School's got to be boring.

FREDO: That's just not true. That's some of the influence that some kids have already about school. This could be a freshmen in high school or even a middle school student because we had all types of kids there. If you have somebody *that* young thinking that school has got to be boring they're not going to want to be there. They're not going to want to come. There are some kids who'll come the first week of school and then they'll never come again. And that's not too cool.

MAURICE: I think we need to elaborate on the word "boring." Different definitions keep popping up every time we say that word.

FREDO: Boredom is not being interested. Not wanting to do something.

MAURICE: Boredom is one person doing most of the talking. You are not doing anything. A lot of kids that we talked to said that teachers make it boring. I think in some cases teachers do make it boring. But in some cases students make it boring. Because if you know you are not getting good grades in that class and you know there is a chance you might fail then you're going to get bored because you don't want to do that work. I'm not going to do the work if I am going to fail anyway. If you know you're doing good in class and you know you've got a chance at straight A's in that class, you're not going to be very bored. You're going to look forward to going to that class. You want to get good grades. You want to prove somebody wrong.

FREDO: He's speaking on a one-kind-of-person basis. Maurice likes good grades. He'll work for good grades. The class will be boring and he'll still try to get good grades. And that's basically what he's saying. And other people—for instance like me—I'll still try. But if the class is boring, I'm going to try only to a certain extent. If the class is real boring, I'm just going to say, "Forget it. Just give me the homework." Not everyone tries that much. But if you help students try then things could be different.

MAURICE: I'm not one of those people. Fredo said I'm going to try and get good grades. I *am* going to try and do that. But I am also going to know if a class is boring. If a class is boring to the point where I just don't want to do anything, I'm not going to do it. But the thing is kids are going into class thinking the class is going to be boring. So when you have that mentality already it's like, "I'm not going to do any work because it's boring." What kids need to know is that it's their responsibility to do work right now. Because at this age, until you're sixteen, seventeen, eighteen or whenever you get out of school, it's your *job* to go to school and to get good grades. Because there's nothing else you're going to do. You can't get a job because they're going to say you've got to go to school. Kids have to motivate themselves instead of putting all the blame on the teachers. It is a fifty-fifty thing from where I stand. How you do in school will eventually determine how you do in life. If you work hard and listen, you will be successful. If you don't work hard and you don't listen, you will have a hard time.

FREDO: What you said is real good. Real good. But the motivation part—again, it's your job to come to school. It's your responsibility. I feel that way. But what I'm saying is a lot of kids don't feel that way. Some people wonder why we have so many "bums" on the corner doing this and doing that. It's because you can say a certain high school teacher didn't want to take that extra time and put that extra effort in to make that kid want to learn. That's all I'm trying to say. What Maurice is saying is that teachers are not supposed to make you want to learn. That is to me basically what he said. Teachers are not supposed to pull you to learn or do this. You are supposed to do this by yourself. Some people can do it by themselves and some just cannot. They just do not have the ability. What I'm saying is if some teachers took that extra time and really tried to pull you in, some things could be different. That's all I'm saying.

MAURICE: You can't blame teachers for causing "bums" on the street. If the teacher did not put that extra effort in then you can't blame the teacher entirely because the student is supposed to want to do good in class. He isn't supposed to say "If the teacher isn't going to do it why should I?" Just because he ends up being a "bum"—that does not mean that teachers made him do that.

FREDO: If they try to make the kids want to learn, kids would come to school more often and try a little harder. But if you make the class boring, some students will try and some students just won't. And the students that won't will just stop coming to school and everything will be messed up.

STUDENT–TEACHER RELATIONSHIPS

STUDENT IN FOCUS: I think one reason why some students don't like their teachers is because some teachers really don't know how to deal with certain classes that they have and certain students that they have in their classes.

FREDO: A point that we should make in the book is that they should start having classes for teachers so that they can learn how to teach and deal with different types of students. Letting them know that not every student is the same. Each student is different. Some may be able to take criticism. Some may not. Some may be sensitive to it.

MAURICE: I think he means that teachers should make class special for students. Students do not like to sit in the class, get lectured throughout the whole class. Kids want to be active in class. Kids like to talk. Kids don't like it when the teacher says "Be quiet. I'm talking to the whole class." Maybe for parts of the class kids want to get involved.

FREDO: How can a student succeed without getting a chance? Some teachers cut you off because of what they see of you in the hallway. Like they see you are hanging with the wrong kids—whatever. Teachers are just looking at you to do one wrong thing and you are out. It could be dropping a pencil or it could be someone else who did something and they say you did it. Some teachers just don't want you there. They may not want it to come out that way but a lot of teachers make it seem like, "I don't like you. You don't have to come to my class." They don't say it to you but the way they talk to you, you can see it. The way a teacher talks to one kid and then the way he talks to you. I have one teacher who will talk to one student with a soft tone. Then when he talks to me he feels that he must bring some force deep inside of his voice to make him sound all tough. I will think in my head, "Why are you putting this front up? Why are you acting this way?" I don't know. There are some teachers who constantly, constantly—I mean they will actually stop the whole class if you are not paying attention and bring you back into the lesson. There are some other teachers who will say, "You can put your head down. Do what you want. Don't bother me." Okay, there are some kids—I can't deny it—who don't come to school for the right reasons. Then again, there are some that do come to school but are not motivated.

MAURICE: And then there are some teachers that will tell you, "If you're not here to learn I'm not going to force you to learn. I'll just help the kids that want to learn." Some teachers will tell you that up front. And those teachers are the teachers that come to school and teach. They don't want to waste their time on the knuckleheads or clowns. I like both kinds of teachers in a way.

FREDO: Sometimes we're told we are not meeting expectations. We are supposed to be leaders of the school. It is like you are almost supposed to be a robot and you are not supposed to make mistakes or have any flaws. Sometimes teachers come in your face and are just talking, talking, talking. It is too stressful sometimes and you just want to get away. In some classes, it is like, "Oh, yeah. We have that guy again." Sometimes it gets to the point where you would like to do work but he is not letting you because he is sort of just yelling at you.

STUDENT IN FOCUS GROUP: If my teacher's not teaching me anything then I'm going to go to [my job and] work. I'm not going to sit here and waste my time and twiddle my thumbs when I could be doing something productive.

MAURICE: Productive is the keyword.

FREDO: Some students don't understand what they are working for. So in a way you have to see and understand what you are working for and what it is you are trying to do. School should be something productive. Like for the future. That's what you're working for—the future—so you can get a better life. I don't think teachers are *that* bad. I was with a teacher today and she was telling me how she is taking a class on how you can engage kids in learning and how you can involve them more. That is already starting and I think it is really good.

MAURICE: I think that teachers care for kids to an extent. Their job is just to teach. As long as they're a good teacher I'm not going to hate them for not spending extra time.

CHANGING GEARS IN THE SCHOOL DAY

FREDO: In a lot of classes it's: doing that, doing that, listening, okay, we are almost done, doing that, doing that, and then the class is ended. Then you have to go to the next one, then you have to do that, do that, do that, then the class is ended. You do that for the whole day, then they want you to go home and do homework, homework. Or you're working hard in one class and they want you to come and switch to the next class. It's not that easy for kids. Some kids can't. When you have English class you might be enjoying it and you are reading something about *Hamlet* or writing a poem or something like that. You might be enjoying what you are doing and then you have to go to math class. Then you switch again. . . . Or maybe you start to doubt yourself: "Maybe I'm not as smart as that kid." Some kids at the conference were talking about alternatives—study halls or two periods together would be less stressful. Sometimes on a Thursday or Friday kids have four tests in one day. I mean, how's that? The night before— even that week—you have to sit and cram for tests. That's not cool! It's not easy! Most adults don't think so but teenagers like to have an outside life and hang out and have fun. Students have lives outside of school. Basically I don't know what teachers who give you 300 pages to read in one week are thinking. But we don't go home and read a whole book, write notes, then go on to our next assignment, do four pages on that, and then write a lab report.

MAURICE: Yeah, because we work all week. We work Monday through Friday. We expect to catch some slack on Saturday and Sunday. You think you have had it good the first five or six classes. Then the last class: "Hey, do a four-page report and it is due on Monday." Kids don't like that. Say a teacher says we have a vocabulary test on Monday. All weekend kids don't do anything. Then they come in: "Oh yeah. I forgot. We got a vocab test on Monday." Students are going to cut that class because they did not study and they don't want to get an F on that test. They might take that Monday to study and take it on Tuesday. They will then have a better chance of passing.

TAKING ADVANTAGE OF SUBSTITUTE TEACHERS

MAURICE: Most of the time when we have a substitute, we have fun.

FREDO: I mean you can't stop cutting but when a substitute's there it's like, why *be* there?

MAURICE: It's like a two-way street. Some kids will go to class and see a substitute and then they will walk right out the door. Some kids see their friends and they stay the whole period. So, either way you put it, they are going to have fun on their terms. Substitutes don't get as much respect as regular teachers do because the students say, "Well, I'm not going to do any work. This is time for me to rest, make up some homework, and go out and get something to eat." They do whatever they want to do when the substitute is there. Basically, respect—well, substitutes don't get it.

FREDO: Students could walk in and the fact that he or she is a teacher or that he or she is an adult—so we should shut up and listen? Most of them are substituting for Spanish class but majored in math. So that won't help us out at all. Maybe if the substitute majored in math and it was a math class and he or she was good at communicating with people, we'd be able and he'd be able to get involved and learn. There are some substitutes who are good and you actually learn when they're there.

PEERS AND PEER PRESSURE

STUDENT IN FOCUS GROUP: One reason kids cut is because the "wrong people" are in the class.

MAURICE: I think that's an interesting point—"'wrong people' in the class." There are kids who go to class because they want to learn and kids who go there just to irritate the teacher purposely. I was just in class. There were some kids like that in there. They want to sit outside and smoke or come in class and be loud. They are disrespectful toward the teacher and that's another reason why kids are stressed out. Some kids are serious about school and the disrespectful kids distract the kids who are interested and want to do the right thing. Kids are more apt to listen to their fellow peers. If there are ten kids in the class who always hang out and eight of them decide that they don't want to go to class, I would say that there is more than a 90 percent chance that the other two are going to go with those other eight kids. Because peers have a real big effect on other kids.

PATROLLING THE SCHOOL

STUDENT IN FOCUS GROUP [in response to the question "What can stop cutting?"]: I mean, you make up a rule or have "sweeps" like in my school. People still cut classes though.

MAURICE: What's a "sweep"?

FREDO: It's what we had last year when security use to come and "sweep" all the floors and any kids that were in the hallway would get kicked out.

MAURICE: Oh. Like it's sixth period and it's thirty minutes after the period started. If you're in the hallway and you don't have a pass, you are asked, "What are you there for?"

FREDO: It's not just like you can make a rule and people automatically are going to stop what they are doing because they're afraid. If students have problems with teachers they're going to find ways not to be in class. Even if it is a really smart or bright student with lots of potential—they will stay out because of problems with a teacher.

MAURICE: If security was around they would tell the kids to get back to class. If security sees that the kids cut a lot then they could just kick them out of school. But cutting still continues to grow. I don't see it lessening any. Security is not a part of the solution, certainly not a big part.

FREDO: I don't think it is a part of it at all. I mean let's say you went to Disney World. Would you see security? Of course there is security, but is there really that much security when you think about it? If kids want to stay in school, we would not even need security to watch the doors. Cutting is not why we have security there. Security is here for fights or kids having arguments and for people trespassing on the school property. Security should not be there to watch who is trying to sneak out of school or who is sneaking back in. If school were more fun security wouldn't even have to worry about them sneaking in or out. Maybe if security happens to be walking around and sees a kid leaving they can try to force him to stay, but if a kid wants to leave, what is the point in forcing him to stay in school? He is either going to be disrupting the class or doing something negative. Disney World wants you to be there. Disney World wants to make their money. Teachers say, "I'm going to make my money anyway. You do what you want." I think there is too much of that. Too much of teachers saying that you can leave if you want. We should not be in the situation right now where this many kids leave school. When I'm in class and there is a door right by, I see tons of kids walking out. Just walking out.

FOOD: ANOTHER PIECE OF THE PUZZLE

MAURICE: You don't eat breakfast at home. If you eat it at home you would be late for school. They don't give you any breakfast that you would want to eat. Bagel or something. At lunch time we'd like to go outside instead of staying in the school all day. We'd like to get out more, socialize, and communicate between classes. Things like that.

FREDO: We get up at 6 A.M. and don't eat anything until 2 [P.M.]. Most people do not have any time in the morning to eat at home. Can't blame the school for that. Maybe the school system but not the school. You need a nice lunch. Cutting is also about food. It is just a different part.

MAURICE: I was going to leave school today for food.

FREDO: Food is a big part. Not just food, but good food. Kids are going to the sub shop because of the school lunches. No one really wants to eat a sloppy joe or whatever. Not all kids who cut are bad. They leave for different reasons. I don't eat lunch in school. I can tell you myself that I have left school to go to the sub shop and get something to eat. If they made an attempt to make the school lunch a little better, in a way, fixing the system.

What Can Cure Cutting?

STAYING INVOLVED

STUDENT IN FOCUS GROUP: You can't stop cutting classes in school.

FREDO: You cannot stop cutting classes, but you can make it less tempting. Sort of on the same line as before. Just make it more—I don't know—just make it better. Cutting is based on being stressed and bored in class and things like that. Make school more active and less stressful. A day like today was a pretty good day: We had a college fair and we got to go down to the gym, and now we're doing this [research project]. You start to enjoy things like that. If we had to do things like this in class it would be cool.

MAURICE: I agree with a lot he said. Kids—we've got this tendency: If we're bored we're not going to hear you. We're not going to be bored for too long before something else comes up. So we've got to stay active. Teachers ought to make class that way. They are in charge of everything. Active is just getting people involved. Everybody wants to be involved, whether it's putting in their little two cents—being able to raise their hand.

FREDO: You know I was in science class the other day and I couldn't stay quiet. I was always talking. But the teacher was doing something or showing us something. He's the sort of a teacher who knows how to handle the class because he'll say, "Fredo, you come and hold this. We'll have Fredo hold this." And then when I held it I just forget about what I was saying and I just get involved in what he's saying. It was like involving me and I just tried a little more.

MAURICE: We've got some teachers we can walk up to, see them in the hallway, and start a little conversation with them. They tell us how we are doing in school, how we are doing in classes. I like that because it shows that the teachers really care about us—not just in the class but outside the class, too. They are leading me toward the right direction, making me want to go to class, and making me want to get those extra grades that I know I'm capable of.

FREDO: Students have to be accountable and responsible for their actions. It is not good to cut at all. Even if you do cut for positive reasons and get a permission slip you still have to come back and make up that work. So you can't say, "It is not fair. I'm not doing this. The teacher does not like me" and all that other nonsense that kids try to say. We are talking about kids that do not take advantage of their education. A student at our conference workshop talked about kids in Somalia who do not have an education. But here we do but we don't take advantage of it.

MAURICE: Somalians, if given that opportunity, might come over here and get straight A's.

FREDO: That is why most foreign kids who do have the opportunity to come here do as well as they can. Everyone would like to be involved but I think that some people learn not to be involved.

MAURICE: Yeah, people who are really quiet.

FREDO: They learn that though. When some kids learn that the teachers are not going to involve them, they are not going to try. And then there is the teacher that comes around and tries to involve you and you are like, "What are you doing? I'm not used to this. Get away from me."

ENJOY LEARNING

FREDO: Not boring is just being interactive, doing things, and having a conversation in class. Like when you get to debate about certain topics that you like. Like in science. It's a really boring class and sometimes you have to take notes. But then when you get to go in the back and experiment with things and do things like that, it's the fun part. I can understand when you have to take notes and prepare for a test and do homework but that's short-term boredom. But then when you get to see this maybe explode or you get to create water or when you get to do all these things that you never knew before, then it's really interesting and fun. And that's the good part—just interacting, engaging, and having fun. Most teachers think it's just about writing out the dictionary and this and that. I mean, you can learn that way but there are so many other ways you can enjoy what you're doing. Sort of like middle school when you do more activities and things like that. Like when I was working at the aquarium last summer, I used to go out to community centers. We wouldn't just go and tell them information. We'd come and bring animals to them, let them see the animals, and let them touch the animals, and let them enjoy it. At the same time that you're learning something new, you are having fun.

INVOLVE STUDENTS IN MEANINGFUL DECISIONS

FREDO: Kids should be involved in decisions made by the school and concerning the school. Kids are the ones using what the school does. Sometimes the school puts money into ridiculous things that we don't like.

MAURICE: Schools make decisions that the kids don't like at all. They might buy a whole bunch of Spanish books when kids need a whole bunch of math books. I don't know a lot of decisions that this school makes but I know that a lot of the kids don't like some of the new things in the school. They don't like the fact that the school fired a whole bunch of teachers that the kids liked—and that they did not bring anyone back in to replace them. So now we have all these substitute teachers in most of our classes.

FREDO: I think students should be the number one priority. I think when something's going to happen the students have to agree with it. If they are thinking about what kind of teachers to hire, they should ask the students. If they want to know what kind of cafeteria food, they should ask the students. There are so many things—like Maurice said—in the school that they're trying to fix, but they're trying to fix it the way that *they* want it. And that makes no sense. It doesn't matter what they want because they're not going to be using it. It's the students. And I think there's a lot of students who want to speak out like we do and they just don't have the opportunity. Maybe if we had more of a student voice instead of just saying that there are class representatives to make actions or something like that. At the beginning of the year they were voting for senior class president. Only seniors were voting. And kids were like, "Why can't we vote? What is the deal with that?" Then they elected a class president and it is just like a name on the wall. I don't see or hear about any meetings. I don't know what it is like in other schools but this is now and it is here.

PEER LEADERSHIP

FREDO: When students first enter the school they are looking for a guide, in a way, a path to take. If you have someone who the students can look up to and they can see you doing this and doing that the right way they don't want to get caught up in doing other stuff. You do not want to get caught up in just preaching at them, but sort of being a big buddy.

MAURICE: Someone you can relate to.

FREDO: Teachers also. Because not enough teachers sit down and talk to you. I mean, it does not even have to be about school—just about life in general. Not enough teachers do that. Maurice and other students my age are not really looking for leaders right now. We are talking about younger kids—when you first come into high school. Because you are coming from middle school and middle school kids do not cut too much because the ones that do get suspended or expelled or things like that. So, when you come to this school and you are fourteen, it would be good to have an eighteen- or seventeen-year-old always talking to you and telling you positive things to help you.

MAURICE: I agree with what Fredo said. We are not robots. We are just human. We don't like to rush to class. I can understand the part about us having to be the role models because we are the better part of the school. But I don't think we should be role models for the kids that don't want to do good. There are some freshmen and sophomores that I talk to all the time, you know. I say, "Aren't you going to class?" when I see them in the hallway. I'm just talking to those kids because I like them. I took an interest in them, you know. I'm not going to go up to the kids who I never see in class and say, "Why aren't you in class?" That's a waste of my time.

FREDO: I could understand the role model part that they are talking about. Think about it. If I was a student, for instance, and got all A's and Maurice was the star player on the football team, kids that come into the school are going to look up to him more than they look up to me. And if Maurice is speaking positive things to them they will sort of go on to those positive things. But if Maurice is speaking negative things to them they are sort of going to lean that way too. And if I'm saying: "You should get A's. You should do this and you should do that. And when you are eighteen you should vote"—they are just going to say, "Shut up! Who are you?"

GET RECOGNITION

MAURICE: My first year I was real good in the math class. The teacher would give us the work but she wouldn't help me because she knew that I already knew it. So she would go to the kids that needed the help. She would put them all in a group and I'd work by myself. And after a while I asked her, "How come you didn't help me?" She said, "'Cause I already know you know the stuff. I just want to get all the other kids, you know, up to your same level." At first I thought that she didn't like me. Then I realized that she was going for the good of the other kids. Because when I gave her my work to check she said, "Yeah, it's all right. Yeah, it's all right." Every time my work was all right. And I liked that.

FREDO: Maurice said that kids like to be congratulated when they do good things. And different kids are encouraged differently. That is true. It is like what Maurice was saying about math class and how he was doing good. The teacher really did not have to do anything to him. She would just work with the other kids. In another way, it can go on in sports. Like last year I was playing varsity and Maurice was playing junior varsity. Maurice was sort of doing all the work and then he felt that he wasn't getting picked. The varsity coach came up to him: "Don't worry. I see what you are doing. Just keep working on your game and you will be up there with us next year." It made him feel sort of good because he thought he was getting no recognition for all his work. And now he was seeing that somebody was noticing him. Kids need that schoolwise, sportswise, work—anywhere. Some kids that don't have support. When they come home their parents don't push them to do homework or their parents don't put college in their minds. It's like they're not really thinking about it half the time. And then when college starts coming around and the teacher starts asking them—"So what are you doing to get into college?"—they're just like, "Wow. Oh, I wasn't even thinking about that." And you could be seventeen or eighteen and still doing that.

MAURICE: It's harder for some kids when they come home and are on the honor roll, get straight A's, and their mother will say, "Okay. That's good." Kids don't want that. When they get on the honor roll they want people to say, "That's a good job. I like what you just did. Keep it up. You can go to college with this. Be whatever you want." Kids need support like that. Especially at a young age because that will stick in their minds.

FREDO: That's right. Like he said, when students get all A's they want to come home and have their parents to say, "Wow! You did a good job." And then when their mother gets on the phone and talks about them and says, "Look what my kid did! Look what my kid did!" But there are so many people—they see you have a bad grade and they say, "Wow!" They start laughing at you. I mean, that kind of puts down a kid a little. Some kids want to work harder. Some kids just want to quit. When you get straight A's you should be rewarded. But I also think kids should be rewarded for more and different kinds of things, like sports accomplishments and outside-of-school community and service accomplishments. Things like that.

COMMUNICATE AND RESPECT

MAURICE: You can't have good communication without respect. If I don't respect you we can communicate. But what I am saying would not be what I am honestly thinking because I do not respect you. So respect and communication go together.

FREDO: Disrespect is talking and looking the other way. If you are not respected you don't want to talk to the person. And there's another way of noncommunication. If you don't respect the person they take it the wrong way. I think a lot of teachers take it the wrong way a lot of times and get into conflicts and big misunderstandings for no apparent reason over something like, "You dropped that." Respect that goes both ways is encouraging everyone to communicate together, resolving conflicts as they arise on all levels of the school, and encouraging students' input and feedback. Without respect, you can be ignorant toward the other person.

MAURICE: We've got some teachers we can walk up to, see them in the hallway, and start a little conversation with them. They tell us how we are doing in school, how we are doing in classes. I like that because it shows that the teachers really care about us—not just in the class but outside the class, too. They are leading me toward the right direction, making me want to go to class, and making me want to get those extra grades that I know I'm capable of. You don't always have to say something to them. Just acknowledge someone. Just know that they're there. When you walk by, give them a little nod or something.

FREDO: I think that teachers work differently with different students. Like when they talk to the student who does so well more than the others. A lot of teachers today try to stick with the students who know what they're doing and don't need any help rather than trying to move on to the students who are having a difficult time. They sort of leave it up to the students to come to them and bring their problem to them. If you think that a teacher doesn't like you, or is disrespecting you in a way, you're going to start disrespecting him or her. "I'll just sit over here doing my work and when I'm finished I'll never take your class again." Communication is something that is getting more complex every day. The respect part is not that big of a problem at the beginning. At the beginning is cooperation and staying engaged. Once you lose that, you'll start to be ignored, and once you ignore a person, that's when you lose respect for them. So then everything is messed up. So I guess at the beginning it's really staying engaged and cooperating. Once you stop being engaged you lose concentration and then you start to ignore the other person. Then there's no more input, no more feedback, nothing. In a way, when you're bored, you're cutting your imagination off, and you're not thinking about anything.

BE ABLE TO ENVISION A GOOD FUTURE

FREDO: I have a real good relationship and a nice time with some teachers. We talk and we laugh. But then when we have to work, we work. Like we said, some parts of school just have to be boring. If you are just in math class and you are just doing math problems or you are doing your homework, it kind of has to be boring. But there's always that fun part that you know you're looking forward to and that you know is going to come. It's sort of like when you were little and there was a real nasty cereal that you had to have but there was always a prize at the bottom. Your mother said you could only get the prize if you ate all the cereal first. That's what you had to do to get it. In school sometimes you have to do the work to have fun. And sometimes you do the work to do the work and to get a better grade to get ahead. There are a lot of prizes in the future for us. We're saying for now, keep the students engaged. Most people who dropped out of school are probably bored by now, maybe from not working at a good job or from having to struggle and do many things that are not fun. People who stuck with it, went to school, and are probably doing what they want to now and are having the best time of their lives. It's almost like when you're bored, then you get stressed out. If you get bored too much, then it kind of leads on to other things. You start getting depressed and you want to leave that place but you'll be depressed going into another place. You carry it with you and it's hard to continue doing good work. I think that's what happens to a lot of people who cut class. The boredom carries on, they get stressed out, they get depressed, and they say, "I don't need this. I mean, this is not doing anything for me." Like I said before, you don't catch too many straight-A students cutting school, or leaving school, or saying, "This has nothing to do with me." Once you stop believing in your own future it's hard to do anything no matter what anyone tells you. They can say you have the ability or you were doing so well before. But it doesn't really matter if you don't believe in yourself or your future.

MAURICE: That pretty much says it all.

Looking Back: How Has the Research Process Been?

FROM THE STUDENT RESEARCHER PERSPECTIVE

FREDO: It's like what we've been talking about. We were always talking about how cutting class did this or that. But when we started doing the surveys and the presentations we found out how and why. And it was real. It was there. Instead of us listening to what the students in the transcripts were feeling, we got to feel it. I guess the research has helped us to come to understand a reality. It makes you understand that it is not just you—that there are other things going on.

MAURICE: Other horizons. Other peoples' points of view.

FREDO: We were not listening to just one. We were listening to a whole lot of different people and then we would compare them. And then we found out that all of them were different and none of them were the same. When you start to hear that over and over, it kind of sticks. Then we noticed what we thought was not what they thought. It sort of grew on us.

MAURICE: Keeps your mind open. When I went over to Africa I was not closed-minded. I was going to try new things. I was not going to be over there like I am over here. Not stay to one group but get out and do more things. I did a lot of things.

FREDO: If we are debating in class we will not just go for what the teacher says. We will try to go a little deeper. Dig out the roots. Like in Mr. _____'s class. He thinks from all points of views and things like that. But then he will say something and I will say something different. He knows what he is doing. He is making us talk. I will say something different and, you know, we are just pulling different ideas up. And he is writing everything we are saying on the board. Then we pull it all together and see how it relates.

MAURICE: Sometimes students have their own little discussions. Like us, the fellows in the class. The class can be getting boring sometimes so we will all talk about what the teacher was talking about. Talk about it among ourselves. And we will have six or seven different opinions on the same thing.

FREDO: All good opinions that they relate to each other but are different. We don't take over. We listen to what they have to say.

MAURICE: We say our part and then it goes to the next person.

FREDO: You do have to start something. Once you start it up they will talk, talk, and talk. So basically Maurice and I will start it off and they will just go on and go on.

LYDIA: Were you already doing that kind of discussion before you ever started this project?

MAURICE: I don't think so.

FREDO: We did not discuss things—maybe sports or something. But now we really get into some good topics about politics or history.

SUSAN: What do your friends think of this research project?

MAURICE: They think it is cool. Sometimes we will go to them after this and start a little discussion. They will ask what we did.

FREDO: Usually right after we come from this we will start a discussion. They will ask, "What did you all do today?" The research was fun. I liked it because it was hands-on. I like debating. I give my part, you give yours, and we each comment some more. You get to learn a lot of things. We talked about some interesting topics. We really got into discussions and broke down why kids cut class. We were really committed. We wanted to know why.

MAURICE: It was a good year. We were doing the same thing over and over but in some way it always changed and we ended up somewhere different. Every time we talked we came up with some more elaboration or more detail. If we just did it the first time it would not have been the same because it would have been done in one time. And every time we came in we had something different. It was the same thing but different outcomes. It got better. Things kept coming out of it. We did get a lot out of it. Not just the research part, but the skills we got out of it: the patience, the reviewing things, just learning things, working with people, accepting other people's views, respecting their views, and trying to get one bigger or better view—trying to pull it all together. Like if I say something you all would listen and maybe you all would have something to add and then things would get better out of that process. We would all add a little something and it was like that the whole time.

FROM THE ADULT RESEARCHER PERSPECTIVE

Lydia Fortune

For me it has been fascinating to observe the journey that Fredo Sanon and Maurice Baxter undertook while working on this research for the past two and a half years. They have moved through stages of initial curiosity and temporary boredom to becoming the central voices in this project. It became clear that they wanted to find creative ways to make the discussion of cutting more useful in their lives. One idea led them to design their own survey questionnaire to explore the reactions of their peers regarding the issue. Soon after, other opportunities presented themselves.

It has been exciting to watch them latch on to such skills as analyzing materials, organizing their thoughts, identifying key points of information, and planning events. Planning seemed to be a new skill and was initially resisted because they viewed it as a potential threat to spontaneity—"going with the flow"—and placing a script ahead of the people present. However, the value of it became clear as time went on.

In coming full circle, the young men have gone from successfully presenting lively and informal workshops for their peers, to discussing critical issues and statistics about cutting with parents and teachers in a more formal setting. The seriousness of their insightful observations, their refreshing directness, and their heartfelt honesty energize this important work.

Their learning experiences speak to the nature of cutting as we have come to understand it under their guidance. The cycle of boredom for many students seems to be, in part, a response to feelings of initial exclusion. Without a clear indication or invitation from teachers that active participation in the learning process is welcomed, inclusion is not possible for many students. The young men disagree as to where personal motivation comes from (internal versus external), but they are both saying that the opportunity to have a voice and to participate is crucial to feeling connected to the learning experience.

Susan Opotow

Fredo and Maurice—classmates, teammates, friends, and coresearchers—see schooling quite differently. Their distinctive perspectives suggest the breathtakingly wide range of reactions, opinions, skills, concerns, and interests that students bring to school. Although the chapter highlights their thoughts and understanding, they are not only expressing their own ideas and experiences; through data collection and analysis and their skill at perspective taking, their dialog takes account of many students' voices.

Fredo and Maurice agree with teachers that students' personality, motivation, maturity, and foresight are an important aspect of cutting (Opotow 1995). Their analysis goes further, however, and focuses on the context in which cutting occurs. They identify cutting as a symptom that a key learning relationship has floundered or is severed. This learning relationship, an unspoken but powerfully motivating compact between teacher and student, depends on mutual recognition, involvement, enjoyment, communication, and respect. They also identify the social context of this learning relationship as important. It is more likely to flourish in schools that value student engagement in the decisions that affect their lives and learning. Schools, in turn, are embedded in a larger society that holds more promise for some than others in career attainment. As Fredo and Maurice point out, when students see a desired future that they can attain for themselves, school has more meaning.

Thus, they identify loss of hope in the future, an inhospitable institutional environment, and the lack of meaningful, collaborative relationships at the heart of cutting. Without a sense of hope, justice, and connection, the difficulties of learning outweigh its joys.

Fredo and Maurice served as our guides and teachers throughout this project. Our relationship could not have occurred without the interest, support, encouragement, hospitality, and bravery of our cooperating school. Cutting is a closeted issue in education and is rarely discussed openly. The school's willingness to host our project and squarely face a difficult issue has, we hope, the potential to benefit many students, educators, and schools.

References

Opotow, S. 1994. "'Breaking Out': Cutting Class in an Inner-City High School." Paper presented at the annual meeting of the American Psychological Association, Los Angeles.

Opotow, S. 1995. "The 'Cutting Epidemic': How High School Students and Teachers Respond and Adapt." Paper presented at the annual meeting of the American Psychological Association, New York.

Opotow, S., L. Fortune, M. Baxter, and F. Sanon. 1998. "Conflict, Coping, and Class Cutting: Perspectives of Urban High School Students." Paper presented at the Society for the Psychological Study of Social Issues biannual conference, Ann Arbor, Michigan.

CHAPTER 5

An Education for What? Reflections of Two High School Seniors on School

Student Authors: Steven Marzan and Amy Peterson

Researcher/Teacher Authors: Ceci Lewis, Scott Christian, and Eva Gold

What is it that students go to school for? The common answer, of course, is to "get an education." My question is: An education for what? To teach children how to think better? Or is the education system a very expensive mass baby-sitting place, as an eighteen-year-old senior whom I interviewed puts it?

　　　　　　—Amy Peterson, Buena High School senior

Okay . . . I'm going to start this with a story, or a type of personal experience that has a major point that needs to be proved. It's about the school system, their curriculum. To clear up any confusion, the curriculum for . . . Buena High School in particular consists of classes, needed credits that are considered to make us the best possible student. . . . The curriculum they chose is teaching the students in the way they think could best help the student along into higher learning . . . in some cases that's not so. My life is a perfect example.

　　　　　　—Steve Marzan, Buena High School senior

Introduction

Eva Gold

Amy Peterson and Steve Marzan were students in Ceci Lewis's senior English class in the fall of 1998. Ceci was interested in what students had to say about the ideas of school reformers for changing schools and the congruence between those ideas and students' perceptions of the strengths and limits of their school experiences. Therefore, she designed a class in which students were asked to write about their school experience and conduct research projects on school reform. As part of this project, Ceci offered several students the opportunity to work on-line with two researchers, Scott Christian of Juneau, Alaska, and Eva Gold of Philadelphia. She had met Scott and Eva through participation in the Bread Loaf Rural Teacher Network (BLRTN), and they were documenting the reform initiatives of BLRTN, which include the use of telecommunications to stimulate and support student writing. Amy responded positively almost immediately to being offered the opportunity to exchange on-line; Steve was more hesitant but decided to participate as well. Both Amy and Steve knew when they agreed to write on-line with Scott and Eva that the expectation was that the students would contribute to a chapter for a book on what students have to say about school.

Amy and Steve started writing for class assignments first and shortly afterward the on-line exchanges with Scott and Eva began. The first class assignment was a personal narrative, in which they were to chronicle their most memorable school experiences. The on-line writing started with Amy and Steve posting a little bit about themselves and Scott and Eva responding, telling them a bit about themselves, similar to pen-pal correspondence. Quickly, however, the on-line writing turned to discussions of themes and issues coming up in Amy's and Steve's writing for class.

Amy's and Steve's sections in this chapter grew out of these two separate but interconnected writing experiences: separate because the on-line exchanges took on a life of their own, exploring personal and other issues tangential but related to class assignments; interconnected because the on-line exchanges added a new layer and depth to the writing for class. Amy, for example, wrote that having the on-line aspect of the project was providing her with another perspective that was helping to further move her ideas for her class assignments.

> I think that being on-line . . . throughout the duration of this project has been good to help stimulate and bring to the surface a lot of my thoughts, and it was good to have you [Eva] help formulate questions that I [then] addressed in my work. I think over all, working on-line with you was a big help, and it was fun to get to know you too.

Steve emphasized that the on-line communication provided him with a non-threatening space to explore troubling areas that he feared could have negative consequences within his school and community.

> It made me feel better that there was actually someone there listening to what I had to say. I could talk about what I didn't like about education. I can't just go off here and tell everybody . . . I can't go around telling them anything like that. But, for someone out there to listen . . . not to just my problems . . . the technical parts, but other parts . . . like being an Asian-American student . . . it's kind of hard . . . it was a good thing.

Ceci, in one of her exchanges with Scott and Eva, echoed the students, observing that communicating on-line appeared to free Amy and Steve to discuss issues related to their school experience that they might have left unexplored and that it also helped them organize their thoughts for class writing.

> It is my belief that [writing to] you is highly instrumental in helping these students formulate their ideas. They really need that to help them structure their writing. The on-line communication helps them "voice" their opinions in a safe place with a person who will listen. This helps to confirm their ideas.

While the on-line exchanges provided an important venue for deeper exploration through writing, it was not a substitute for personal contact. Ceci's close interactions with the students mediated the facelessness and abstraction of the on-line exchange. Often, before posting comments on-line, Amy and Steve would use Ceci as a sounding board, talking through with her both personal and educational experiences, including topics like comfort zones for learning and different teaching styles they had experienced. Ceci noted that this kind of conversation with students enabled her to step back and observe her students' writing process. She wrote to Eva and Scott about the differences she was discovering in Amy and Steve as writers.

> For Amy, the [on-line] writing appeared to come easily and effortlessly. She jumped at the chance to write on-line to Eva. Every day she would come in to check the conference folder to see if she had any mail. If there was a message for her, she would immediately sit down and write back. Steve, although excited to read his mail, was extremely hesitant to answer back. He would spend time discussing the message from Scott and then he would procrastinate in writing his reply. The usual excuses of "I don't have enough time," or "I'm not sure what to write," always seemed to come out of his mouth. Ironically, Steve could spend hours seriously discussing these issues one-on-one and face-to-face while Amy appeared to be a bit more distracted if the conversation dragged on. The more informed Steve became, the more closely he guarded his written words. It was as if he realized the importance of what he needed to say and he became increasingly frustrated searching for the right words to convey his meaning.

A visit Scott made to Buena High School midsemester also helped to counter the remoteness of on-line communication. Ceci wrote Eva following Scott's visit that, "when Amy and Steve met Scott, it seemed to cement the project [to write a chapter together]."

Amy wrote her section in January 1999 after she had graduated from Buena. To help her assemble her section, Eva posted "organizing questions" on-line.

Amy then pulled from both her writing for class and her on-line writing to compose her section. In her section, Amy explores her valuing of interactions that foster the ability to communicate, which she believes can help students "function" better in the "real" world. She finds too many classrooms geared toward narrow academic assignments, ostensibly to prepare students for college.

In contrast to Amy, Steve had just completed the first semester of his senior year and following winter break had plunged into second semester. Scott and Eva helped Steve compose his section by excerpting for this chapter writing he did for class, on-line, as well as from a face-to-face interview Scott did with him when he visited Buena. Particularly important to Steve's section was his writing for his final class assignment, a personal reflection on himself as a student and his discovery through his class research on school reform that there are educational approaches that incorporate "hands-on" learning with more traditional, academic approaches. Steve writes about the experience of being a visual and hands-on learner in school and home cultures that highly value academic tradition.

As an introduction to Amy's and Steve's writing, Ceci presents Buena High School and its students. Amy's and Steve's reflections on their high school experience follow. We conclude with a few thoughts on writing together, focusing particularly on the kinds of changes Ceci observed in the students and our collective thoughts on what a dialogic on-line network contributed to the kinds of writing Amy and Steve were doing for school.

Buena High School

Ceci Lewis

Buena High School in many respects is typical of high schools across the nation. Overcrowding, lack of available funds, and the push for state-mandated achievement testing all combine to work against me as I try to find a way to make writing relevant to my students. Many of my students have learned just to suit up and show up. The spark for learning has been extinguished. I am still baffled when a student is elated to receive a 61 percent. This grade translates in the student's brain as "passing." The wish to participate in their own educational experience seems unnecessary.

Buena is also atypical in some respects. Our school, located in a rural section of Arizona, services a student body with teenagers from two ranching communities, a military installation, and a booming town that the *Arizona Daily Star* once referred to as "a suburb in search of a city." As a result, our student experiences range from those who have literally lived all over the world, to others who have never lived anywhere but in Cochise County. Also, due to the transient nature of this community, some of my students have been to several high schools before they reach my senior classroom. Interestingly, both Amy and Steve have lived in this community for the majority of their lives. They have been students in the public school system here since elementary school.

My Own Path of Colors

Amy Peterson

Hi, my name is Amy Peterson, and I am a graduating senior in Mrs. Lewis's sixth-hour English skills class. As a student, I have a very knowledgeable outlook as to what is expected of me and how to go about fulfilling the expectations of the system in place here at Buena. I am an honors student involved in many extracurricular activities, such as speech and debate and American Legion Auxiliary to name a few. I will be graduating in December, and traveling to Thailand in April as an exchange student for one year. When I return, I have hopes of going to Seattle University and majoring in journalism with a minor in European history.

As a social member of Buena, I have a very positive attitude toward my peers. I have many friends, and authority figures look upon me as a model student. It is my belief that students gain more knowledge and skills for the outside world within the social spectrum of Buena than within the confines of the classroom.

I am an energetic pupil who has soared through school leaving my own path of colors. During high school, I was very lucky to have been able to know the right people to allow me to do things my way, within certain conventional rules, of course. I'm not one to completely conform to rules, or be confined by boundaries; my personality and character just won't allow it. I always try to infiltrate my creativity and vivid imagination into assignments. As I do not like to see the world as black and white, I live from day to day in a world of a hundred thousand shades.

At school, I thrive as a social chameleon, always knowing the most recent gossip, who is dating whom and always yesterday's history assignment . . . only because I just did it last hour. To me, school does not hold much validity. Of course, come report card time I have high marks and pleasant teacher comments, but I find that conventional schooling is not something that I much care for, the reasons being that I don't feel I learn much that will help me later in life and the rules are at times unbearable. High school in general, as I see it, is trying to gear students toward college, when college is not the answer for all students. I see the need in my life for a transition period between high school and college, which is why I have chosen to travel to Thailand as an exchange student following high school.

I feel that going to Thailand will better benefit me as an individual in the everyday working world, because it will help to better sharpen my "people skills" that are critical later in life without the cushions of Mom and Dad to fall back on. Throughout the stages of my life, beginning with my entering the classroom, I have grown more and more independent of my parents, therefore it is becoming crucial for me to communicate with others. I have learned to communicate with people and express my ideas in a manner that allows me to get things done. It is through this type of social learning and interaction that I have been able to attain an open mind and high level of respect among my peers and older generations.

Looking back through my school years, the experiences that have best managed to shape me as an individual have taken place during social interaction with my peers. Therefore, I feel the most educational grade to students is kindergarten. It may sound ludicrous, but it was in kindergarten that I learned to share, talk to my peers without anger, and basically get along with people in general. When I entered the first grade, I remember the transition to be quite dramatic. I was all of a sudden expected to sit in a desk, in an assigned row, and feel some sort of "connection" with a teacher at the front of the room, lecturing to thirty-plus students at once. The basic rules were not to move from my seat unless first given permission, not to talk unless I had first received permission, and not to interact with others during class time except with the teacher. Recess was the biggest relief to me! Ever since kindergarten, I have become increasingly disappointed with the lessons taught within the classroom. Of course a certain amount of math, English, history, and science is necessary for later in life, but so is a certain amount of interaction with other people.

My classroom education has fallen short of giving me the most vital skills needed to survive in the world today. It has failed to teach me that effort ought to be rewarded, regardless of the overall product; it has failed to teach me how to communicate with others; in short it has failed to teach me any type of social skills. The reason I am well spoken and outgoing, and not afraid to voice my opinions is because I chose to learn how to speak and communicate with people. I joined the speech and debate team at my high school my freshmen year. Before that, I had never been taught how to speak in front of people, or that it was okay to voice my opinions. I chose to take a speech class as an elective and in that class there were only twenty people. Twenty students out of a school population of over 1,000 chose to take that class. The first day of class we were all apprehensive, and practically terrified that we would be speaking for durations of up to ten minutes at a time in front of each other. Many of the students in the class were seniors, and I was appalled that these students did not have the skills to speak to one another without fear. How, I asked myself, were these people to survive in a working environment if they did not even know how to communicate with their peers without fear of ridicule? In that class, we were graded upon our effort; we were not compared to one another, but instead graded individually. This is how I feel all classes ought to be taught.

The effects of the teacher on students could be the most critical component of a good education. If a student and a teacher have a personality conflict or if the teaching style is hard for the student to understand, the student is less apt to learn at the same level of ability. I can recount through my own educational experience that this rings true. In a class I once took, the teacher ran the class as a sort of military installation. Each day, as we filed in, we were to sit down, get out pencil and paper, and wait for him to begin class; any noise was harshly scolded. When class began, he would get in front of the class, and "teach" the lesson. Everything the teacher wrote on the board was supposed to be taken down in notes, we were not allowed to ask questions until after he was finished. Multiple times I found that halfway through the lesson I was troubled by a question, but by the time he was finished had forgotten the question since it had been so much earlier in the class period. I found myself afraid to even ask the questions I did remember because of the seemingly exasperated tone that he used when answering pupils' questions. Unfortunately I struggled through the class, not managing to learn at the same level I was capable of. I "passed" the class, but am still disappointed to know I did not do as well as I could have, had the teacher taught in a more friendly manner.

I have been lucky in my high school career to have had parents that took part in my educational experience. They took the time to care about what I was learning, and how. If there were problems at school, my parents were not apprehensive to speak with administrators, or teachers. They played a large role in my education, in the sense that they made sure the teachers teaching me were of high skill and ability in their profession. When I was put into a class that my parents did not want me to be in, they made sure I was switched out of it. I was basically given the liberty to choose my teachers because of whom my parents knew in the school system. Yes, I was given an advantage over other students, but this goes to show the importance of teaching people at a young age that through communication, things get done in a proper manner.

I Do Have a Voice

Steven Marzan

A little background information. I'm eighteen and not very into schoolwork. I'm not saying I'm incompetent, it's just that some subjects don't catch my attention like others do. It's sort of hard, coming from an Asian household, where education is held as "top priority" and not really wanting to do it.

My mother was born there [Korea] . . . giving me my *han-gul-mal* heritage, and my father is Puerto Rican and Filipino. There is a lot of pressure, growing up in school and education when you're always pushed to the highest you can, and be expected to go even higher.

Things I want to learn, I can learn very easily, but things that don't interest me very rarely get accomplished. I know I can do it, I just don't have the interest to. Anyway, taking after my father, I'm one who needs to work with my hands, those things dealing with vocational activity, or "blue-collar" types of jobs.

At this moment, I am here writing a compilation of thoughts of what I think goes on . . . in hopes that I may change things, or help in some way, how people may learn. Everyone has a different style of learning. Some people can take a book, analyze the content, and take a test on the information and pass with flying colors. Others have trouble with this method, and need some sort of "hands on" experience to intake the knowledge. The way of teaching subjects at my school (as well as others) is the way, I think, I just described. In that it's for those that are book smart, and can learn by traditional "fed information," learning by a literature way and lectures. A lot of people cannot learn this way.

It almost seems like there's "one in every family," someone who doesn't like to do schoolwork, and would rather learn about a trade. In my house, yes, there is some tension. Actually, all of the tension comes from being expected to do better. From when I was little, my parents have pushed me to strive to the best of my abilities, learn all there was to learn. I don't shun my parents for this. I'm glad they've made me settle for nothing less, but it's hard to always be expected to shine out, academically. . . . Being Asian, it's like I'm supposed to be a whiz at everything.

I remember in biology. We were working on atoms. I was totally lost in that class. Then the teacher pulled out these little things, like tinker toys, and told us how they fused together, and stuff like that. And all of a sudden, I was like all right, now I'm understanding it. I took the test and got a B on it. Without that I would have been lost. He tried to show me on paper how they connected. I was like, "What are you talking about?"

I envy some people that I'm sitting next to. They are just taking notes and everything. Reading the book. Understanding everything. And I'm like, no way, it's not happening. Once we got into that section in biology, my grade just soared up. We had been doing all this other stuff I couldn't remember, most if it was like atoms and cellular division. I almost got kicked out of that class. I was doing so poorly. But then, once we started doing dissecting, and anatomy, that's how I passed it. My grade got so high when I could see it. I don't like dissecting. I don't like cutting things open. But once I saw it, I knew what it was.

I won't be able to tell you the mathematical equation of the calculus persuasion, but I could tear apart an engine, and rebuild it, or run a press like a mad man to reach an abruptly made deadline. I guess it just depends on what someone's definition of a "smart person" is. I guess "smarts" don't have to pertain to studies. . . . I've been in printing for three years now. I'm in "advanced three," and it takes up two hours. So that's the only elective I've had for almost my whole high school years, because I've had to take all of my [academic] requirements. I have a job with the district print shop here. I work, just like a normal job. I get paid, but it's also a learning experience, meaning, I'm experiencing what it's like to be in a print shop—to do orders and everything, to actually do the labor work and the designing of forms. I do these things and also learn.

I guess what I'm trying to say is that I know there are different ways that people learn. Some people learn through book work, some from hearing it. Some people can learn from reading it. Some learn by experiencing it. There are combinations. . . . My question is, who is to say what is the best way to learn? Why is it that the book work type of learning, basically [that] our school is mostly book work? . . . If we learn a different way, if there are students that learn differently, they should have the option of, given a chance to learn their way. . . . I'm saying for those who want the alternative, those who want to take another route, it should be there.

Writing Together

Ceci Lewis, Scott Christian, and Eva Gold

Shortly after their sections for this chapter were written, Amy and Steve moved on in life. Amy left for Thailand for a year as an exchange student; Steve became enmeshed in the last semester of high school and making plans for postgraduation. Ceci had a new class of students to teach. Neither Amy nor Steve, given the different directions in which their lives were going, stayed connected to the writing of this chapter. Ceci, Scott, and Eva, however, are tied through their shared association with BLRTN, and were able to come together in the summer of 1999 for discussion about this chapter.

In looking back at the writing experience, Ceci reminded us that Amy began the semester with great confidence about her ability to affect change at school and beyond. Scott commented that when he interviewed Amy she spoke as if she were "the voice of her generation." Amy told Scott that she was interested in participating in writing a chapter for a book because:

> I would love for people to hear me, what I think as a student. I know
> that there are a lot of students and that we are not necessarily heard as
> much as adults are. And no offense, but I think that a lot of adults don't
> quite see what kids are going through. Because they have been out so
> long. And they don't understand, don't know where we're coming from.

Despite this confidence, Ceci noted that Amy's research into school reform paradoxically led her to a more complex understanding of the difficulties of making change, which in turn made dimmer her views for actual reform, and she seemed to grow less confident. In talking together, however, Ceci, Eva, and Scott believed Amy's struggle resonated with some of their own experiences and began to think about her experience in terms of the phases in a personal change process. Amy, when she first went to Thailand, continued using Ceci and Eva as sounding boards, e-mailing to them her thoughts about schooling, student life, authority roles, and life in general in Thailand.

When Steve began the study, it was with a strong feeling that he was "outside" of the schooling process, that he was "not a student." Scott discovered when he interviewed Steve that the classroom inquiry into his school experience and school reform had become a personal journey of discovery for Steve. Scott wrote to Eva that he had learned that Steve "wanted to know why he was failing and how he could explain it to his parents." Scott found that Steve was slowly growing more hopeful about himself and the possibility of change. Steve told Scott:

> Actually there are more people than I thought there would be who learn through experience. But still you know . . . if we change the system . . . to being all experience, the people who learn by reading would suffer. I have no solution to everything. I guess this is the best way because most people learn from reading and sitting. If there are students that learn differently they should have the option of learning their way.

Ceci noted that when Steve began reading about school reform, "he virtually lit up reading about other learners just like himself." She said his enthusiasm was particularly evident in an oral presentation he made to the class about his research, where his interest spilled out to engaging other students in talking about themselves and how they learn. Two weeks before graduating high school, Steve stopped by Ceci's classroom to tell her about a major change in his postgraduation plans. He had decided to attend a community college rather than the technical school he had been thinking about earlier. His obvious excitement, coupled with pride in his mother's approval of his decision, demonstrated to Ceci that Steve had, in the past year, begun to understand himself differently than he had at the beginning of the school year.

When Ceci, Scott, and Eva thought back on the writing process for this chapter, the contributions and difficulties of the on-line exchanges became more evident. Communicating across time and space was awkward because of Scott's and Eva's lack of up-close, personal interaction with Amy and Steve, mitigated largely by Ceci's regular interactions with Amy and Steve, and by Scott's visit to Buena. However, the on-line exchange also helped to remove Amy and Steve from their immediate realities, enabling them to ask questions and explore issues differently than they usually did. When she was ready to write for this chapter, Amy had had the opportunity to be a bit more reflective than usual, having explored the topics she was writing about several times—in class writing, through on-line writing, and by reviewing the "text" of her on-line exchanges. Steve, in his section, was able "to open up a topic"—expectations he felt as an Asian young person—initially too "hot" to discuss freely in his school or home but which he was able to explore on-line and which became part of his section. Ceci, Scott, and Eva were left to think about the "spaces" adults create for student writing, the combining of different kinds of spaces and the difference these spaces make for how, when, and what students write.

CHAPTER 6

Caught in the Storm of Reform: Five Student Perspectives on the Implementation of the Interactive Mathematics Program[1]

Student Authors: Dorothy V. Holt, Emily Gann, Sonia Gordon-Walinsky, Elissa Klinger, and Rachel Toliver

Researcher/Teacher Author: Edward (Ned) Wolff

Introduction

Ned Wolff

I am a full-time faculty member in the mathematics department at Beaver College and am also a codirector of the Philadelphia regional center of the Interactive Mathematics Program®. IMP is a reform mathematics curriculum created in response to several major national reports published in the late 1980s that pointed to the need for a major overhaul in mathematics education. As advocated by these reports, IMP minimizes routine manipulation of symbols and procedures and emphasizes problem-solving, conceptual understanding, communication skills, the use of technology (such as graphing calculators), and cooperative learning.

One of my responsibilities as codirector was to pilot IMP at Central High, Philadelphia's oldest and most prestigious public special-admission secondary school. From September 1993 to June 1997, I taught all four years of the program. Each year I team-taught one IMP class with one of the two Central teachers who first volunteered to teach IMP. (These teachers also taught their own solo sections of IMP.) As a strong believer in IMP's goals, I spent considerable time promoting the merits of the curriculum to the students, their families, and the school administration. I also did my best to protect the students from IMP's opponents, including a few teachers who were vehemently opposed to the inclusion of IMP at Central. Mocking IMP's student-centered pedagogy and de-emphasis of algebraic manipulation skills, these teachers believed that the program was lowering standards. They openly disparaged IMP and belittled students who chose to participate in it.

Three of the student authors of this chapter—Emily, Elissa, and Rachel—were members of the original cohort of IMP students at Central, and each had me as their math teacher for at least three of their four high school years. These three students are currently college sophomores.

The other two authors, Dorothy and Sonia, are two years younger and are in their senior year at Central. Their experience has differed significantly from the others' in that for their first two years, they had newly trained IMP teachers who, even from the start, felt uneasy about the curriculum. Early on, they began modifying both IMP's content and teaching methods, often, for example, providing their classes with short-cut formulas to solve problems rather than adhering to IMP's philosophy of encouraging students to construct their own solutions. By the middle of their second year of teaching IMP, these teachers had become totally disgruntled. They announced to their classes their intentions of leaving the program, abandoned the IMP text in favor of their own traditional-style handouts, and advised their students to change to the traditional curriculum when registering for their junior-year courses. While not sure about what to do, Sonia and Dorothy (and roughly half their classmates) decided to remain in IMP. Fortunately for them, their junior-year teacher was an experienced IMP teacher (one of the teachers with whom I had team-taught) who fully believed in the curriculum and provided the students with a far more positive experience.

In what follows, the five student authors reflect on their experiences as math students before, during, and, in the case of the three college students, after IMP. Despite my own allegiance to IMP, I made it clear that the students should "shoot from the hip" regarding their true feelings about the program and its teachers. While not always agreeing with the students' perceptions of the program, I resisted, at times with great difficulty, all impulses to engage them in a conversation that might lead to their modifying their expressed opinions.

The writing of this chapter proceeded as follows. The original student writing team consisted of Dorothy and Sonia who, at the time, were beginning their senior year at Central. The three of us met approximately once a month throughout most of the academic year. We found that an effective technique to help them make headway was to tape informal sessions wherein I asked them to reminisce about their IMP-related experiences. I then prepared transcripts of those sessions for them to use as the basis for their writing.

By late spring, Dorothy and Sonia had completed their contributions. The three of us decided that including the perspectives of former IMP students, now in college, would enhance the chapter. Accordingly, early that summer I invited Elissa, Emily, and Rachel to join in the project. Based on interesting issues raised by Dorothy's and Sonia's writings, the two of them and I drew up a list of topics for the newcomers to address concerning their pre-, during, and post-IMP experiences. The challenge facing us was that all five coauthors were either spending the summer out of town (indeed, two were overseas) or had very limited availability due to previous commitments. Thus, all subsequent communication among coauthors took place via e-mail.

Credit for the editing of this chapter goes to Rachel and Elissa. Rachel provided editorial assistance to her coauthors, organized everyone's contributions into logical sections, and wrote headings for each. Elissa then meticulously reviewed and further edited the manuscript to give her and her coauthors' voices maximum clarity.

Early Experiences

At the time we enrolled in IMP, we came to the class from every imaginable skill level and educational background. While some of us had been extensively exposed to and highly successful in traditional math, others had received weaker math instruction as elementary or middle school students. When the time came for choosing a math class as freshmen at Central High School, our decisions to take IMP were largely influenced by our reflections on our previous math experiences. The following are the accounts of our math histories leading up to the time of our enrollment in IMP.

DOROTHY: Throughout my elementary school years, I was always interested in math and science. It fascinated me how everything tied together. Unfortunately, the math and science programs offered in my parochial grade school were not very interesting. In eighth grade, my math experience was a total disaster. My teacher was Filipino and couldn't speak English very well, let alone teach math to thirty-three students. The class was always out of control, and my teacher could never get anything done. He never tried to have fun with the subject. He would just write things on the board and assign homework. There were no group projects and no fun.

EMILY: As a student in the Philadelphia Public School system for all but two and a half of my years as an elementary and secondary student, I was subject to the old-school, traditional math curriculum found in schools all across the country. I do not remember having particularly strong feelings about math either way—that is, until I first collided with the "low math self-esteem" bug that seems to inflict so many girls. I was a sixth-grader and was asked one day by my teacher why I was "so good at English, and yet so poor at math." As far as I could tell I was just fine at both, but after that, my visceral reaction to math class was henceforth one of slight fear and definite frustration. It was not a complete coincidence that a few months later I transferred to a local private Quaker school. There, I had good math teachers who were dynamic and effective, and I completed algebra in eighth grade. However, my interests had already turned to art, drama, and history, and the math stigma remained. Coming into Central as a freshman, I was prepared for the generally uninspired and drill-oriented math curriculum that I had left two and a half years before.

SONIA: I attended Philadelphia's most selective middle school. It is important to my situation to point out that I entered ninth grade IMP after having already completed courses in algebra in seventh grade and geometry, introduction to trigonometry, and elementary functions in eighth grade.

RACHEL: My earliest memories of math classes resemble those academic stress dreams, where you unexplainably appear in a class and don't know anything about the subject—and, what's worse, everyone else knows that you don't know anything about the subject. One experience in particular illustrates the feelings of incredible insecurity which the traditional math classroom, coupled with a teacher's insensitivity, can instill in some students. The game was called "Beat the Clown." I suppose my teacher thought that she was providing us with a fun math game and harmless competition. But what was challenging competition for students who were stronger in math was humiliating for me—and, I assume, many students who, like myself, were not as strong in math.

"Beat the Clown" operated on these rather simple rules: every day (or every week, I can't remember) we were handed slips with about nine or ten problems on them. It started on the lowest level, with simple addition problems, and moved up from there to (I think) division. We were timed, and had to complete our lines of problems before the teacher called out for us to turn in the quizzes. If we completed our slips perfectly in the time allotted, we would get a clown body part—a construction paper arm or leg or torso—pinned up on the board with our name on it. If we did not complete the problems correctly, we would be handed the same slip of paper over and over again, until we got them right, while the other students moved on to other problems of higher difficulty. The object of the game was to assemble an entire clown. So, while some students had bright, proud, neatly assimilated clowns up on the board for the entire class to see, other students' [clowns] hobbled along, maimed, missing a leg or an arm, their development embarrassingly arrested. A few clowns were sorry sights, deformed beyond all recognition—simply a sad, floating disembodied leg, which remained week after week while all the other clowns developed and flourished. With help from my parents, my clown, although a bit stunted, eventually was completed. The next year, I left that school and entered the world of Quaker education—at a small, local Friends' elementary and middle school.

Things were rather different for me in Quaker school—instead of endless purple mimeographed "ditto sheets" (work sheets) we played with Cuisenaire rods. At my first school I had been taught that it was wrong to count on my fingers, while at my new school, using tools (fingers included) for learning was accepted. However, that school was something of a mixed blessing for me, especially as I progressed through the later years of middle school. The school was quite advanced in the humanities, especially social studies and English. Math and science, however, were far weaker, and as I became friends with students from other schools during my eighth-grade year, I realized that the level of my math achievement and education was lagging far behind that of many of my peers. By the time I had graduated from middle school, I think that I had covered very little beyond basic algebra skills.

ELISSA: I had always been in the "fast track" math classes in the two public schools that I had attended as an elementary school student. During eighth grade I was given the option of joining four other students in a "faster track" pre-algebra mini-class. We sat outside of our prealgebra class at a designated time and worked through the class text at our individual paces, without the constant supervision of our teacher. I do not recall how frequently this separation occurred, but I do remember being with the rest of the class for a portion of time, presumably for sessions of instruction and testing. Our teacher was highly regarded at the school, I would say partly because she emphasized a more hands-on approach to learning mathematics than other math teachers. She even wore smock-like attire that, in recollection, made the class feel like a laboratory of learning. She broke the mold, so to speak, by assigning a challenging problem to each student that was to be presented to the class, but the overall structure and expectation was generally traditional in scope. At the conclusion of eighth grade I fully expected to enroll in algebra that fall as a freshman at Central High School.

Interest in IMP

Since we came to the program from varied backgrounds, each of us had a different reason behind her initial interest in the program. However, there are some similarities among our motives for enrolling in IMP, most notably frustration with or fear of traditional math as we had experienced it in elementary or middle school. Here we share our recollections of the first time we heard about the program and our thoughts on why we elected to enter IMP rather than a traditional math sequence.

SONIA: At a freshman orientation prior to my attendance at Central, an introduction IMP caught my attention and sparked my interest because of its creative alternative to learning. My mother and I spoke with Ned (who gave the IMP presentation) after the orientation and presented our concern that IMP would be an easy repeat of seventh and eighth grade for me. But he supported his case and I was pretty much convinced. I proceeded to take the math placement test for the traditional math classes. Nevertheless, in the end, taking into consideration that I would not need comprehension in math to pursue my career path of becoming a rabbi, I chose IMP.

EMILY: At the parent's orientation, my mother was "IMPressed" by a presentation about IMP, explaining the new math offering for students. I don't remember much of this presentation—I was busy checking out my future classmates. Nonetheless, I was intrigued by the idea of a creative, writing-oriented math class, and had enjoyed working in small groups in middle school, so I decided to give IMP a shot.

DOROTHY: When it came time for me to choose my subjects for freshman year, I was very nervous about whether I would be prepared for high-school-level math. This is why I chose IMP as my course. I figured that since IMP was a fairly new program, I would have no problem with adapting to the new course. I was very intimidated by the traditional math courses at Central because I had heard that all of the teachers were very demanding. They wouldn't slow down just because I had a bad teacher in grade school. When I heard the different things about IMP such as group projects, presentations to the class, and students and teachers working together to solve a problem, I felt that IMP was for me.

ELISSA: When I was in eighth grade, I spent a day at Central, and knew immediately that I had been right in thinking that I wanted to go there all along. However, I attended a traditional geometry class and considered it rather dry. Perhaps the seeming inevitability of sitting through such a class for an entire year caused me to think seriously about another option when one was presented to me some months later.

When I went to a freshman orientation at Central before actually commencing my education there, I heard a presentation (by Ned) about IMP. The program sounded like it was innovative and challenging, so I decided to pick up the paper with which to enroll. My parents thought that I should stay with the traditional sequence of math, but they ultimately left the decision up to me.

RACHEL: In order to be admitted to Central High School, all students had to take a standardized test. My parents recollect that I scored only slightly higher than the cutoff point in the math section, although my score was far higher in the verbal. My parents were somewhat worried about how successful I would be in high school math, but they were even more concerned about the fact that I did not enjoy math and always wrote myself off as simply "bad at it." So, when Ned introduced IMP during my freshman orientation session, my parents were intrigued, especially my mother, who was then working on a master's degree in education. I didn't expect IMP to be "easier" then regular math, and since I had never taken a formally organized traditional algebra or geometry course, I really had no standard for expectation. However, I was terrified by my perception of what the traditional math courses would be like; most of these perceptions were lifted from TV sitcoms where a teacher who looked eerily like Albert Einstein would scrawl incomprehensible equations across five blackboards, while lobotomized-looking students would stare blankly. I figured that anything else, even though it was unknown, was a better bet than that intimidating fate. I always say that it was providential that IMP started up the year that I started high school. While I might have muddled through traditional math, I would have never excelled at it, and sometimes I even think that traditional math courses might have been a serious impediment to my success at Central.

Out with the Old, In with the New

Before encountering IMP, we had spent most of our previous school years in traditional math programs; consequently, we were somewhat perplexed and astonished by the innovative program. This section contains our first "IMPressions" of the program as well as some comparisons between our new experiences in IMP and the math education that we had been accustomed to in middle school.

SONIA: In consideration of both my negative and positive experiences with IMP I feel that the style of teaching/learning was more beneficial to me in a well-rounded/long-term sense than a traditional schedule of math classes would have been.

RACHEL: Since I had come from a very small private school, I was probably a good deal less shocked by the IMP classroom than my counterparts who had attended public schools. I remember the perplexed raised eyebrows and quizzical questions from my classmates—"So what do you think of IMP?" But ironically, for the first time, the math classroom was a "safer" place than many of my other, more traditionally run classrooms, since it recalled my middle school experience.

ELISSA: When I started at Central I remember thinking how new and different everything was, especially IMP. I was surprised by the seating arrangements of groups of desks facing each other, as well as the presence of two teachers in the classroom instead of one. Our thin workbook units filled with stick-figure graphics and assignments featuring a cast of diversely named characters made the class seem even less traditional. In elementary school, most of my math classes consisted of the teacher going to the board and teaching, with the students expected to be in a state of enrapture brought about by the dynamism of the teacher and the sheer pleasure of watching the manipulation of numbers at the front of the classroom. This ideal situation often fell short of its intended goals.

The IMP classroom seemed to be the anticlassroom. The desks were clustered together in groups of four (two sets of desks facing each other), meaning that the classroom had neither a designated front nor back. An overhead projection device in the center of the room became the "front" of the class, shared equally by teachers and students explaining or presenting ways of thinking about problems and solutions. Teachers and students taught the class in a kind of team effort. Students would present their solutions to problems either individually or

in groups (with full group participation), and no one method of solving a problem was emphasized over another. In fact, by the end of a unit students often had
many different ways of solving the same problem. In its entirety, the IMP classroom experience was significantly different from all previous classes.

EMILY: From the beginning, it was clear that IMP would be different. Gone
were the heavy, old, incomprehensible textbooks of years past, replaced by unit
books that looked like the teachers had just run them off on the school copy ma-
chine. Instead of sitting like traditional classes in neat rows facing the teacher, we
sat in groups of four and five—enabling us to talk freely amongst ourselves. The
projector in the middle of the classroom was for presentation of our math findings—either by group or individually, and the colorful posters that eventually
decorated the walls were remnants of important discoveries related to the even-
tual solution of the unit problem. For the first time, math seemed purposeful to
me. Each month or so we were given a new unit problem—a new goal to head
toward. These were practical problems, taken from real life, and involving students as characters in the stories that accompanied them.

Above all, the IMP focus was on real problem-solving skills. It wasn't a matter of memorizing formulas or drilling equations, but of learning the reasoning
skills to get from point A to point B. I thrived off of the creativity that IMP not
only allowed but encouraged. We built giant pendulums, designed probability
games, and wrote papers on population control. I also felt that IMP was less
competition-oriented than traditional math classes as well as many of my classes
at Central in general. I greatly enjoyed collaborating with other students and not
feeling as though classmates were vying with each other for the highest grade.
With a few key changes, I would be delighted to see IMP replace traditional
math entirely—it is far more capable of engaging students' interest and respecting their ability to learn by discovery.

You Can't Teach an Old Dog New Tricks

*Although IMP is a cutting-edge program fueled by the larger trends toward educational
reform, we found that some traditional math teachers seemed to have a very difficult time
adjusting to the challenges of a new teaching style. This often frustrated both our teachers and us. We perceived this conflict between old and new and, while still loyal to the
ideals of the program, realized that a complete overhaul of curriculum without a complete overhaul of teaching styles and teachers' attitudes would be worthless.*

SONIA: As I began to understand the program itself and became more critical of
it, I found that I was an advocate more of its fundamental principles rather than
of the execution of the program.

EMILY: For many of my friends in other classes (not taught by Ned), IMP was an innovative curriculum being taught by traditional math teachers in the most traditional way possible. I think for many teachers it was just too difficult to adjust to the new way of thinking that IMP required. It wasn't just that we were asked to solve longer, more wordy problems, or that we sat in groups, or sometimes engaged in mathematical arts and crafts; I think it was more the adjustment to a student-centered class that was so hard for teachers to make. I think that a teacher who has spent enough time in the system adjusts his or her teaching style to make room for a certain amount of class-management and disciplinary action. I think that for IMP to run effectively, teachers must be trained in the curriculum and student-centered philosophy early on in their careers, or as separate, nontraditional teachers.

The Old Dogs and the New Dogs

This tension between the old and the new is symbolized well by the dramatic differences in our classroom experiences, depending on whether our teacher was truly committed to the program. Elissa, Emily, and Rachel, the pioneer IMP students, thrived under Ned's dedication and expert guidance, while Sonia and Dorothy had very negative experiences in the classrooms of traditionally trained teachers who were reluctant to teach the program. The contrasts between the experiences of our two groups vividly illustrate the importance of matching visionary teachers with a visionary curriculum.

ELISSA: For the four years of IMP I had dedicated teachers who believed in the merits of the program and sought to defend its place at Central. This made all the difference.

EMILY: I felt extremely lucky (and still do) to have had Ned as a teacher for all four years. I was aware at the time that it was his teaching as much as the IMP program that I responded to positively. The "team-teachers" that we had in the classroom were traditional teachers whose grasp of the IMP philosophy and purpose unfortunately ranged from bad to worse. This is not to say that they were not competent math teachers. The traditional-turned-IMP teachers seemed to be incapable of trusting us students to lead ourselves through the curriculum. I felt that they were generally quicker to admonish or criticize us, and less willing to step back a bit and allow us to discover things ourselves. If I had it to do all over again, I would still have chosen to participate in IMP—though with the singular caveat that Ned be my teacher all four years, as he was.

DOROTHY: Now that I look back I realize that my first year in IMP was a disaster. The year as a whole seemed to me to be a success but I didn't really know what wasn't a success. To top it all off, I was deathly afraid of my teacher. Not only was the class nothing like a real IMP class, but also our teacher was *extremely* temperamental. Many of the topics included in the first-year curriculum were skipped over and the class even started to do "worksheets" in class—a definite no-no in IMP.

Our first impressions of IMP were that it was unorganized, and overall a confused compilation of homework and class assignments. Our teachers haphazardly flipped through the book, assigning what seemed to be random homework and class assignments.

SONIA: Dorothy and my experience for our first two years in the program was with two teachers who were themselves not true to the essence/values of the program. They had been classically trained in math, and our freshman year was their first year teaching IMP. This was our first exposure to IMP so we were aware of the problems in the classroom but not that these problems were really with the teachers. These teachers left the program after our sophomore year when we then found out that they themselves had not been enthusiastic for the program and wanted it to be adapted to their styles of traditional teaching. They were only in it for the money, not for the excitement of a new topic and subject to teach to eager students. We were not a bit aware of what was going to happen this year or of any qualms the teachers were having. About halfway through the year, our teacher was making up his own worksheets for us. The teacher also made us switch from our group thing to traditional rows.

After a very bumpy ride with those teachers, in addition to the possibility of the program shutting down due to a lack of interest and funding, we finally had one of the original IMP teachers in our junior year. As our new teacher and our classmates tried to find a common ground for our knowledge we realized that we had missed many of the lessons in IMP. Our first IMP teachers took shortcuts, which defeated the whole purpose of the more extensive routes the problems in IMP were intended to take. Over the year that we had her (the original IMP teacher at Central) as our teacher we had the opportunity to delve into the methods that IMP was intended to be based on.

Outside Reactions

As well as there being a conflict between new and old teaching methods, a larger controversy rages outside of the IMP classroom. We IMP students leave that classroom and are confronted by hostile teachers and administrators, and are sometimes even mocked by our fellow students. We are also faced with national standards and expectations, especially those posed by the inevitable SATs.

ELISSA: My IMP class was the first ever to go through the program at Central, and because of this there was some less than smooth sailing. First of all, I recall there being many outside visitors who attended our classes. These were most often educators who were interested in seeing the program in action. The visitors joined a group and were interviewed and introduced to the class by the group. Although having attendees provided for fun and interesting diversions, some class time was wasted in having them interviewed and introduced to the class. After a while it began to feel as though IMPsters were living their math lives in a fishbowl. But visitors to our classes were not the only reasons why it seemed as though all eyes were on us.

Science classes at Central, particularly honors and advanced placement classes with competitive entrance exams, were heavily math based. In these classes there was often open criticism of IMP, making me feel caught between teachers for and against the program. Confidence that was being built up in IMP was being broken down in other classes. IMP students were definitely wedged between teachers and administrators with strong personalities whose opinions about the program should have been kept out of the classroom. Traditional math students who knew very little about IMP firsthand were critical of the program, no doubt, because of these inappropriate remarks and attitudes of their teachers.

RACHEL: Not having taken any additional math courses or higher-level science courses, I wasn't often confronted with teachers who looked down on the IMP program. However, I recall that one IMP student (Gina Calderaio, now a math major at Bryn Mawr College) had an experience in her calculus class that clearly exemplifies the conflicts between IMP students and uninformed teachers. After her calculus teacher handed back the first exam, he commented that half of the class did well and the other half did very poorly. He said that the half who did poorly were probably the IMP students, and he asked to see those students after class. When the IMP students approached him, he reacted with surprise and said that they were his best students. However, even after that point, the teacher still made disparaging comments about the IMP program. To me, this anecdote demonstrates how many teachers viewed the program only through their own biases, ignoring even hard evidence to the contrary.

Every so often my friends in traditional classes, or even other IMP students, would make fun of the course or criticize it. Sometimes I felt bad about the judgments that were being made about IMP, especially when my friends made IMP students out to be somewhat intellectually inferior, or made it seem like we were receiving an inferior education. Now that I think about it, I'm not sure how they were such authorities on the program, since they had never been in an IMP classroom and probably had never even looked at our course materials or homework assignments (except, perhaps, by being confused by the fact that there were more words than numbers on our homework assignments). I felt that my defense of IMP was very limited; the only thing that I could really say about IMP was that I liked it and that I knew that I was doing better in IMP than I would have done in traditional math. But most people's responses were, "Of course you like it if you couldn't have made it in a traditional class." Also, the fact that I was still, by traditional standards, "bad" at math made everything that I had to say less valuable, since I was living proof of the fact that IMP students couldn't "succeed" in the "real world." (Of course everyone knows that one encounters those very practical SAT-style algebra problems on a regular basis in the aforementioned "real world.") Most of my friends came from traditional math backgrounds in Philadelphia public schools, and many of them excelled in that environment. It was sometimes difficult to dialogue with my friends about IMP and math in general because their backgrounds, expectations, and needs were so different from my own.

Women in Math

Some studies have confirmed that women tend to feel inferior and intimidated in math and science courses. It is possible that the discrepancy between male and female students' performance in traditional math classes might have more to do with the structure of these classes than with any inherent differences between the math ability of men and women. Two of us considered the question of whether the IMP program was more equitable than traditional math programs.

SONIA: In thinking about what part our two male teachers played in our education for the first two years of IMP, I became aware of the numbers of men versus women involved in teaching IMP. Mental note: two male teachers, both unsuccessful with teaching IMP; one male teacher (Ned) who has made IMP his own and is as enthusiastic and true to the program as can be; three female teachers, two of whom I know from personal experience and word of mouth are very successful IMP teachers, and one of which I know nothing except that she has a roaring temper. So far, the count is one to two, maybe three if the temper does not interfere with her teaching success, with the women in the lead. However, these numbers are too close to show any significant pattern. When I asked Ned about these numbers, he added to my knowledge that out of thirty or so national leaders of IMP, twenty-two to twenty-five of them are women.

My next question is, is IMP a women's course? My first response is that there are so many different variations of men and women that it is impossible and unfair to generalize what kind of math is for women and what is for men. As this century has surely shown, women can certainly do what was traditionally considered "men's math." But can men do "women's math"? As a young woman, I am quick to say "no." IMP requires one to stand out from the rest, to take all of the insults thrown your way from conservative math and science teachers who say they do not approve of the method, but are probably just too set in their ways to take a good look at the program and recognize its good merit. It takes flexibility to change your own ideas of what math classes "should" be. Most of all, it takes a different mind-set; to go into class and know that today you will only work closer to your goal, but may not solve the overall problem. Is this something only women can do? No, but I think women tend to be more flexible in their thinking, more open to alternative approaches, and more patient to prolong the instant gratification of solving a problem. In all three of my IMP classes, the three most outstanding students were all girls. It is difficult to analyze this though, knowing that there are girls who perform poorly in IMP, as well as boys who perform well.

RACHEL: Until I read Sonia's piece about the role of women in IMP, I had never thought about whether women or men are, in general, more receptive to the program. Of course, it is telling that all of the students Ned asked to write for this project are women. In our IMP class, some of the best students were men, but they generally did well because they were talented with math and not because the program enabled them to learn better, whereas many of the women who did well in IMP were successful by IMP's unique standards. For example, although my math skills were below some of my classmates', I did well in the program by virtue of the program's unique makeup (group work, writing, thinking about thought processes), whereas many of the men that did well in our class would have done just as well, if not perhaps better, in a "regular" class.

Although I prefer to shy away from stereotypes about "male" and "female" characteristics, I do believe that many of general qualities which make good IMP students are more common to women than men. Women tend to be more relational, so they react well to working in groups, while men can sometimes be more competitive. IMP relies on intuition, common sense (not to say that men don't have common sense, or that all women do) and a general understanding of the world more than the traditional math class, which tends to be more removed from real-life experience. And finally, IMP is more verbal and pictorial, rather than being mere abstract number crunching. All of these factors, coupled with the fact that (hopefully) all students in IMP classes are given equal chances to be an active part of every project and are required to present their findings to the class, make IMP classrooms a place where girls have a more even footing and can acquire the self-confidence needed for any task.

Looking Back

At Central High school, students have far more freedom in designing their schedules as seniors than in any previous year, since senior year is the only year in which there are no math and science requirements. Sonia's and Dorothy's unique choices for that key year, and the way IMP influenced those choices, are significant in that they illustrate a great deal about their reactions to the program, what they took away from it.

DOROTHY: This year I am taking calculus in addition to IMP 4. Ironically enough, I have the same teacher for calculus as my freshman IMP [class]. Two other students from IMP (they were also in my freshman class) are also taking calculus. We agreed that we feel that we are discriminated against by our teacher because we take IMP and because we didn't bail out as he did. The things he says in class are definitely a smack in our faces because he asks everyone in the class if they remember their "algebra 2" and "elementary functions." Then he gives me this look that just makes me think he's saying inside, "Well, of course you don't remember because you take IMP." This has definitely motivated me to work even harder in the class because now I have something to prove to both him and myself: that an "IMPster" can take on any subject, anytime. It turns out that I have a better grade than most of the others in the class who had taken the traditional classes. I sort of have the best of both worlds since I have taken IMP courses and am taking a traditional class as well.

SONIA: Entering high school I knew that I wanted to minimize my math and science studies so that I could focus on the arts and my other interests such as music, language, and social studies. When senior subject selection came around I decided to take printmaking, world conflicts, and woodwind ensemble, and to play in the school orchestra, in addition to fulfilling the two required government and English courses. Although I value the experience I had in the three years of taking IMP, I was also very happy to get out of there; to be finished with the POWs, the politically correct word problems, and the group assignments.

College Experiences

One criticism of IMP and a major fear of IMP students (especially seniors) is that the program does not adequately prepare students for the challenges of college math. The three of us who are college students—Elissa, Emily, and Rachel—are all enrolled in prestigious colleges and have each come across some form of math or math-based class during their time in college. The following accounts are reflections on what aspects of IMP were helpful preparation for college math, and critiques of what IMP could have done to better equip us with the skills required for college math.

ELISSA: One of my roommates my freshman year was taking calculus, and sometimes I heard her talking about aspects of her class that she did not understand. She went to my other roommate for help because she knew that I had not had a traditional calculus class in high school, which both she and my other roommate had taken. When I heard her ask questions, I realized that I had a better conceptual framework for thinking about derivatives than she had, even though I could not necessarily understand the symbolic language of her calculus class.

During my freshman year at Bryn Mawr College I decided not to take calculus, postponing the requirement for my course of study until later in my college experience. Ned suggested that I take calculus at Haverford College, a neighboring institution at which Bryn Mawr students can take classes, and vice versa. Professors in the math department at Haverford use the Hughes-Hallett Gleason calculus program which, like IMP, places more emphasis on conceptual understanding rather than correct answers. I took his advice and enrolled in one of these calculus courses after having been in college for a number of semesters.

As of now I have completed one semester of calculus. While I found my prior knowledge of conceptual thinking about derivatives to be helpful, I had difficulty with many symbolic manipulations that are essential to calculus. I believe that I would have had less difficulty with the course had I taken it immediately after high school. One of my biggest problems was the inordinate amount of time it took me to do some problems, which I think might have been more routine had I a stronger foundation in algebraic manipulation. I found that IMP's emphasis on different ways of thinking about the same problem was somewhat of a mixed blessing. I definitely found it helpful to think about problems both graphically and algebraically, or to use guess-and-check when solving some types of problems, but it was difficult to bring all of these methods into play when under the time constraints of a test.

When I think about IMP in relation to calculus in college, I really miss the hands-on approach that IMP institutes in its classes. I know that a college semester contains only so many weeks, and there are a certain number of topics to cover, but no amount of quality teaching can replace what students learn by guided discovery.

I believe that taking IMP helped me in other disciplines. For example, during my freshman year at Bryn Mawr I took a challenging chemistry class with a significant lab component. Lab write-ups caused a great deal of stress, but I found them to be much like what we had been doing for IMP "problem of the week" write-ups. In fact, I have found that the structure of writing problems of the week is fairly widely practiced in a number of disciplines, both in the sciences and the social sciences. This weekly exercise proved to be invaluable. Now that I am in college, I realize just how helpful IMP was in terms of developing the skills of reasoning and problem solving.

RACHEL: I must say that when I got to college, I intentionally stayed away from anything mathematical. While most of my friends were taking calculus, I cringed at the thought of taking any math courses voluntarily. I honestly can't imagine what I would have done if a calculus course or some similar horror had been required of me. I did, however, have the insurmountable obstacle of Barnard's "quantitative reasoning" requirement, which was mostly fulfilled by math courses as well as a few math-related courses like statistics.

In order to get as far away from math as possible, I enrolled in a logic course for my second semester; since it was offered by the Columbia University philosophy department, I figured that it involved relatively few numbers. I was shocked and dismayed to find that my professor had actually gotten his Ph.D. in math, and that, although he was one of the most renowned logicians in the country, he had a reputation for being one of the most difficult teachers in the school. This, coupled with the fact that he had a completely traditional and almost militaristic teaching style (every day without fail he would call roll, barking out our names like a drill sergeant, with last names before first names—even now people from that class call me "Toliver, Rachel"), nearly scared me away from the class. However, I was shocked to have my first quiz—one that centered on algebra-style simplification of problems—turned back to me with a 96 on it. Eventually I grew to enjoy the class and the challenge it presented. I was greatly helped by smaller group meetings with a very patient TA [teaching assistant], who presented a number of different ways of thinking about and solving problems, a teaching style which was very analogous to the IMP program and philosophy. While my professor simply threw out formulas and rules for us to memorize, my TA taught us the logic behind logic, often sharing the intellectual and philosophical history of the subjects we were studying. My TA was also similar to an IMP teacher in that he used real-life examples which symbolized the concepts; he was especially fond of representing problems graphically through Venn diagrams and illustrations.

In studying for our intimidating final, I worked with groups and studied one-on-one with friends as much as I worked on problems by myself. I was not afraid to push my classmates for explanations that I could understand, and was not afraid to "think out loud" until I understood ideas for myself. When studying, I was strongly motivated to wrestle with understanding why a simplification worked out, rather then simply being content to memorize it. This experience reminded me strongly of my IMP days, bringing home once again the validity of the IMP philosophy: that knowing the reasoning behind the formulas, rather then simply memorizing, is vital to true learning. In some ways, logic was the ideal subject for an IMP graduate, because the entire discipline focuses on ideas and language represented by symbols. IMP taught me that math is exactly that—symbols representing ideas—and it taught me to delve behind the symbols for the ideas that they were illustrating. IMP also taught me to work the other way, to represent symbols with concrete ideas and to express what I had learned through language, in order to remember it better. I feel that IMP prepared me for studying for this class because it taught me two important tools in the learning process: how to understand derivations and how to verbally express difficult problems in understandable terms.

EMILY: Having completed my sophomore year at Harvard, I've had the chance to continue to reflect on my experiences with IMP. I've found that most of the concerns I had in high school played out in my first two years of college. I felt generally prepared for the math that I would face, and had no problem passing the required math exam for freshmen that was given the first week of school. However, the economics course that I took that year posed more of a challenge. Not only did we encounter complicated algebra on our exams, but we were also not allowed to use calculators. This was not the best situation for me, and I again felt that I could not answer the problems as fast or as well as I would have liked due to my meager algebra training. The lack of a calculator was also significant, as we had relied upon them heavily in IMP. The true test of my IMP preparation, however, came this past year when I was required to take statistics. As a social studies concentrator, I had the option of enrolling in Statistics 100 offered by that department or a statistics management class at the Kennedy School of Government. I chose the latter, having been advised by other students that it was more user-friendly. The class itself turned out to be quite IMP-like, with its practical focus on problems concerning the chi-square of a public health study, or poll predictions for an election. I found that much of what I had already learned in IMP—probability, basic statistics, etc.—was repeated in the class. The atmosphere also mirrored the IMP style. The lively professor encouraged questions from the hundred or so students, who seemed more focused on *why* a formula would be used rather than *how* it would be used.

Now that I am free of the shackles of math education (kidding, of course!), I look back and am pleased overall with my choices.

General Feedback about the Curriculum

How effective and comprehensive is IMP's curriculum? What skills and knowledge do IMP students take away after their time in the program? Here are our thoughts about the value of the materials that we covered in IMP: what we could have had more of, what we could have had less of, what was good about the curriculum, and what could have been "IMProved."

EMILY: I clearly remember talking to friends in other IMP classes who were not nearly as pleased with their decision to enroll in the program. They felt that they weren't learning the math that they should have been—and I suppose it took a good amount of faith to believe that we were indeed going to learn all of the math that the traditional students were. . . . As for the curriculum itself, there were several concerns. My first is that the unit booklets often went out of their way to obscure the "real" math topics that we were learning. Instead of identifying a concept as "linear algebra," "trigonometry," or "elementary functions," the program would choose to avoid these proper labels in favor of story-related terms. While I understand that the emphasis was on learning the concept and not falling into traditional terminology, it was frustrating to feel that the wool was deliberately being pulled over our eyes. There would be no harm in telling us what we were learning, and I believe that it might make students completely aware that they were in fact learning the same things as students in the traditional track were learning. My other curriculum concern was over the limited algebra instruction. Even though I had taken algebra before coming to Central, I still remember having difficulty manipulating algebraic equations on standardized exams like the PSAT and SAT. I felt like it took me twice as long to manipulate an algebra problem than it took friends in the traditional track. I think that this has to do with the tendency of the IMP curriculum to shy away from any form of math drilling. In the case of algebra, though, drilling could have been useful.

Overall, as far as I am concerned, IMP restored in me a feeling of math competency, above and beyond the material that I learned. Had I remained in the traditional track, I feel certain that I would have continued to be discouraged with and uninterested in math.

RACHEL: While I found many of the topics covered in IMP to be difficult, I enjoyed the writing aspect of it, and the chance that I had to make up for my deficiencies in math by using the skills that I had in writing. I almost felt like I was getting away with something, like someone had said, "Here, you can take an English class instead of a math class." I remember that I had a very difficult time with the more "traditional" topics, especially ones related to algebra (the thought of which still makes me break out into a cold sweat), while I did better with the topics which required more creative thinking (i.e., trigonometry problems involving surfers, probability problems involving ice cream cones, and—my favorite—an especially literary unit which was modeled after *The Pit and the Pendulum*). While I had some rocky times in some of the subjects, I was always pretty grateful that I wasn't in a traditional class. I often needed help from my father with the problems of the week (the question of getting outside help had been addressed early on in the class, and we had been told that collaborative work was fine as long as credit was given where it was due and as long as we wrote it up ourselves), but once he had provided me with the answer I went back over the problem and made sure that I could solve it again myself, so that I would be able to explain it thoroughly. Doing all that writing sometimes felt tedious, but I was glad to have the chance to express and explain myself. Sometimes I really felt like I was fooling my teachers though, and I was afraid that a moment of truth would come where they would peel away my fancy writing and say, "Aha! See, I told you! She has no clue about math!"

It was true that some students in my class who were better at math were dissatisfied with the program and felt that what they were learning was too easy and wouldn't help them in college or on the SATs. I wonder why these students preferred traditional math to IMP, since from my perspective, having an opinion like that would mean that a CAT scan should be in order. For one thing, these students always seemed aggravated with having to explain their answers and thought processes, either verbally or in a written form. Perhaps this proves that there is something to the pervasive myth that some math people can't function in the humanities world (and, of course, vice versa); many of the students that disliked IMP also hated English and felt that they had been duped into taking an extra English class. It is ironic that perhaps those same IMP students who mocked IMP as being "too easy" might have actually felt insecure because IMP challenged their verbal skills. While I understand that many students who are stronger in math would want more difficult, traditional material—which leaves students to flounder on their own by not giving what I guess they might consider "free handouts"—I would hate to see IMP become a sort of remedial classroom for students who could not survive anywhere else.

ELISSA: If I were to be critical of IMP, it would be that algebraic manipulation was not emphasized enough. We were guided in creating for ourselves the thinking "software," but the necessary hard-core algebra skills were somewhat lacking. Sometimes more abstract and traditional kinds of lessons were introduced, only to have a few assignments in a unit reinforce the concepts. There are times when a certain amount of practice is necessary in order to give students a level of comfort or proficiency, out of which can come creative thinking. I think IMP students were asked first to think creatively, without being given the traditional mathematical language. This allowed for the "discovery" of theorems, or essentially the unpacking of them (a demystification of math), but the proficiency with symbolic manipulation was never mastered.

I enjoyed the way IMP drew from physics (the movement of pendulums) and the biological sciences (population growth, geometry of beehives). I thought the use of literary works ranging from *Alice and Wonderland* to *The Pit and the Pendulum* as backdrops for problems was quite unique. This multidisciplinary approach, combined with presentation practice and a familiarity with technology, are definitely what I consider to have been the strong points of the program, as well as the dedicated teachers who taught my classes for four years.

DOROTHY: For me, IMP wasn't just a math course, it taught me how to approach problems in every subject. Fortunately for me, at Central I have experienced both four years of IMP and one year of traditional calculus. I worry a little about my all-IMP classmates who haven't been exposed to certain topics that the other students have had. It is comforting for me to hear from my collegiate coauthors that they fared well in their first math-related college courses.

I sometimes think back to the end of eighth grade when I first heard about IMP. Back then, I thought that IMP was for me. As it turned out, I was right: IMP *was* for me.

A Last Word

Ned Wolff

At the time the five student coauthors first chose to enroll in the Interactive Mathematics Program, their math backgrounds ranged from highly successful to math phobic. Some years later, as they looked back on their IMP experiences, all said they were glad they participated in the program. Of particular benefit, they suggest, was IMP's emphasis on problem solving, group work, and communication skills. They also identify areas of the program they felt needed strengthening. These included a need for more practice doing algebraic manipulation and increased exposure to traditional terminology.

While this feedback will certainly be of interest to the program's developers and other math educators considering its adoption, other issues raised by the students are relevant to all educators. One is that no single curriculum can be an automatic "silver bullet" that solves all problems. Indeed, a new program can be successful only when taught by enthusiastic, well-trained teachers who fully buy both into the program's content and pedagogy and who teach at a school whose culture is supportive of their and their students' efforts.

In a section heading, Rachel used the familiar saying "You can't teach old dogs new tricks" to summarize the students' frustration over the difficulties that arose when teachers, long accustomed to traditional methods of teaching, attempted to remake themselves as facilitators of a student-centered classroom. It should be noted, however, that one of the teachers about whom two of the original students complained, because she seemed "unable to adjust to the new way of thinking," is precisely the same one who later taught Sonia and Dorothy in their junior year and whom they credit for finally showing them what IMP was really meant to be. Thus the students' experiences can be interpreted to support the optimistic view that, over time, teachers can indeed become successful practitioners of new pedagogical strategies. (Of course, motivation, administrative support, and professional development opportunities all play key roles in making this transition possible.)

One final issue raised by the students' writings merits emphasizing. When the students signed up for IMP, they had no idea they would soon be immersed in an ongoing, heated battle between traditional and reform-minded educators. Their articulate, thoughtful reflections serve to remind us that when educators become embroiled in acrimonious conflict, it is the students who are caught in the middle.

Notes

The Interactive Mathematics Program is a four-year college preparatory mathematics program published by Key Curriculum Press. For more information about the program, visit the Web site at www.mathimp.org.

1. The first part of the title is used by permission from Janice Bussey, outreach coordinator of the Interactive Mathematics Program, who wrote an unpublished essay, "Caught in the Storm of Reform."

CHAPTER 7

Reflections: Writing and Talking about Race in Middle School

Student Authors: Darreisha Bates, Noah Chase, Chris Ignasiak, Yvette Johnson, and Tina Zaza

Researcher/Teacher Authors: Tricia Niesz, Patti Buck, and Katherine Schultz

Introduction

Tricia Niesz, Patti Buck, and Katherine Schultz

This chapter, written by a multiracial group of middle school writers, is composed of three parts. Each section represents a facet of the students' perspectives on race relations: a play the students wrote, a discussion of why and how the students chose to write a play to represent race relations, and excerpts from students' writing about race. The students attended a suburban middle school located in a school district that recently rescinded its court-mandated desegregation plan. This chapter grew out of a writing project that was a part of a longitudinal research project at Skyline Middle School. That study, initiated by Katherine Schultz and James Davis in 1996, was designed to document students' perspectives on race and race relations in this postdesegregation time period. The researchers noticed that students' voices were missing from debates about the future of the district under the new court order. A goal of their project was to document students' understandings and reflections about their schooling at this historic moment. Patti Buck and Tricia Niesz joined the research project as ethnographers and initiated a writing project with a group of students. As another way to elicit students' perspectives on race relations in their school, the researchers invited a multiracial group of friends to meet together after school to write about race and schooling in the context of their own middle school. The students immediately agreed to participate in this writing project.

In the beginning, our writing group meetings took the form of informal discussions about the student writers' experiences and perspectives related to race at

Skyline. This proved to be unfamiliar territory for the students. At Skyline, as in most of the country, there is an unstated rule to avoid talk about race. Too often, talk about race is interpreted as racist and to notice race and name it as a topic for discussion is seen as divisive. While it was difficult, the students were willing to participate in these discussions. Writing proved to be harder for them. After a few meetings, students told the facilitators that they wrote so much in their classes, it was difficult to muster the enthusiasm to write after school. The group leaders had to help students find a bridge to writing about race. Searching for a way to enliven our work together, researchers suggested writing a play and the group responded positively.

The play gave the writers an opportunity to make interesting and important connections to the topic of race. Each student began by focusing on a different topic: Tina wrote about the role of race in multiracial friendship groups; Noah wrote about teacher treatment; and Darreisha wrote about interracial dating. In addition, the writers each drew on different types of material to compose their first several scenes. Darreisha surveyed her white and black girlfriends to ask how they would approach a boy they liked. The responses differed by race, and these differences were incorporated into the play. Yvette picked up on this same theme of interracial dating and wrote from the perspective of black girls who commented on but were not a part of interracial couples. Noah reflected on his own experiences in school as a multiracial student and exaggerated these events to create a poignant scene about teacher treatment. Chris wrote about being teased for being white when he played basketball with a group of black boys. Rather than drawing on her own individual experiences, Tina used group discussions to write her first scene. Students eventually worked their individual perspectives into a single script that contained each of their voices. After they completed the play script, the student writers discussed its fictionalized nature and the ways in which it represented an exaggerated version of reality. We begin the chapter with introductions from the student members of our writing group. These are followed by the final version of their play.

Introductions

So you wanna know about me, huh? Well, my name is Darreisha Bates and I'm a fourteen-year-old girl who lives in Delaware. I live with my mom and my older brother. I enjoy long walks on the beach and sunsets. (That's a joke, I just felt like putting that.) About everyday I practice/play my clarinet. I've been playing for three years. As far as sports go, I'm pretty good at volleyball and basketball. When I get to high school I would like to run track and play the sports that I just wrote. I prefer to read mystery/horror books but I'm glad to read just about any kind. I enjoy the out of doors and I love *Rugrats*.

I am Noah Chase, a thirteen-year-old multiracial boy who is in the Penn writing group. I guess when I accepted the invitation to be in this group, I didn't know what I was getting myself into, but now that I think about it, it was a good thing. This group made me more aware of the race problems or issues that affect people around my age. I think of my intelligence as above average. But I'm not a prodigy or a nerd or anything. I make honor roll about three-fifths of the time, even though I used to make it every marking period. I think the problem is I'm just lazy and I get too engrossed in the Internet. Next year I'm going to Charter and my goal there is to make excellent grades every marking period, every year, because it is really important to my parents that my twin brother and I make not good grades, but superb grades. The thing that concerns me most in school is my twin brother, Useff. He is at least as smart as me, but hardly does any of his work. And I don't want him to mess up but he does often and it's like he doesn't care.

I'm an eighth-grader in Skyline Middle School and my name is Chris Ignasiak. I am a wiz at computers and play computer games on a daily basis. When I grow up I want to be a NASA space engineer and I like astronomy. I got a telescope last summer and have found Jupiter, Saturn, Mars, and the Orion Nebula. I wish I could get the more powerful telescope but it costs over $300. In my younger years I built models and built things with my K'Nex and Steel Tek. I also like *Star Trek*. I watch the TV shows and movies and buy the figures, but I'm not a geek. I also like soccer and almost all of the sports we play in my gym class. That is pretty much me.

My name is Yvette Johnson and I am currently an eighth-grader at Skyline Middle School in the 1998–1999 school year. I am fourteen years old and a few things I like to do in my spare time are travel, read, and write, which is one of the reasons why I decided to contribute to this chapter. Even though I don't pay much attention to race differences or discrimination, I feel as though my views on these particular subjects will benefit students and teachers nationwide.

Hi, I'm Tina, a.k.a. Shorty, Taz, Lil' one! I live in Wilmington, Delaware and attend Skyline Middle School in eighth grade. In school this year, I enjoy art and social studies classes as well as phys ed because I love sports. You could call me a tomboy from birth! Currently, I am in a bowling league and travel to tournies along the East Coast called JBTs (Junior Bowling Tours). That makes bowling a large part of my life and it's where most of my friends originate. I also enjoy soccer and basketball, but I'm not very good. I'm not too sure why I was chosen for this particular writing group; you'd have to ask Tricia or Patti that. I mean I'm not a really good writer and I don't have too many ideas but I guess I can be creative and artistic sometimes. Lastly I enjoy being on-line at home.

Reflections: A Play about Race Relations

REFLECTIONS

A play written by
Darreisha Bates, Noah Chase, Chris Ignasiak, Yvette Johnson, and Tina Zaza

ACT 1: FALL

Scene 1: The first day of school

(Primary authors: Noah Chase and Chris Ignasiak)

STEVE [to himself]: I don't know whether to be mad or glad. School, ugghh, why
   do I even bother. Sometimes I don't know how I keep these good grades.
STUDENT 1: Hi, Steve.
STEVE: Hi.
STUDENT 1: What classes do you have this marking period?
STEVE: Science, honors L.A., algebra, social studies, technology, and gym for
   electives.
STUDENT 1: Wow, you must be pretty smart; honors L.A. and algebra?!
STEVE: Yeah, I guess—
STUDENT 1: Are you sure there wasn't a mistake?
STEVE: Shut up.
(Steve is instantly offended and walks off to his next class.)
(In the hallway)
STEVE: Science class might be all right this year, huh?
ZACH: Maybe. First I wanna try and get through the day. I don't want to be here.
STEVE: Guess what happened to me over the summer?
ZACH: What?
STEVE: I went to camp in Cecil County at the Y.
ZACH: Cecil County? Is that where all those hillbillies live?
STEVE: Yeah. It was a crazy experience. All the girls loved me, but all the guys got
   all jealous!
ZACH: Oh.
STEVE: And on top of that, I got people gettin' angry at me, and calling me names.
ZACH: Names?
STEVE: Yeah. All the jealous guys were calling me stuff like nigger.

ZACH: Jeez, that sounds really messed up! If I were you I wouldn't go to camp there ever again! Why were all those girls so attracted to you?

STEVE: I guess everyone down there was white. That's what it looked like anyway. I was new and different to them.

ZACH: That's pretty strange. Lemme tell you about my summer. I went to basketball camp for the first time. When I got there I noticed that there were only a few white kids.

STEVE: Really? I thought there would be a lot of white kids there.

ZACH: There were so little of us that none of us were in the same cabin. Not that I have anything against that, but I thought there would be more white kids.

STEVE: God, there were so few of you.

ZACH: Well I was always picked last for teams and the only time I got to play was when the counselors were teaching lessons. They called me whitie behind my back when they thought I couldn't hear them.

STEVE [teasing]: Maybe I should start callin' you whitie.

ZACH: Don't even. The time my summer turned around was when we were playing a tournament game and everyone was being covered except me. The ball was passed to me, I dribbled under the basket, and did a reverse lay-up. After that I was picked first for the teams and the ball was passed to me a lot.

STEVE: Uh huh.

ZACH: They still called me whitie, but it was a nickname. I didn't mind it when it was meant as a good thing.

STEVE: Yeah.

ZACH: My summer was great and I forgot all the negative stuff that happened and I made lots of friends. I'm going back next summer.

(Bell rings.)

STEVE: I got L.A. next. See you later.

ZACH: I'll see ya in second period. Hey, Mike, wait up.

(Walking into honors L.A.)

STEVE [to himself]: Why are classes so far away from each other this year? (walking into class) Oh god, everybody here is white.

MRS. CRABTREE: What class are you here for?

STEVE: This one.

MRS. CRABTREE: What? Did a teacher send you with something for me?

STEVE: No, I'm supposed to be in this class right now!

MRS. CRABTREE: Really? Lemme see your schedule.

STEVE: Here.

MRS. CRABTREE: Okay, but tomorrow I want you to check with the guidance counselor to see if it may have been a mistake.

STEVE: Whatever. [to himself] Gonna be a long, long year.

ACT 2: WINTER

Scene 1: Second period of the day, in Mr. Joe's class and Mrs. Freedman's class.

(Primary author: Darreisha Bates)
(A black girl likes a biracial boy, and a white girl likes the same boy. Observe the different ways they ask him out.)

KATHY: Steve is sooo fine. He is the best looking guy in school.
STEPHANIE: He ain't all that. He's just okay.
KATHY: Are you kidding. He's not just all that. He's alllllllllllll that! Hmmmm.
STEPHANIE: Whatever. (sigh) Brian is much cuter.
(Kathy shrugs her shoulders and starts daydreaming about Steve.)
(Same time in Mrs. Freedman's class)
JANELLE: I want to go out with Steve so bad. I think about him all of the time.
TAY: You are one sick puppy. You're obsessed. Why don't you just ask him out?
JANELLE: I don't know. I just think that he won't like me! I heard it through the grapevine that he only goes out with white girls.
TAY: Well, you'll never know until you try.
JANELLE: You're right. I'll ask him out today during fourth period.
(Back to Mr. Joe's class)
STEPHANIE: Omigod, look at Brian, he looks hmmm great today. Are you looking? Ah too late, you missed it. Hey, what's wrong with you?
(Kathy is daydreaming about Steve so she doesn't even take notice to Brian as he walks in.)
KATHY [surprised]: W-w-what did you say?
STEPHANIE: I said, what's wrong with you? Brian just walked past and he was looking . . .
(Steve walks in late as usual.)
KATHY [interrupts her]: Omigod, look at Steve. Doesn't he look good today? [That beautiful body of his (sigh).] I've decided I want you to ask him out for me.
STEPHANIE: What!! Are you crazy?!?! Why don't you ask him or write him, send him a videotape for all I care.
KATHY: I'm too nervous to ask him. I can hardly pick out a pair of shoes without going crazy. Besides, what if he says no? What if he says yes? (Starts to bite nails nervously.)
STEPHANIE: If he says no, you go on with your life. If he says yes, you jump up and down like a maniac and say yes back. I don't think Janelle would be nervous. Oops. (Covers her mouth realizing her mistake.)
KATHY: What does Janelle have to do with it?

(Stephanie shrugs her shoulders.)

KATHY: Don't tell me she likes him too! Oh my god. Now you definitely have to ask him for me. Pleeeeeese, Pleeeeeese, Pleeeese, please.

STEPHANIE: No, I won't. (Shakes her head no.)

KATHY: Pleeese, you've got to. If you were a true friend you would.

STEPHANIE: (Huffs and puffs) Ohhhhhh alright! I will. What do you want me to say? (Stephanie whispers for about five minutes, and then she walks over to the table where Zach, Brian, and Steve are working.)

BRIAN [smiling]: What's up baby! Watcha want?

STEPHANIE [flirty]: Nothin' much. Just came over to ask Steve something.

BRIAN [winking]: Oh, okay.

STEPHANIE: So, anyway, Steve, do you wanna go out with the beautiful and magnificent Kathy?

ZACH: Who?

STEPHANIE: Kathy and besides I wasn't talking to you so [shoo–shoo]. Anyway, (to Steve) what do you think?

STEVE: I think I need to think about it, okay?

STEPHANIE: Okay, see you later.

(Later on before lunch)

JANELLE [walking]: Hi, Steven, wuz up?

STEVE: Nothing, just chillin'. How about you?

JANELLE: I'm fine. I just wanted to ask you something.

STEVE: What?!

JANELLE: Well, I was just wondering if you like me and if you wanted to go out with me.

STEVE [confused]: You're asking me out? I thought we were just friends but I need some time to think about it, okay?

JANELLE: Okay.

Scene 2: Lockers and class

(Primary author: Tina Zaza)

ZACH: Hi, guys!

BRIAN: Hey, Zach. What do we need for our next class?

TAY: Just bring some paper and a pencil. We hafta take notes on Mrs. Crabtree's big speech, remember?

BRIAN [sarcastically]: Oh, yeah. Sounds like fun!

STEPH: Yeah, really. That teacher's always going on and on about something stupid.

BRIAN: Yeah, I know, and she's always mean to me for some reason.

ZACH: Really? She's never mean to me.

STEPH: Me either.

TAY: I think I might know why . . .

ZACH: Why?

TAY: Oh, never mind. You wouldn't want to hear it, and you wouldn't believe me.

ZACH: Tell me.

TAY: No.

STEPH: Yea, all right, let's go. We're gonna be late.

BRIAN: C'mon, Mrs. Crabtree's gonna be bustin' on us about how we never get there on time.

TAY: Uh huh. (Starts to walk away and everyone follows her.)

(The bell rings just as they walk into the classroom.)

MRS. CRABTREE: Looks like you four just made it in time. Take your seats now. Today we'll continue our study of civil rights.

TAY: (Whispering to Brian) Yea, I wish we had some.

BRIAN: (Whispering back) What do you mean by that?

TAY: Oh, nothing. (She quiets down as Mrs. Crabtree looks toward them.)

STEPH: (whispering to Zach) What does Tay keep whispering about?

ZACH: Something about not having civil rights I think.

STEPH: Oh, that's ridiculous. She has as many civil rights as anyone.

ZACH: I know . . .

MRS. CRABTREE: Now we're going to talk about the "Little Rock Nine." Quiet everybody. (She continues to explain about the Little Rock Nine.)

ZACH: (whispering to Steph) Man, this is so boring. We're all treated the same.

STEPH: Yea, nowadays. But they insist we learn this anyway.

ZACH: Yea, but why? We won't ever use it. Just like language arts.

STEPH: Oh well.

(Mrs. Crabtree walks toward them still talking. She motions for them to be quiet and listen. Then she continues talking and the children look bored.)

BRIAN: (Whispering to Tay) I'm glad I didn't live in the 1960s. I'd have busted those people in their lip if they didn't let me go to school there.

TAY: Yea, me too. (They giggle.)

MRS. CRABTREE: (Walking toward them with a mean look on her face) Is something about my speech funny?

BRIAN: Nope, sorry.

MRS. CRABTREE: Well, then I'd like to know why you were laughing? Or should I send you out?

TAY: We were saying what we would do in the same situation as the, ummmm . . . Little Rock Nine. Yeah, that's it.

MRS. CRABTREE: Oh? And what would that be?

BRIAN: You don't want to know . . .

(The class giggles.)

MRS. CRABTREE: Oh, really? Well, let's just say if you interrupt me again, not only will I want to know, but the principal will too.

CLASS: Ohhhhhhhh . . .

MRS. CRABTREE: Quiet, class, back to the lesson. (She goes on.)

(They all walk back to their lockers without saying anything until they get there.)

TAY [angry]: That was messed up!

BRIAN: (agreeing quickly) Yeah . . .

ZACH: What? About how Mrs. Crabtree got all mad at you guys?

TAY: Yep, it's not right. I mean, I know we shouldn't have been talking but she didn't do that to you and Steph, Zach.

ZACH: Well, I don't see why she couldn't have. I wouldn't have been surprised if she did.

STEPH: She's a wacky old lady. I'll bet she's racist.

TAY: That's what I've been trying to say all period!

STEPH: Oh, well, it makes sense. She's from the South and was a teen in the '60s. I bet she learned a couple things then that are still in her head now.

TAY [sarcastically]: That makes it real good for us now.

BRIAN: Yeah, tell me about it.

ZACH: A'ight, if this is the way she thinks, what can we do? Just forget about all this and let's go. We're gonna miss our buses.

TAY, BRIAN and STEPH: I guess not . . . bye.

(They all leave.)

Scene 3: The lockers after class

(Primary author: Yvette Johnson)

(Tay and her friend Crystal are standing in the locker bay.)

TAY [with disgust]: Oh, my god, I guess Brian asked Stephanie out.

CRYSTAL: (Places her hands on her hips.) Are you serious? Another black boy taking scoops in vanilla.

TAY: (Pokes Crystal in the ribs) Look. Here they come.

(Brian and Stephanie were walking down the hallway, holding hands. Tay walks over to Brian and shakes her head.)

TAY: You're a traitor.

BRIAN: Don't start with me Tay.

(Crystal rushes over to Tay's defense.)

CRYSTAL: (Sucks her teeth) What, black girls ain't good enough no more? You gotta go to white girls?

(Crystal and Tay and one of their friends form a circle around Brian and Stephanie.)

STEPH [angrily]: I guess he has no choice. Who would want to go out with girls as ugly as you?

(She flips her hair and continues down the hall. Brian follows after her. The bell rings and Crystal rushes to class. Tay runs up to a group of white girls. Tammy and Kathy are standing by the classroom door as Tay walks over to them.)

TAMMY: Hey, Tay. How—(She stops when she sees Tay's angry expression.)

TAY: Yo, you need to get your girl.

KATHY: What's wrong?

TAY: She and Brian are going out.

KATHY: Oh, that. So?

TAMMY [yelling]: What do you mean, so? They shouldn't be going out.

KATHY: Why shouldn't they?

TAMMY: (Shifting uncomfortably) It's not . . . right.

KATHY: (Rolls her eyes and sighs) I don't know what planet you're from but here on Earth, hardly anyone cares about interracial couples.

TAMMY: (Stamping her foot) Yeah, right. You and Stephanie ain't nothin' but nigger lovers.

(Tay walks over to Tammy and yanks on her hair. They start fighting and a teacher rushes over, pulling the two girls apart. Scene ends with the two girls breathing heavily and glaring at each other.)

ACT 3: SPRING

Scene 1: In the cafeteria

(Primary author: Chris Ignasiak with Yvette Johnson)

(Janelle and Tay finally get called up to the lunch line by Mr. Brown after a thirty-minute wait. As Janelle leaves the lunch line with spaghetti on her tray, she sees Steve. Mr. Brown is quietly observing the lunch room. He takes notice of a particular conversation.)

JANELLE: (Talking to a friend in the line) So, what do you think of Steve? Isn't he blazin'?!

TAY: (Facing Steph) I know! And—

JANELLE: His butt is so nice . . . (Trips over Steph's foot and falls into the plate while wearing her new cashmere sweater. She gets up.) I just bought this sweater yesterday. You gonna pay for this!

STEPH: (Giving her a dirty look and saying under her breath) I think you need to take it back.

JANELLE: You hoochie!

TAY: You wigger.

KATHY: (Standing up for her friend) Don't call her that!

STEPH: (Standing up from the table) So? Your point being . . . ?

JANELLE: Her point is you ain't black! Oh, and I think this was yours. (Picking up the spaghetti from the floor and throwing it at Stephanie and missing, hitting Steve.)

STEVE: What the heck are you doing throwing spaghetti at me? These are my good clothes. You lucky they're already dirty. (Throwing his spoonful of pudding and missing, hitting Zach and Kathy.)

ZACH: Steve, I know you my boy 'n all, but it's on now. (Throwing a big, fat plate of spaghetti and meatballs, missing and hitting Tay dead smack on the chest.)

TAY: Oh, no, he didn't! (She picks up a glob of spaghetti from Janelle's plate and throws it at Zach.)

JANELLE: Yo, here comes Mr. Watson. I'll catch up with you at the dance. You all better watch yourself.

Scene 2: The dance

(Primary author: Darreisha Bates)

(Before the dance at school)

JANELLE: No, you're not!

KATHY: Yes, I will and you can not stop me from dancing with him.

JANELLE: Steve doesn't like you, he likes me.

(Steve comes up to them)

STEVE: What's all the fuss about?

JANELLE and KATHY: You!

STEVE [shocked]: I'm tired of you girls fighting. I'll make my final decision at the dance tonight, okay?! (Walks away.)

JANELLE and KATHY: Fine. (Walk away.)

(At the dance. Janelle and Kathy give each other dirty looks. Steve comes up and dances with Kathy.)

STEVE: Kathy, this dance has been fun but I really don't like you like that . . . I'm sorry.

(Kathy starts whimpering and walks away. Steve goes and dances with Janelle. After the dance he walks away. Janelle is excited and happy because she thinks he likes her. She goes outside for air, where Kathy is crying.)

JANELLE: What's wrong?

(Kathy swings at her but misses.)

JANELLE: Why did you do that?

KATHY: Because I felt like it.

JANELLE [with aggression]: Why the **** did you try to hit me?

KATHY: Because Steve doesn't like me, he likes you. You stole my man you jerk!

JANELLE: How can I have stolen your man if he wasn't your man? I told you I would get him. (Snickers and walks away with a swish.)

(Kathy cries to herself and it starts to rain.)

KATHY [yelling]: Why is everything bad happening to me today?!?!

(She walks back inside and into the bathroom, fixes her hair, and goes back to the dance. Steph walks up to her.)

STEPH [lying]: Where have you been? I've been looking for you.

KATHY: Well, Steve just said that he didn't like me and I was upset. But at least he told me and didn't just go out with me because he felt he had to. Anyway, I'm over it now so let's do what we came here to do—Dance!

(Confused, Steph shrugs her shoulders and starts dancing.)

(Back to Steve and Janelle, who are dancing. They stop dancing and sit down.)

STEVE: Alright, Janelle, we need to talk.

JANELLE: About what, babe?

STEVE: Well, I'm sorry to tell you, but I don't really like you in that way. I hope we still can be friends . . .

JANELLE: (P.O.ed and annoyed, gets up and slaps him in the face) Forget you, you, you, you . . . stupid, big-headed, no-brainer idiot who thinks he's a playa but he's only playin' himself. (Walks away.)

STEVE: Janelle!!! Wait, come back! Don't leave me. I still want to be your friend. Awww, man!!

(Janelle walks by Kathy as she exits the dance.)

JANELLE: What'd you say to him, now he don't like me either!

KATHY: Really, that's cool.

JANELLE: No it's not, it sucks!

KATHY: That's true! I know how you feel.

(Silence)

JANELLE: I can't believe it. We both actually agreed on something.

KATHY: Yeah, that's right. We used to be good friends but what happened?

JANELLE: Steve happened.

KATHY: We never should have let a boy come between us!

JANELLE: I'm sorry.

KATHY: Yeah, me too.

(Later on, Janelle runs into Crystal.)

JANELLE: Hey, Crys. What's up?

CRYSTAL: That's what I should be asking you, you traitor!

JANELLE: How am I a traitor?

CRYSTAL: I saw you talking to that white trash!

JANELLE: How could you call her that? She always nice to you and never mean or nasty to you. She did nothing but respect you.

CRYSTAL: She hangs out with Stephanie and she took my man.

JANELLE: He was never your man.

(Silence)

CRYSTAL: He could have been.

(Tay walks in on them.)

TAY: What's all the commotion about?

JANELLE: Crystal's being a real . . . She's making rude comments about Kathy, and she's being narrow-minded. (Pause.) I'm going back to the dance because I'm not gonna let you ruin my night. (She leaves.)

TAY: Did I miss something?

CRYSTAL: Not really. Janelle is just taking up for that hoochie trash that you call Kathy.

TAY: You know what, Crystal? I can see now why I stopped being mean to white people. I realized that I was being rude and nasty to people who obviously didn't have any problems with me. (Pause.) I can't believe I actually used to act like you. In the beginning I didn't like the thought of black people going out with white people. But after I got in the fight with Tammy, I realized how many friends I was losing over something that didn't really matter.

CRYSTAL: What are you talking about? I thought you were my friend.

TAY: I am your friend, but I changed and situations have changed. You are the only one who is being the same.

(Crystal becomes teary-eyed.)

TAY: The truth hurts, doesn't it?

(Silence for a minute.)

CRYSTAL: Yeah, I guess you're right. Are we still cool?

TAY: Yeah, I guess so.

(Crystal walks over and begins talking to Kathy. The music is blasting. Crystal is making wild gestures with her hands. After a moment they hug. Tammy walks over while they are hugging and tries to separate them.)

TAMMY: What are you doing Kathy? Don't you feel dirty after hugging them Negroes?

KATHY: What are you talking about? In case you haven't noticed, it's the '90s and we refer to African Americans by their names, which in this case is Crystal.

TAMMY: Well, whatever their names are they need to get away because they're making me sick.

(Zach appears through a thick artificial mist.)

ZACH: What's up?

KATHY: Well this THING (pointing to Tammy) is being prejudice.

ZACH: About what?

KATHY: She thinks people can't be together if they're different.

ZACH: What's wrong with people going together if they're not of the same background? I've gone out with Lainna—she's Asian. So what's the problem?

TAMMY: There's something wrong with you. I don't care what you do but I think interracial mixing—whether its friendship or dating—is wrong.

KATHY: Who told you that?

TAMMY: My parents.

KATHY: Well, here's an idea, maybe for once your parents are wrong. And since when do you listen to what your parents say anyway?

TAMMY: Forget you! (She walks away.)

(Later on that night Steve, Zach, Brian, Crystal, Tay, Steph, Janelle, and Kathy are all on the dance floor dancing together. Mrs. Crabtree walks up to them, unaware that Mr. Brown is slowly approaching behind her.)

MRS. CRABTREE: I think you guys need to separate because you know I won't allow this black and white dancing to go on.

STEVE: Well, I think you're disgusting and a big racist. We see how you treat us differently during class.

MRS. CRABTREE: How dare you call me that?! Different races get treated differently because they act differently, they go to different places, and they read different things. Besides, it's your word against mine. Nobody's ever going to believe you anyway.

(Mr. Brown makes his presence known.)

MR. BROWN: I will! I will make a formal recommendation to the school board that you be relieved from your duties immediately. There will be no racial discrimination in this school.

(Mrs. Crabtree stomps off.)

EVERYBODY: Yes!

TAY: She's finally gone!

ZACH: So lets get our groove on! (Starts doing a disco dance)

STEVE: Ah, look at that fool! He can't dance.

(Everyone laughs and points at him, and starts dancing together in a circle.)

"The Truth Wouldn't Create Conflict Enough to Write About": Back to Realities of Race at Skyline

Our final meeting for play revisions fell on a sunny day in June, only days before final exams. The writers and the researchers negotiated with teachers to get the writers excused from classes in order to finish up a project that lasted longer than any of us had anticipated. Tying the scenes together was proving to be complicated, especially since most of the early scenes had single authors. How could we—as a group—figure out how to bring disparate story lines and writing styles together? Before getting to the tedious work of revising those final scenes, we debriefed the project and our work together. Chris was missing from the group to attend an important exam review session. The rest of us sat around a too-large conference table in the principal's meeting room. Tina sat at the far end of the table, insisting on typing up the notes of our conversation on a laptop computer. The rest of us spread out around the small tape recorder with books, notes, and copies of the play sitting in messy piles.

Although our conversation that day drifted among many topics—from the group's working relationship to exam worries to the fast food picnic lunch planned for later—Patti and Tricia pushed the writers to compare their own experiences of race in school to the fictionalized account in the play. What follows is a second representation of race by the students in the form of an excerpt of the conversation in which the comparison is highlighted. It has been edited for readability. This excerpt reflects where we ended up at the conclusion of the play writing process. Patti had asked the writers if they thought that they had been able to put their own personalities into the characters that they had played during our readings of the play in public forums. The conversation began with Darreisha's discussion of her character, Janelle.

DARREISHA: Personally I know [that unlike] my character, I would never fight over a boy like that where I'd be like [in] confrontation—especially with a friend [from] before. I was just like, you can have 'im. I wouldn't fight.

TRICIA: So, how come, do you think, it worked in the play to make them have a confrontation?

YVETTE: Because in a play you need action.

Others agree.

DARREISHA: And plus that was the topic—race, identity and everything. . . . I'm nice to everyone. I'm always happy. I'm not usually down like Janelle was. She was kinda there. She had no niceness emotion. And she was boy-crazy. I'm more nice than [she is].

YVETTE: [Tay's] underdeveloped.

PATTI: So what about you could develop her character?

DARREISHA: You're not mean like that.

YVETTE: I know, I'm nice.

TINA: (reading from her computer screen) There's a lot of stuff in there that I wouldn't say, like when Darreisha wrote a scene with my character in it, I found it hard to read because it wouldn't be something I'd say to a guy. I'm also more quiet than what was shown in the play. I'm more into sports and stuff than into obsessed with boys at school.

TRICIA: Were there reasons why it was easier to write a play than the others—the just regular stuff you were writing?

DARREISHA: If we had to write individually and we get like four pages each [of] just plain writing about race, so we figured that a play would be easier because you can make up stuff. It's easier to write fiction than write the truth sometimes. Because it comes out of your imagination, it comes out of your brain. It's hard to write truth—when you say truth it has to be true, so everything you say has to be true. So we do fiction you can mix make-believe, your imagination to the truth.

TRICIA: What's the difference between, um, I mean the topic of race, right? What's the difference between the truth of your experience of race and the fictional?

DARREISHA: Well, you mean everything in our play? Like as far as our school goes and stuff? Well we don't have as much racial-like stuff like that happening at Skyline—at least not now—and no one has racist teachers, as far as we know. They don't show it like they do in the play and, um, not as harsh in our school as in the scenes.

TINA: I agree.

YVETTE: One thing I hear from other people who come from different schools like King and Brookings.[1] They come here and they say they're surprised at how we act. 'Cause we're not that talking about races.

DARREISHA: Yeah, we're not separated as much.

YVETTE: Yeah.

DARREISHA: I mean, you should—oh my goodness, you should see—this is why I'm not going to a Sheridan school just because of that one thing. Because I live out right next to Sheridan Mall and I would have to go to a Sheridan School District and they're just so separated, it's terrible.

NOAH: What's it like?

DARREISHA: Well, I went into one with my mom. [She] just took me there and you could tell that different types of people and how they hung out with people and how they, just everything, how they acted around people, talks of conflicts.

TRICIA: Why do you think that [Skyline's different]?

DARREISHA: [It hasn't been] always perfect. But like they got rid of all the bad people who started the conflict. And it's just it's gotten better I think. . . . We don't get bad people.

PATTI: And those bad people—

DARREISHA: Or they, yeah, or they fight.

TRICIA: Yvette, would you agree with what Darreisha said?

YVETTE: About what?

TRICIA: About how, um, why there seems to be less conflict here than—?

YVETTE: Yeah, the bad people couple years ago went to DSC [an alternative school for students expelled for behavior problems].

DARREISHA: Yeah DSC. . . . I saw Monique.

YVETTE: I saw, um, Shaquan.

NOAH: James Watson.

PATTI: Darreisha, you said that the teachers here, the teachers here aren't as bad . . . the teachers aren't as racist as they are in the play and they don't show it as much anymore.

DARREISHA: Yeah.

PATTI: Have you thought about ways that they do show it?

DARREISHA: Well, they don't show it. If they have racism, they don't show it basically at all. If they do show it, you don't notice it. I haven't noticed any teachers be racist because it's too hard. I don't know how people could be racist; it's too hard, especially for teachers. It's really hard to be racist if you have to deal with all the students. I don't think I've seen any—I thought, you know, if you get yelled at—like my friend, whenever she gets yelled at . . . well not anymore, but at the beginning of the year she thought one teacher was racist but it was, she just got yelled at so she got mad, so she just said, "[she's] racist"—and then, later on you find out it's not [true].

TRICIA: Do others agree with how Darreisha characterized it, or do you think, do you have a different opinion? Different ideas about it? Noah.

NOAH: I agree. I'm not all here right now. I'm kinda—

DARREISHA: We need some fast food.

NOAH: Fast food won't help. I just want another bowl of cheerios.

TRICIA: Well, if a lot of the things you wrote about aren't that likely to happen at Skyline, where did the ideas come from for each of the—think about the scenes that you wrote? If it was a scene that just really wouldn't probably happen here, what made you think about it to write about it?

NOAH: Why did we write it? Um . . .

TRICIA: Well, Noah, in your first scene about the teacher, when we did a one-on-one interview, you said that that really hasn't happened to you.

NOAH: It just seemed like something that's possible to happen. It probably happens in many places.

DARREISHA: Can you repeat that question? I got it but I was thinking too hard.

TRICIA: Just thinking about the difference from what really goes on at Skyline versus what the play is like, where did the ideas come from?

DARREISHA: Everywhere, personal experiences other places, not here but experiences like with the shopping mall or something. Or you hear it from friends at other schools. Just, you know, experiences.

PATTI: Has it, has being part of this group, talking about race issues, made you think about your experiences at Skyline differently?

NOAH: I think I noticed a lot more stuff.

TRICIA: You noticed it before?

NOAH: I guess it made, a lot of things made me more aware.

TRICIA: (to Darreisha, after she told of a friend in a love triangle similar to the one in the play) I don't understand what you just said. Somebody was mad at somebody?

DARREISHA: She wasn't mad at him but I guess you could say she was jealous.

TRICIA: Kinda like the story [in the play]?

DARREISHA: Yes, it wasn't as upfront and they didn't confront each other . . .

PATTI: So if there's like a theme it's that the play—

DARREISHA: Overexaggerates some of it, acknowledges everything.

PATTI: And race issues in real life are [subtle]?

DARREISHA: Yeah.

Writing about Race and Writing: Some Final Reflections

As the researchers watched students collaborate and compromise to write the play in a single voice, students were periodically asked to write individual pieces that reflected their own views on race, identity, relationships, and school. What follows is an edited collection of this writing. This third and final representation includes students' reflections about the experience of writing this chapter together.

RACIAL CATEGORIES

When teachers, strangers, students, or people in general stamp a label on me by just looking at me, is when I don't want to be seen as my skin color. I don't want what I look like to determine where I am to be placed or how I am stereotyped. It's my personality that makes me Darreisha!

On the other hand I'd like people to always see me as who I am. For example, when people talk about my race and they stress the word black, it kind of makes me mad. It always irks me that people don't think before they speak.

—Darreisha, 9/22/99

I don't think anyone likes to be put into categories, whether they belong to that category or not. Especially categories based on race and appearance. Even though most times they don't show it, many people get offended when they are categorized. One reason may be that that particular person's appearance doesn't reflect their heritage. If you want people to remain positive toward this kind of thing and if it is absolutely necessary to categorize by race, ask every person who you are using for statistics what race they are, and/or, if needed, what race they identify with.

Me, being biracial, most people would probably take a look at me and almost instantly categorize me as black. I would not appreciate this at all. I was never really fond of categorizing, but if it had to be done I (and I'm sure others agree) want to be asked what my race is. From what I know, people are categorized into four races—white, black, Hispanic, and Asian. Maybe even less than that. But I believe that there should be as many racial categories as there are actual races.

—Noah, 2/25/99

I don't categorize people I meet by their race but by the ethics and personalities. To me each person is different and each person has a different way of doing things, whether black or white. Instead of asking people their views based on their race, they should be asked based on their own beliefs. As long as people are categorized we'll never get past our racial differences.

—Yvette, 9/22/99

ON TEACHERS AND PEERS

I think that most teachers have a little bit of a premonition on what a black student is like. However, once they meet some of them their premonition just about disappears. Although some teachers tend to prejudge students that they end up wrong about. I think that a teacher, who expresses themselves toward everybody and not just toward one set of people, gets more respect from everybody. When a teacher acts shady, they tend to express all their thoughts and feelings toward one group. Some teachers don't understand that students can pick up on that.

—Darreisha, 1/14/99

From the black guys I know most of them are good students, or at least my friends are. The ones in *some* of my classes seem to act out a little more than others do. Mostly, only if they get yelled at or are in trouble. I think we need some black male teachers; I haven't ever had one of those. But most of the music we listen to is black guys.

I think that being a black boy in the school makes you seem pretty dominant. That's the impression I get. The black boys usually do a lot of the school's fighting, if any. I guess some people look at them as being stronger or threatening. They could probably easily beat people up. Most of them idolize black male rappers that are sometimes very negative and/or gangsters. They wear a lot of brand-name clothes. And that's about it.

Even though, on the surface, we seem pretty unracial at Skyline, underneath there is some racism. It only occurs in extremely odd times, I think.

—Tina, 12/19/99

REFLECTIONS ON WRITING THE PLAY, REFLECTIONS ON RACE

My name is Yvette Johnson and as a former student of Skyline Middle School (1998–1999) I feel that personally racism wasn't a big deal but to those around me it was like an everyday reminder about how different we really are. (Not so much as in race but in our personality and how we approach the issue of racism.)

Because I've never been really faced head-on about race, I haven't much opinion on it but as to my African-American peers they were constantly aware of the differences in whites and black based on beliefs, cultures, and racial tendencies.

In the future I suppose I'd feel the same as I do now but as an adult I suspect I'd have to be faced with it every day in the workplace and everyday life. I can't say that I'll be able to convince biased ideals of racist or prejudiced people but it won't be because lack of trying.

So in the future I'll approach race with an open mind and an open heart.

—Yvette, 9/22/99

I believe that I will approach racism, in the future, just as I have been in the past. I'll have my eyes open and aware that it's there, but I won't harp on the issue or let it place me in life. To me it is only skin deep. What tells the most about a person is their personality. When I decide who I'd be interested in dating, I rarely look at their color. That issue just doesn't determine anything in my life. Now, of course, I'm not perfect, and yes, I've thought that a waiter or store clerk didn't help me because of my race. But I always feel that that is their ignorance against me and usually I'll just let it go, like a feather in the wind.

Over all, I'd say that this project unlocked a little storage shed in the back of my mind. I was able to let out some of those feelings that had been locked in there. I felt better to have my voice be heard, as well as listen to the rest of the crew's voices. It was an exhilarating experience that I was glad to be a part of.

—Darreisha, 9/22/99

In the future, I plan on approaching race in the same exact way as I've always done. I never have tried to let it be a problem and wouldn't confront it unless it absolutely became necessary, like this group. I think, however, that being a part has helped me realize that there must be more racial conflict than I thought and also now I am able to more freely address the issue and talk about it. Though it was "strenuous" at times and hard to get out opinions, I think we produced a good finished product, whether fictional or factual.

From this point on, I will most likely acknowledge the racial existence in school. With teachers, I try not to care what they think of us, and just assume everything is equal (because that's how I see it.) Within my peers, friendships, and boyfriend, I basically think about the same way, in that if they want to be my friends and haven't treated me wrongly before and are willing to associate openly with me, then that's great and I'd be willing to make that work. My opinion on this will most likely never change because that is how I keep friendships strong but, hey, you never know. I now, and probably always will, put my friends above everyone no matter what race they are. I hope to keep it this way and would like to see others also make it known the importance of races, and the conflicts that should be resolved. I would like to be seen as a white girl only on the records of a survey when it is completely necessary. All other times I would not care what color I am. I could be rainbow-colored, have everyone stare at me twenty-four–seven, and I would not care. I'd make it known that I didn't care or mind and that they shouldn't either until it gets engraved in their brains. This is all just my opinion though.

A lot of times we did not have an answer for things, some things can't be put into words, but I still believe we got a lot out of the writing group.

—Tina, 9/22/99

In the meetings I've had with Noah, Tina, Yvette, and Darreisha, we've touched a lot of issues in today's world, from interracial dating to friendships. In the whole time I did this I've always approached race with open arms. Something I've thought of is, "It isn't the race, it's the individual person that does the negative thing." I've thought a lot about this over the last couple days; for example if you ask someone (regardless of color or race or gender) for help on a math question and the person says stuff like, "You don't know that, how stupid can you be" and gives you dirty looks versus the person who says, "I'll be glad to help" and shows you exactly how to do the problem. That is an example of "it's the person, not the race."

Another thing I've learned is that people tend to hang out with people that have same interests and that think the same. The thing we talked about with the blacks and whites sitting at different ends of the cafeteria has to do with who they are friends with and not that we dislike white people or black people. I have a couple black friends that I talk to during class but at lunch they have friends that they've known a lot longer and know more about so they tend to sit with those people just as I do in the cafeteria.

The thing is we just have to accept each other as equal.

—Chris, 9/22/99

We conclude with a poem by Yvette Johnson that expresses both her talent for writing and a deeply felt desire to transcend the sociohistorical boundaries of race. We believe that it is a fitting end to this chapter, given the resonance of this theme throughout our work together.

AS ONE

I hear the heartbeats of my ancestors. With every throb their echoing cries vibrate in my mind. I hear their powerful voices, the voices of Harriet Tubman, who believed that every slave should be free; Martin Luther King Jr., who had a dream of black and whites living in unity.

I also hear my voice. My voice knows we are all a part of one race. In order to survive we must come together as one: black man, white man, yellow man, red man. What is a color? It is only the icing that stands proudly on the cake.

If we could look past the skin and see the person you and I know they could be, people's outlook on the world would change drastically. Like a slave clinging to its master the world hangs viciously onto the past, refusing the future's arrival. We must let go before the past forever claims us.

In the midst of the fog that hovers heavily over our eyes walks the great and small. Kings, queens, slaves and peasants. They are of one mind: separate we must be. They give no thought to freedom, individualism and democracy.

Here we are facing a new millennium; we should also be facing change. For we are all a part of one race, black man, white man, yellow man, and red man. We must come together and act as one.

—Yvette, 2/5/99

Note

1. The names of these schools are pseudonyms.

CHAPTER 8

Writing the Wrong: Making Schools Better for Girls

Student Authors: Margo Strucker and Lenelle N. Moise

Researcher/Teacher Authors: Vicki Magee and Holly Kreider

My heart is racing but I keep my head down. . . . It's a wonder I can even hold my head erect today. For all those years it hung loosely, downward always.

—Margo Strucker

Once upon a reality there was a little girl who sat in the very last seat in the very last row of the classroom. There, where her little heart sang with the sounds of incoming and imagined escapades; there, where her soul sank at the screech of the worn-down piece of chalk, wondering on the blackboard—there, she waited like a hungry bitch for her master—there she waited to be noticed, at least, and then, perhaps fed. Waiting is the first life lesson.

—Lenelle N. Moise

We write in this chapter about our experiences in middle and high school. Through freewrites, we present our feelings of satisfaction and disappointment in school. We elaborate on and consider the issues these freewrites raise in the context of school reform, and we focus on ways to improve relationships in the classroom and bring girls' voices into conversations about school reform.

We are four women who bring our specific personal and cultural lenses to this work. We are intergenerational, ranging in age from younger than twenty to fifty years old. Lenelle is Haitian American, Vicki and Holly are of German and Irish descent, and Margo is of Scandinavian, Eastern European, and Native American descent. We also represent working and middle-class backgrounds and various regional perspectives, including the Northeast, Midwest, and West. All of us are self-described writers who have used freewriting, poetry, playwriting, short stories, and journals in our personal lives.

When we began this chapter, Margo and Lenelle were finishing their final semester of high school. Both are now in college. In nearly each case, we knew each other before this chapter began, through the context of school, graduate school, and special projects. As we discuss later, this relational history set the stage for honesty and trust in our collaborative writing.

We have made a deliberate and artistic choice to use the collective voice in this chapter, and we do not deny the different psychological implications of that choice. First, in our collective experience, we have found that our individual voices have been disregarded in the classroom; *we do not want to risk being ignored by our readers*. Second, at one time or another, each of us has felt intimidated and unheard when speaking in our individual voices, and we do not want to be intimidated by this endeavor. Third, all four of us have felt lonely, misunderstood, and excluded as students and are using the collective to remind ourselves that *we are not alone*—that we have never been alone and that other students need to know that they, too, are not alone.

The Context of Our Work

WHAT WE DID

We began thinking about what we would write for this chapter by meeting several times at Vicki's or Holly's homes to freewrite together. Freewriting is a writing exercise that often involves a set period of time and the use of a prompt, for instance, words, phrases, photographs, objects, or music. Freewriting is meant to express one's "wild mind" through a kind of writing that is an uncensored, uninterrupted act of pen to paper (Goldberg 1986).

Our meetings always included several ten-minute freewrites. We used various word prompts to get us started. Among all of the words that we brainstormed, we finally selected five words/phrases as prompts: *hallway, purgatory, boys, sex education,* and *better.* Our selection of prompts and our group agreement of reading aloud only when one felt comfortable was meant not only to keep us focused, but also to create an environment where we did not have to reveal anything that felt uncomfortable. We discovered that we were comfortable sharing all of our freewriting with each other.

The freewrites in this chapter reflect both our positive and negative memories of school. Many of these memories focus on the quality of our relationships with teachers and with other students. Three relational themes emerged from our writing and conversations: teachers' absence, peers and pain, and silence and writing.

Our freewritings serve as the central material of the chapter, but the act of collaborative writing and discussion helped to organize our freewrites and distill our ideas further. So we also offer a description of our collaborative writing process for others to consider.

Finally, we draw conclusions from our freewrites and our relational experiences in school, including the value of girls' voices in educational reform and the need to find ways to bring students' personal writings into the classroom. We suggest freewriting as one activity for welcoming students' personal voices in the classroom and for building student-teacher relationships.

It was during our truthful meetings that our collective voice was first born. Our choice to write this chapter in the first person plural was an obvious extension of this experience.

OUR CHOICE TO WRITE IN THE COLLECTIVE VOICE

Do not be deceived. Margo and Lenelle, the younger aspect of this chapter, have not been disregarded, brainwashed, or spoken for. Very early in the writing process, we realized that although we differ from each other in many ways, one of the things we share is our educational experience in this country.

In reading this collective voice, know that Margo and Lenelle are intelligent, articulate, opinionated, and capable young women. Our voices have been qualified by Vicki's and Holly's, and likewise, their voices qualified by ours. We are using the collective voice to further qualify the voices of our fellow students and writers and, more importantly, to qualify the voices of those who have remained silent. We are using the collective voice to break the cycle of silence.

We conversed in this writing process—in meetings, phone conversations, and e-mails, challenging as well as supporting each other. In the past, many of our teachers have been surprised by our proficiency or doubted us and underestimated us. In reading this chapter, we are asking you to respect us, trust us, and join us. Keep an open mind.

WHY WRITING?

We are convinced that girls' writing holds tremendous potential for revealing truths about girls' psychological, social, and educational experiences. We know from other sources that girls' writing can be essential psychological data. Common knowledge points to diary and letter writing as part of many girls' lives. A number of diaries, including that of Anne Frank, stand out as examples of girls' personal writing throughout history. Some scholars have also noted the important role of personal writing in girls' lives. Even Sigmund Freud (1921) brought attention to girls' diary writing when he wrote his preface to *A Young Girl's*

Diary. He called this diary a "little gem" that would be of great interest to psychologists and educators. Most recent research has shown that through freewriting and other forms of personal writing, many girls who approach adolescence and might otherwise struggle for a safe place to express a full range of thoughts and feelings are able to sustain their authentic voices in writing (Magee 1999).

This chapter adds important contributions to the discussion of educational reform and girls' writing. It considers how writing can be a source of valuable information in educational reform efforts. Specifically, it shows how girls' written voices can be instruments in that reform, by treating girls as experts of their own educational and writing experiences. Much of what is known about girls' writing comes from the reflections of academics, or at best draws partially from the personal writing of girls themselves. But this chapter relies exclusively on girls' and women's writing, and written and spoken reflections about that writing.

Thoughts about Collaborative Writing

Our writing process was as important as the freewriting itself. The history of our relationships with one another, the freeform nature of our method, and the shared power of our voices created the supportive atmosphere that we needed to write truthfully.

Part of the success of our collaborative writing was the history of our relationships. We knew each other, to some extent, before we sat down together to write this chapter. Margo and Lenelle had participated in a research study on girls' writing with Vicki. It was during this research that all three first discovered the power of collaborative freewriting. It facilitated trust and lessened anxiety so commonly present in research relationships. It also allowed us to raise more and different topics, feel more free to explore our creativity and choice of words, use more metaphors, be more personal, self-disclosing, and playful, and feel more understood.

That first experience also left us with a sense that we had made a profound connection and a desire for a deeper connection to each other. So when the opportunity to write this chapter arose, we chose freewriting to help us build an even greater trust, overcome fears that come from exposing oneself through personal writing, and stimulate our thoughts about bringing student voices into the story of educational change.

Other aspects of our history together also contributed to our ability to write and speak truthfully with one another and resulted in the realization that we are not alone in our experiences. Lenelle attended a girls' summer program that both Vicki and Holly evaluated. Vicki and Holly have been colleagues in graduate school and work. We, Lenelle and Margo, experienced a minimal connection in the two years that we shared in high school. We shared a class period or two, a homeroom, and little else; certainly not our pains and triumphs chronicled in the logbooks of poems and journals we kept throughout school. I, Margo, felt at times that I walked alone in those hallways carrying secrets, carrying a voice that made no audible sound into the ears of all those bodies passing around me and into me. I, Lenelle, on the other hand, put on a façade. High school, for me, was all about multiple personalities. I knew how to play the social games of high school: the pretentious "hallway love," the meaningless conversations with meaningless people at lunch about who "liked" who. I laughed, and gave high fives to random people I didn't really care about. And in between the giggles and the in-class notes, I'd be writing in my journal about how DISGUSTED I was with the whole thing. I, Margo, felt at times that I walked alone in those hallways carrying secrets, but there was someone else out there, who even if she did not have the same voice, had the same secret: writing. It was Lenelle. We wish we had connected then.

Another important aspect of our process was its freeform nature. Our conversations and our writing led us in new directions and guided our next steps, rather than arising from a preset structure that might be found in typical classrooms or educational programs. Our "reform" was literally a constant re-forming of our plan and our process. We began with no rules, and allowed ourselves to adapt our process in ways that helped us connect to one another. First this freewriting experiment was random. We wrote for ten minutes, each of us, with one designated as a timekeeper. We did not use any words or phrases to guide us. Someone simply said, "Go," and we all began. The sound of pencil on paper was at times soothing and at other times annoying. Always it felt like we were leaving our comfort zones in exchange for the discomfort of something more complex than the simple surface we had painted for ourselves. We then introduced prompts or words that brought us even closer and served as triggers for our elaborate, honest, and metaphorical accounts of pain and survival in school.

This loose structure led to several rich outcomes. First, our freewrites emerged from a different part of ourselves than other writing did. The content of our freewrites focused much more on the pain of school than we might have expected. This in itself was a really important realization. But second, it led us to ask a lot of perplexing questions about our experiences and our writing process: "Was school that agonizing? Does writing somehow tap the darker side of our emotions? If we tried to write about the positive aspects of school, what would happen?" We have no answers to those questions, but we are relatively sure that the act of collaborative freewriting, teenagers with adults, is what generated these questions.

Common Themes

Our freewriting told of school experiences, good and bad, that centered on relationships with teachers and students who we saw every day at school, most often not by choice. With few exceptions, we could not relate to our teachers, who remained mostly faceless and inhuman. Common sense might suggest that we could turn to our peers for relationships, but in our experience, they often offered nothing but criticism and animosity.

Though they were few, we each recalled at least one positive experience in school with a teacher or student that reminded us that good relationships could happen in school. For example, one of Lenelle's male teachers shared his personal life and his own desire for relationships with students. He held students accountable. One day he sadly and quietly mentioned in class: "Hey, I am a person. You know who I am. You don't acknowledge me when I see you in the hallway. Won't you say hello next time I see you in the hallway? You can call me by name."

One of Margo's important friendships spontaneously formed out of chance conversations that revealed a shared sense that most of school was depressing and overwhelmingly disappointing. To get a hint of her agony you only need to read this:

> High school is purgatory between childhood and life . . . they stick you into this social asylum—the misfits, losers, psychos don't get any better because of high school, no epiphanies or fond memories, support groups that make you want to improve yourself. If you're not happy with yourself before high school I think you should take some time to adjust to liking you . . . there aren't a lot of people that will like you right off the bat in secondary school—secondary to what? Was life just one section "part I" before ninth grade?
>
> —Margo Strucker

Margo and this newfound friend, in naming their sense of isolation at school, formed a common bond that helped reduce their loneliness. They developed a strong and supportive relationship through nightly conversations by telephone. This common ground allowed them to reach across the loneliness to connect. In one of Margo's freewrites, this connection is mentioned:

> Then I met him. First he was my best friend, like no friend I ever had, boy, girl, sister . . . a part of you falls in love with people you can relate to and feel comfortable around. No matter if they're boy or girl.
>
> —Margo Strucker

Numerous other themes emerged from our collaborative writing. We have chosen to focus on three main themes: teachers' absence, peers and pain, and silence and writing.

TEACHERS' ABSENCE

Mentioned more than any other topic in our freewrites was the feeling that teachers really did not care about us as people. We do not deny that some of our teachers showed some interest in us, but our writing showed how much anger and loss we still had toward teachers who rendered us invisible and silent. We discussed how our relationships with teachers were different from those of our family; with our family members we typically suffered brief disruptions in our communication through hurt feelings that were soon remedied, but with teachers we were never in relationship with them, so the disconnection was perpetual. Our freewrites reveal these feelings of disconnection:

> We think of time . . . we actually think of race and love more, but for this page: we think of time. We think of patience. Like waiting to be noticed—waiting to be noticed—waiting to be seen for more than race—waiting to be acknowledged—waiting to be felt like true love. It's all the ties that bind. I am angry and impatient . . . however. I am tired of having to gain respect. I am tired of having to prove myself to some prick in a gray suit with a pen ready to red-mark me back into the ghetto. I automatically give him his respect. It is expected of meheismyprofessormyprincipalmyheadmaster (maybe slavery ain't over) my doctormyminister (my mister). Who am I, and does he care? Is he aware and waiting?
>
> —Lenelle N. Moise

> I want to tell the teachers reading this that you are important too, or you could be. The psychology teacher who made me finally see that school learning could actually be meaningful and personally relevant, interesting. The writing teacher who forced shy girls like me to read aloud and bring our voices and our work into a room full of the most intimidating critics . . . other students. Or the language arts teacher who shed a real tear while reciting a poem about war. A REAL tear. One moment of realism and it sticks forever. Be vulnerable. Be real. And this is not what I intended—an honor to my teachers, because I also want to shake you for being so clueless and students for being so cruel. And that cinderblock that made up the walls and fences of that strange prison. . . . I lick my lips but keep them sealed. Still trying to unseal them—a lifelong act to counter the one command I learned too well: "Shut up." And now I say shut out shut on shut or open. No sense, I can't even think of the opposite of shut up, it's so impossible.
>
> —Holly Kreider

> "Absolutely," I said to my heart, "absolutely," I shouted through my teeth "absolutely don't whisper," I cautioned to my eyes, "absolutely don't whisper past the smokin gun held to my head." How many times will I rise? Like Maya Angelou says: I rise, then I rise again, and

fall, and rise, and no one noticed, not a teacher, not anyone. Would I be surprised if a buck-toothed Mrs. Green wrote a letter to me to say: I saw you rise, and then rise again, and fall, and rise and I thought you'd like to know—someone smiled at you when you were running fast, back and forth along the backyard fence, near where the yellow roses bloomed in such bright light that now it seems like nighttime again with a full moon. I smile at what you have become.

—Vicki Magee

PEERS AND PAIN

Developmental psychology tells us that adolescence is a time of breaking ties from parents and investing in our peer groups (for example, Blos 1967; Freud 1970; Selman and Schultz 1990). Yet our writing did not tell a story of supportive or confiding friendships in adolescence. Instead, we wrote about boys and girls who did not understand us, who bullied us, and who left us feeling alone. Some of our freewrites express our sentiments toward boys in school:

> I had this fascinating high school sweetheart. He was the only one in four years that allowed himself to enter my deepness. He conquered intimidation—the fear of a strong black woman—and we were relatively on the same page . . . I think about the talks we had: falling in and out of love and in and out of the Black Panthers versus the Ku Klux Klan and getting married "to" the role of women in society "to" having children "to" our fathers and their and theirs. . . . And I think about how important it was for me to impress him with my voice: to match his eager philosophical ramblings: to feel like we could hold intelligent conversations. . . . And as much as I think he knows me— as much as he has seen my artistry and my analytical tendencies—he has never really seen me laugh. I mean really laugh: to the point of tears showing and stomach tightness—laughing to the point of losing weight in a healthy way. I never let him see me "act the fool" because he was the only one who saw beyond my inviting figure (what does that mean?) and my kissable lips and my feminine graces (how redundant, right?).

> —Lenelle N. Moise

> Encountering the meanest kid in my whole class as he comes around the corner, he couldn't hear me coming and I didn't know he was approaching because our footsteps were muffled by the carpeting— there is a look of shock and surprise—no time for him to think of some stinging word. No one for him to show off in front of . . .

> —Margo Strucker

bad bad bad bad boys: they make me feel so . . . they make me feel worse, damn it! Why are they allowed to be so STUPID? I'm not male-bashing, but seriously, in an age of attempting equality, we're allowing our young men to pee side by side in urinals—being one in the "men's room" striking conversation about famous jocks and jock envy . . . and they meet us chicks at our special table (after we just came from our private stalls in the "girls' room" talking about how cute one of them is) and we flirt and we leave this situation red and blushing but certain of their cluelessness—And we get to class and they answer all the questions. They raise their unwashed, urine-stained fingers and they are seen over my head, which is flaming with ideas and intensity—my head that is my center, my stimulator, my imagination, my being. He rules with phallic symbols in the classroom.

—Lenelle N. Moise

Sex education is a classroom full of giggling adolescents? But wait that also describes gym, math, history, science, music class? Were all my classes really sex-ed? Just because there wasn't a teacher up there saying the words doesn't mean that we weren't all secretly thinking them. Interacting with boys was hard enough in language arts class much less in a classroom that explicitly pointed out our hormonal and biological differences. We felt the differences . . .

—Margo Strucker

Other freewrites tell the story of our disconnection from other girls in school:

girls are as mean as boys, sometimes worse. Girls were all I knew. They taught me to be ugly and alone. Boys taught me to wonder. Boys aren't so bad. Not the ones that pull their heart out and give it to a safe girl, a safe girl, a safe girl, a mature girl, a girl who has removed her heart and put it on the exam as Question #1.

—Vicki Magee

Then inevitable annoyance accompanies required patience. Women, as tiny, unseen brats, wait to be received by perfect Prince Charming, away from the cold, damp and elevated tower in which our cold, evil and "BITTER" old hags of mothers imprison us. We wait for our eagerly raised hands to be called on, but that's not important. We wait for Daddy to say we can pierce our ears (or tongues) after Mommy says no. We wait for Shirley to tell April to tell Kenny that we think he's cute. We wait for someone to read our short story about flying, but that's a bit irrelevant because we wait to use the bathroom after bigger, badder babes with hair bangs get busted smoking cigarettes and blunts. . . . We wait for any opportunity to cry and kiss and get your attention . . . by peeing in our panties 'til we're ten, or by wearing black and rambling about death by drowning or by shutting out and shutting up until something ANYTHING reacts or triggers and HAPPENS and leads to the incomplete and never ending final phrase, "happily ever after."

—Lenelle N. Moise

Still other freewrites pointed to the cruelty and distance that we felt from bullies and popular kids in school:

Where do these kids get this endless supply of cruelty? Why don't teachers do anything? I would not be complaining if it only happened at recess because recess has come to mean to me "survival of the fittest." I can take care of myself at recess—read in some hidden place—the mean ones, truly mean ones, don't really even bother you if you keep to yourself. What I feel defenseless in is the classroom. The taunts can't be dodged when you are sitting next to, in front of, or with the attacker.

—Margo Strucker

hallway, hall of horrors. Steel lockers in a darkened hallway. . . . My locker, my locker combination. My small piece of the school pie. My box to shove my books into. The meeting place for friends. My one friend. Noisy hallways. Passages between classrooms. Entries to escape, to break, to lunch, to somewhere. Somewhere else. No stopping place, no personality. No place for little girls. A place for little girls with a voice box, a box of books, a clenched fist, a creepy feeling. Hall way. All the way. Hall of fame. No, famous kids stayed outside, in the sun, well-lit kids to be admired from afar. Kids on the stage, out of the halls, perched on the wall, like Humpty Dumpty.

—Holly Kreider

SILENCE AND WRITING

The silence in our freewrites was deafening. Our writing and our conversations returned again and again to the experience of silencing our real feelings in school. Like many adolescent girls whose voices are not invited or heard in school, we were faced with the choice of taking our voices elsewhere or raising the volume. But we knew the consequences of the latter choice—girls who resist the urge to quiet themselves are often singled out as troublemakers.

So instead, we shouted out in our writing. We used our writing in school as a way to hear ourselves and to be heard by others. We even wrote for unknown audiences who might find our writing years later and be touched by our words. We wrote everywhere, and often. Writing took place before school, during classes, in the hallways, in the restrooms, at our lockers, in the cafeteria, on the steps outside—anywhere we could grab a piece of paper and write. Just as in the freewrites that we wrote for this chapter, our anger poured out in our school writings through reflections on current events and persistent memories. Everything fell out in these mysterious freewrites. We discovered that the emotions that made us silent also made us scream on the page.

We suppose you could say that our silence kept us out of trouble and held each of us together through the loneliness and lies of high school. But we wonder: Do you survive if you never express the truth of an idea or feeling? Did our silence really make us stronger or did it make us weaker? The contradictions abound. We thought silencing our voices would provide breathing room, but instead it suffocated us. We constantly faced impossible choices: Is it better to try to shut up and hold things together until the next school vacation, or let them fall apart and then try to put them back together, or just leave them alone? We didn't know the answer then. We are confused by the question now.

What seems evident to us now is that without communication there is no connection. And without connection there is loneliness. Being lonely at school felt crushing. Yet authentic relationships seemed futile. One difficult choice we faced was whether to interact with teachers or with our peers, because we felt we couldn't have both. Students often conspired to keep student-teacher relationships shallow and meaningless. It was taboo among students at our schools to really like a teacher or to admit that you actually learned something from him or her. Actually speaking with teachers outside class triggered cruel responses from other students. The traumas of student-to-student cruelty and self-silencing show in our freewrites:

> It comes to a point where you don't answer even if you know what the teacher is asking for. The pain afterward is not worth it. Why be teased all the way to your next class . . . just because you know the North won the Civil War. But today it does matter. It wasn't the grade you got, or the check plus for participation that mattered. That's all crap—what mattered was that you silenced yourself. That asshole next to you didn't put their grimy hand over your mouth, that teacher with the penetrating stare didn't touch you—it was your hand over your mouth, down your throat, stealing the very soul of your thoughts.
>
> —Margo Strucker

Today is the day.
You want answers and I have no idea what they are.
Answers come with questions and questions are formed with the

thoughts of brilliant little girls with tape over their mouths and
pencils in their hands . . .
So maybe I do know the solutions—and maybe you know I
do—you: Mr. Tape Holder.
Is it scotch or is it clear and what does it matter?
Listen to my mumbles fall onto paper like the sound of the word
articulation.
I digress like I'll continue to throughout this written cry out.
You should know: my belief is that all random, irrelevant things
are subconsciously linked . . .

—Lenelle N. Moise

My pink skirt is full of my blood and I can't get it out with the cold
water from the faucet. I throw my slip away, I walk down the hallway
full of students, stained, deaf, and alone. Schoolwork captured the
still fear of my "not-learning" and how I craved the song of my heart
to sing a song with words not written yet. I can't say what the journey would have been like if a teacher had come to me and said: Who
are you? There was no safe place for my voice. My voice was my
blood, blood around my teeth, blood around my fingertips, blood
dripping from my shoulders, blood gagging me, blood swelling up in
me, blood thirsty to be free from the fear of my own voice, blood
thirsty for a calm voice to sop up the blood squirting from my arter-
ies, wishing wishing for soap strong enough to clean my pink skirt
back to it's store-bought shape.

—Vicki Magee

They tease you for speaking, not speaking, looking at them, ignoring
them. They come while the teacher is lecturing or sitting miles away
at their desk "doing paperwork." I've never felt so powerless since
then.

—Margo Strucker

don't tell me that I'm not smart. Once I get down into that barrel I
know it's dark and the current is strong so strong that I bob under
hold my breath, open my eyes, swallow my own blood, lift myself up
with my own arms, weak from doing it the day before and the day
before but I'm a come-back kid. Give me a good night's sleep and a
good friend to hear my story and watch. I will come back to purgatory's gate and say: suffer not the little children.

—Vicki Magee

Three Observations about Making School Better

We argue in this chapter that girls' written voices often contain their truest voices and their most silenced voices. To our surprise, our own freewrites contained many dark memories from grade school through high school. In fact, we are not sure, to this day, how to interpret all of the pain uncovered through our freewrites. We obviously do not have any new answers to complex questions about school reform. We have, however, arrived at three observations about what would have made school better for us.

GIRLS (AND BOYS) ARE KEEN OBSERVERS OF SCHOOL LIFE

As we discovered in writing this chapter, girls have a great deal to say about schooling. Yet student voices are typically missing from school-reform efforts. Because girls do a great deal of writing, this can be one way to bring their ideas into school-reform conversations. We see collaborative freewriting as one tool for tapping into girls', and probably boys', opinions and creative solutions.

COLLABORATIVE FREEWRITING IS NOT JUST ACADEMIC

We observed that we felt better after writing with one another. Collaborative writing can serve many purposes beyond the academic, including an intervention to support girls' sense of themselves. Lenelle and Margo, for example, both agreed that their personal writing literally helped keep them sane through their school years. We can only imagine how much happier and more productive our school days would have been if we had been able to share what we wrote with an adult who cared. We believe that relationships in school really do matter and that freewriting might be one tool for improving such relationships. Freewriting could be offered as electives. We realize, however, that the freewriting process that we used to bring us together may not work for everyone. Strengthening relationships, whether across adults and adolescents, or among adolescents, requires a commitment of time for collaborative writing during school hours and, more importantly, a commitment of the heart, of one's self. Teachers and students need to be willing to take the risks necessary to establish meaningful relationships. We learned that it is well worth the trouble.

Seven Concrete Recommendations

We end with four freewrites written to the prompt "better." We selected this prompt to help us press into our best thinking about improving schooling. Read them aloud—the message is stronger.

School would be better . . . maybe if everyone had some time alone each day. The teacher forces everyone to sit quietly and think about anything they want—what would the classroom be like if everyone stepped into it after not talking to anyone else for a few minutes? If no one spoke and could share that same feeling of thinking to themselves, to someone like me it would be a reward and would soothe me.

—Margo Strucker

Reach me with more than words from textbooks—but words from the soul and the mind connected to the heart. What got you to teach me? Wasn't it to reach me? Didn't you love the thought of knowing children and letting them know you through a topic loved? That's what we're missing and dissing: the passion. Being my role model has to be desired in the deepest way. Whatever happened to chemistry teachers that treated elements like poetry? They stayed in my memory. Relate to me, debate with me, Respect me. Stop neglecting me. I get nothing but tired empty wordswordswords . . . make them real.

—Lenelle N. Moise

Better better batter up. Be the best, above the rest. Let's start with that . . . that whole grade-driven, norm-based (whose norm anyway?) system of determining how well you've learned. The only way I could get approval, attention even, was through grades, and all it took was shutting up. Staying sweet and silent and complicit on the surface. Let's start with that, making learning a self-curve, a curvy ride, a ride worth taking. Let's make a cake, let's bake bread. Let's smell our work and eat our work but not our words. Let's feed the world. Let's make it real. The real deal. The raw deal. Hard and tough isn't bad, but boring is. So is invisible. SO is silent. So is "super duper." Duped by school.

—Holly Kreider

Better would be warmer. Better would be the feeling of satisfaction that comes from love. The loving act of learning. Should we love at school? What is that? A commitment to push me. Push me by loving me. Love me by pushing me. Figure out how to love me. Criticize me with a lit candle in the dark. Know that the red-flush up my neck is my scream for a soft tissue. But don't piss me off and if you do allow me to curse you and fall down naked like Melanie let me run out of the gymnasium doors and scream. Let me be like Lenelle who has wisdom in words. Let me be like Margo who sees everything. Then let me be me. And please, at the end of the day help me figure out an occupation, dammit.

—Vicki Magee

Embedded in the above freewrites are hints about how school supported or could have supported our development. In these freewrites, we write about seven specific recommendations for improving schools:

1. *Offering overall support to students,* for example, by finding time for students to quietly reflect on their thoughts and feelings in writing.
2. *Offering support to teachers,* through professional development that helps teachers keep their passions alive.
3. *Strengthening teacher-student relationships* through teacher authenticity, love, guidance, and challenging work for students.
4. *Strengthening student-student relationships* by reducing rivalries and building collaborations among students.
5. *Reaching all girls,* especially engaging with those who are silent.
6. *Being relevant* through curriculum that connects to students' everyday lives and to their futures.
7. *Risking to care* by actively evaluating and researching what stands in teachers' way to engaging more fully in caring and authentic relationships with students.

Our experience shows that girls can be engaged through their writing. We have tried to imagine how our middle and high school education would have been different if the above recommendations had been part of our school experience. Even to be in a conversation about the possibility of enacting one of these recommendations would have given us great hope as students.

We believe firmly that all students are capable of engaging in meaningful dialogues about how to improve their education and know that most would be glad to do so. We hope that we have shown through this chapter that the generations can come to a common discourse. An important next step in school reform ought to be the inclusion of student voices—girls and boys, urban and rural youth, students from upper-, middle- and lower-income-generating families, and students representing different races, cultures, and sexual orientations.

References

Blos, Peter. 1967. "The Second Individuation Process of Adolescence." In *The Psychoanalytic Study of the Child*, 22, edited by Anna Freud. New York: International University.

Freud, Anna. 1970. *Research at the Hampstead Child-Therapy Clinic, and Other Papers.* London: Hogarth Press.

Freud, Sigmund. 1921. *A Young Girl's Diary.* Translated by Eden and Cedar Paul. London: Allen and Unwin. (Note: Freud's original supportive foreword to this book was later retracted when the authenticity of this book came into question.)

Goldberg, Nancy. 1986. *Writing Down the Bones.* Boston: Shambhala.

Magee, Vicki. 1999. "Making up Their Own Minds: A Psychological Study of the Role of Personal Writing in Adolescent Girls' Resiliency." Unpublished dissertation, Harvard Graduate School of Education, Cambridge, Mass.

Selman, Robert L., and Lynn H. Schultz. 1990. *Making a Friend in Youth: Developmental Theory and Pair Therapy.* Chicago: University of Chicago Press.

CHAPTER 9

Negotiating Worlds and Words: Writing about Students' Experiences of School

Alison Cook-Sather and Jeffrey Shultz

When we embarked upon the project of editing *In Our Own Words,* our goal was to create a place for students to write in their own ways about their experiences of and perspectives on school. As far as we could tell, no one had attempted this before, yet the project seemed straightforward enough: identify the students, ask them to write something, put it in the book. Each of these steps proved to be more complicated than we had anticipated, however, and the enterprise as a whole was more challenging than we ever thought it would be.

We have come to think about these challenges in terms of differences among worlds and differences among the words used in and about those worlds. We as editors work within the worlds of higher education, academic conferences, and publishing. Used to offering our opinions and used to writing for various audiences, we knew that we wanted to make a place for students' voices in discussions of school and that we would need to give serious attention to the question of how best to present those voices. The student authors lived and drew on the worlds of the urban, suburban, and rural middle and high schools that they attended or from which they had recently graduated and the communities in which they lived. Unaccustomed to writing formally for audiences other than their teachers and rarely asked to offer their opinions on school, their focus was on expressing themselves. In the position of mediators were the researcher/teacher authors. They created worlds that had not previously existed—somewhere between their workplaces and the students' schools—and within which they could write collaboratively with the student authors.

Although editors, researcher/teacher authors, and student authors came together from different worlds, the challenge to everyone who contributed to this book was to find words that would accurately convey the students' perspectives on their middle and high school worlds. In this concluding chapter, we bring together the words of the different contributors to reflect the different worlds from within which each of us worked.

In what follows, we describe some of the negotiations that led to the production of the chapters in this collection. The unifying thread that connects the different perspectives we include in this chapter is the question of authority: who has it, what it looks like, how it is negotiated. In writing this chapter, for sources we drew on the following tape recordings:

- A conversation among the editors and several of the researcher/teachers early on in the process of planning the book.
- A symposium at the annual meeting of the American Educational Research Association in Montreal in April 1999 that included the editors and several of the researcher/teachers.
- A session at the Ethnography in Education Forum at the University of Pennsylvania in March 2000 that included the editors, several of the researcher/teachers, and the student authors.
- Written responses by the student and researcher/teacher authors to questions posed by us, the editors, related to the process of writing the chapters.

Getting Started: Identifying Student Authors

As college-based researchers and teachers, we did not have access to a wide range of middle and high school students. With the exception of the chapter coauthored by Alison Cook-Sather, for which she had contact with potential student authors, invitations to students to contribute to a chapter came from the researchers and teachers with whom we had contact and whom we knew were working directly with middle and high school students. Although this chain of communication was unavoidable, it created, from the beginning, a gap between us and the student authors, and hence a need for someone to mediate across these different worlds.

We felt it was our job to offer some guidelines to authors regarding how to frame student perspectives on school. Therefore, at the outset of the project, the authority we had as the editors took the form of suggestions to the researcher/teacher authors that they provide brief contextualizing introductions to their chapters and, if necessary, clarifications and transitions throughout the chapter. We emphasized, however, that the majority of the chapter should be written by the students. We did not negotiate directly with the students; the researchers and teachers assumed the authority for inviting and initially shaping the participation of the student authors—of inviting them to prepare their perspectives on school for publication to a wider audience.

After this initial offering of guidelines, we had virtually no role in the composing of the chapters. As far as the student authors were concerned, in fact, we basically disappeared until the editing phase of the project. For the researcher/teacher authors, however, the negotiation of worlds and words was only beginning.

Making Progress: Composing the Chapters

As the student and researcher/teacher authors embarked upon the process of composing chapters, two issues arose: logistical challenges related to how the researcher/teachers and student authors could find time and space to collaborate; and authoring and authority issues.

THE LOGISTICS OF COMPOSING TOGETHER

The logistical challenges of composing the chapters in this collection were a result of the tightly structured schedules of school days, the fullness of students' lives, the lack of space conducive to conversations outside of class, and/or the geographical distance between coauthors. These are not insignificant challenges, and a brief discussion of them provides an uncommon insight into the worlds of students.

About finding time, R.J. Yoo, one student author, commented, "I really think the only challenge [we faced in working on this chapter] was to write the stories while being involved in many school activities and academics. This also made it hard for our group to find a scheduled time that everyone was able to meet" (written response to follow-up questions, June 1999). The researcher/teacher authors felt this time pressure, too, but they faced the additional challenge of wondering whether and how to disrupt students' school days.

Explaining the dilemma of wanting to work with students but having trouble finding time and space, Rebecca Freeman said, "Twenty minutes at lunch is difficult, but I don't want to pull students out of class" (discussion among researcher/teacher authors, November 1998). Rebecca's comment highlights both the dearth of time and the potential disruption of making time. Diane Brown explained how disruptive making time can be: "Just the issue of taking the girls out of their regular routine . . . it's a pattern and a rhythm, and sometimes the girls were not comfortable with being taken that day or that particular time out of that rhythm of what felt right in their school life" (ethnography forum, March 2000).

Even when the authors could find time to meet, finding space wasn't easy. Diane Brown commented on "the physical [challenge of] finding a place to work in an urban school where you can write. We had to negotiate for library space . . . we had to turn the lights off so that we weren't interrupted fifty times in the process [of working]" (ethnography forum, March 2000). And student author Sharita Stinson explained that, for her, "the difficulty [of working on this chapter] was when we were in the library and I kept on talking but I couldn't write anything down on paper; I had writer's block" (ethnography forum).

Other authors faced very different logistical challenges. Eva Gold, a Philadelphia-based researcher, explained that her student coauthors were "students in Arizona; I've never heard their voices . . . I've only corresponded with them electronically. This whole chapter was written through electronic communication" (ethnography forum, March 2000). While this meant that Eva had good records of the writing process, it also meant that she did not have a personal, face-to-face relationship with her coauthors.

These logistical difficulties offer us a glimpse of how highly structured and how full students' school lives are. Finding time and space to meet presented major challenges. As Diane Brown put it: "What seems like such an easy thing to do isn't always that easy" (ethnography forum, March 2000).

ISSUES OF AUTHORITY

The challenges around issues of authority included questions about the content of the chapters, about composing processes, and about who had the final say in editing. Speaking from an early stage of meeting with her student coauthors, researcher author Jody Cohen posed the following question: "If we are saying this is about schooling, what do we mean by that? What about if the stuff that is of most interest is not going on in the classroom?" (discussion among researcher/teacher authors, November 1998). Jeff Shultz clarified that "Schooling is anything that happens in and is related to school" (discussion among researcher/teacher authors). These are neither as simple a question nor as simple an answer as they appear. Part of our intention as editors was to let the answer to the question of what counts as stories of schooling emerge from what the students chose to write about, but those choices were influenced by a variety of factors.

Authority issues born of the power dynamics among students, teachers, and researchers informed the question of what is important to students about school, and there was a danger of second-guessing from both sides. As Rebecca Freeman described it, "Part of what's hard about [asking students to write about what is important to them] is that they want to tell me whatever it is that they think I want to hear" (discussion among researcher/teacher authors, November 1998). Alison Cook-Sather added: "They have an idea of us as teachers and what they should be saying. Our student coauthors worried at one point that they were 'teacher bashing.' And yet our question is, 'What is it that they are understanding that we want to understand?'" (discussion among researcher/teacher authors). That both student authors and researcher/teacher authors wanted to figure out what the other group thought was important foregrounds the challenge of attempting to position students as authorities and authors.

Just as it is not simple to ask students to choose what is important to them about school and schooling, it is not enough to ask students just to write. Teachers and researchers who write about their work are used to structuring their own composing processes. Generally, students have support for such activities. Therefore, how much the researcher/teacher authors should structure the composing process for students was another authority issue that arose. These issues resulted from the gap between the different worlds of the student authors and the researcher/teacher authors, and the words each would choose to describe those worlds. The central question was how much to push student authors to use the conventions of composing used in formal writing and/or help them to produce writing accessible and compelling to an external audience.

Thinking about how to frame the writing task for the students, Jody Cohen pointed out that "it's a funny tension between assignments, like school, and really self-generated writing" (discussion among researcher/teacher authors, November 1998). Even if the students decided fairly quickly on the focus of their chapter—as was the case for the student coauthors of "What's Your Bias?"—they still felt uncertain about how to proceed with the composing. Researcher/teacher coauthor Ondrea Reisinger explained that at first the student authors had "felt kind of paralyzed by the idea that they were going to do research. . . . We had to do a lot of reassuring" (discussion among researcher/teacher authors).

Reassurance was important, but the student authors needed more concrete support as well. Alison explained that she and Ondrea didn't want to come up with frameworks "that the students probably wouldn't have come up with on their own, but when we talked about it, they said, 'Well, we need a research question'" (AERA symposium, April 1999). Alison experienced this tension as one between "inviting and honoring [students'] ways of speaking and knowing but then figuring out how to render that in a way that an academic audience would pay attention to" (AERA symposium). All the researcher/teacher authors struggled with how much to frame and how much to let students say whatever they wanted to say in whatever ways they wanted to say it.

As the researcher/teacher authors spent more time with student coauthors, listening to them talk and watching them write, discrepancies between oral and written fluency surfaced as another issue. Reflecting on their work for "Speaking Out Loud: 'Every Woman for Herself,'" Diane Brown commented that "it seemed that when girls talked to one another and we taped them there was such a depth and a richness, but then when they went to write, I personally felt that

that was lacking in their writing" (ethnography forum, March 2000). Wondering about "the relationship between spoken and written words and how students express themselves," Jody Cohen suggested that Kathy Schultz's approach of sharing transcripts (of students' conversations) with the student authors seemed to give them the opportunity to "use their own voices as data" (discussion among researcher/teacher authors, November 1998). Kathy clarified: "Once they see things written down, they can play around with it" (discussion among researcher/teacher authors).

DIRECTING AND MONITORING THE COMPOSING PROCESS

As the composing process proceeded, questions were raised about who was in charge. Fredo Sanon, one of the student authors, said, "At the beginning you [the researcher/teachers] were in the driver's seat. [But] because you guys were always asking us what we want, things like that . . . we have more say now" (written response to questions, June 1999). This kind of negotiation of authority characterized all of the collaborations to one extent or another.

Some coauthors felt comfortable coauthoring from the beginning. This was the case for the group of students with whom Alison Cook-Sather and Ondrea Reisinger worked, perhaps in part because they had collaborated previously on a project that focused on listening to high school students' perspectives on issues of school and schooling. It was Ondrea and Alison who worried about their role, posing to themselves such questions as those that appeared in chapter 3: "Who should lead and who should follow? How much did Ondrea's and Alison's identities and presence as teachers influence what Kristin, R.J., and Sara wrote and said? How honest should the students be? How directive should the teacher-researchers be?" But the students did not feel this uncertainty. As student author R.J. Yoo explained: "I do not think our group had a problem cooperating and communicating with each other. We all agreed on mostly everything that we discussed and we all thought the stories we compiled were great for the topic at hand" (written response to questions, July 1999).

Other chapter coauthors had neither the proximity nor the personal connections to ensure ongoing participation in working on the chapter. Eva Gold explained that her student coauthors were "very interested in the opportunity to have a broader audience to hear what students had to say, but not interested in the way that made them stick with this particular project; their lives moved on" (ethnography forum, March 2000). Therefore, the researcher/teacher authors had to do much of the editing of the chapter themselves.

On the opposite end of the continuum, the group that wrote chapter 1, "Our World," went through a series of negotiations that moved them from a point of having Rebecca Freeman, the researcher/teacher author, feeling that she would have to do a lot of framing and even editing of the chapter, to the point where she was barely being included when the student authors took over the chapter and reduced her to a footnote (she was subsequently reintegrated a bit more). This erasing of the researcher/teacher from the text was the most extreme example of these negotiations. However, it is emblematic of the sorts of struggles over authority that occurred, particularly regarding what sort of presence the researcher/teacher authors should have.

A final challenge was how much to revise and edit student writing. Rebecca Freeman articulated her concern about how the students would sound to an out-side audience: "You don't see too much reading and writing in the school [my student coauthors attend]. One of the things I was concerned about was not just reproducing an image of Puerto Rican kids not able to do certain things. But I have a very real constraint that they don't have a lot of experience" (AERA symposium, April 1999). So the question was, how much to push? And underlying that question was a tension between researcher/teachers imposing their expectations on students and students having the authority to decide for themselves. Describing her group's work, Diane Brown explained that "there were times when I said, 'I know what you're saying, you're getting there . . .' But they had to make the decision: do I want to interact with this [text] again?" (ethnography forum, March 2000).

Both researcher/teachers and student authors had notions about what the writing should sound like. Ned Wolff said that he wanted the students "to sound like students, to sound like themselves. And yet they want to write as perfectly as they possibly could, and they wanted me to help revise [the writing]" (AERA symposium, April 1999). Susan Opotow explained that the student authors of chapter 4 made a similar request. The chapter is "a synthesis of transcript-based discussions. It translates spoken into written language, the result of [student au-thors] Fredo's and Maurice's request that we 'clean it up' so that it reads well" (this volume). Ned stated the issue concisely: "Do we have the students write to the best of their ability and revise and revise and revise, or do we keep the spon-taneity that student voices would normally have?" (AERA presentation, April 1999).

This presented a challenge to the writing teams, whether it emerged within the discussions the coauthors had or as a result of our editorial suggestions. As Holly Kreider explained, "The revision process was a challenge sometimes, try-ing to write and respond to editors' comments, but also maintain the poetic and relational components of our work" (written response to questions, July 1999).

What the chapters should focus on, how to negotiate students' and researcher/teachers' expectations about writing for an audience, how much to structure and guide student writing, who is in charge of the composing and editing processes, how present should researcher/teachers be in the chapters—these are among the issues of authority that had to be negotiated throughout the time we all worked on the book. We as editors, the researcher/teacher authors, and some of the student authors were concerned about the form in which to present student perspectives on school, and as the discussion above illustrates, contributors took different approaches and had different feelings about how formal to be. Another important aspect of the authority question, however, is the decisions students made about the form of their writing.

The Choices Students Made As Authors

It is interesting to note that for a book about school and schooling, student authors chose forms of writing not routinely associated with or asked for in schools, except, perhaps, in English or creative writing classes—autobiography, narrative, drama, short story/vignette, dialogue. Although they were interested in writing about their school experiences, the student authors were not interested in writing about those experiences in the ways that they are generally expected to write in school.

Students were able to convey their immediate and deeply felt experiences and perspectives through the particular forms they chose. For some student authors, this meant selecting an explicitly personal style of writing—such as first-person narrative, autobiography, or freewrites—that would allow them to be present explicitly in their writing. For other student authors, it meant choosing forms that would allow them to say what was most important to them but in a semifictionalized, and thus more distanced, way, such as in a play or in short stories/vignettes. These forms, in which the students' experiences and perspectives were embodied in "characters," allowed the student authors to re-present their experiences without having to claim them with the explicit first person pronoun.

In the introduction to chapter 7, "Reflections: Writing and Talking About Race in Middle School," the researcher/teacher coauthors explain how and why the students selected a play as one of the focuses for presenting information in their chapter: "After a few meetings, students told the facilitators that they wrote so much in their classes, it was difficult to muster the enthusiasm to write after school. In addition, and probably more importantly, they had not yet connected the issue of race to their own interests and concerns. Searching for a way to enliven our work together, researchers suggested writing a play and the group responded positively." The positive response to the researchers' suggestion that the students write a play seems to have been guided by the same impulse that directed all the student authors—to write in ways that were meaningful to them and not generally invited in school.

WRITING THEMSELVES IN NARRATIVE FORM

Six of the eight chapters were written using an autobiographical-narrative form. Writing in both English and Spanish, Maribelis Alfaro, Lornaliz Letriz, Maritzabeth Santos, and Mariela Villanueva (chapter 1) told the stories of their lives as they intersect with school. Reflecting on past experiences and how they affect current ones, Dorothy Holt, Emily Gann, Sonia Gordon-Walinsky, Elissa Klinger, and Rachel Toliver (chapter 6) narrated their experiences and offered critical commentary of an innovative math program, while Steven Marzan and Amy Peterson (chapter 5) wrote reflectively about how their peers, teachers, and administrators affected the development of the students' selves in school. Quentina Judon, Jessye Cohen-Dan, Tyeasha Leonard, Sharita Stinson, and Tara Colson (chapter 2) focused on their development as women and issues of gender they encountered in school, while Margo Strucker, Lenelle Moise, Vicki Magee, and Holly Kreider (chapter 8) met regularly and created a forum for expression they felt was missing in their schooling. They participated in freewrites—a writing exercise that often involved a set period of time and the use of a prompt—and drew extensively on those in narrating their experiences of school. Finally, Fredo Sanon and Maurice Baxter (chapter 4) tape recorded other students talking about cutting class, recorded their own thoughts in a kind of dialogue-response to those recordings, and then drew on all of those sources to compose their chapter.

In all of these cases, use of the first person pronoun and reference to and interpretation of their own experience in their writing was the primary mode the students chose: a mode which is, unfortunately, not generally elicited in school. One of the recommendations the authors of chapter 8, "Writing the Wrong," offer for improving students' experiences of school is "finding time for students to quietly reflect on their thoughts and feelings in writing."

WRITING THEMSELVES IN FICTION

The other two chapters used fictional forms of writing. As mentioned above, the students from Skyline Middle School chose to write a play about how race influenced relationships in a fictionalized middle school. Darreisha Bates, Noah Chase, Chris Ignasiak, Yvette Johnson, and Tina Zaza (chapter 7) drew from their own life experiences, writing group discussions, and popular culture, but they used the format of a play to write about issues that often were silenced in their daily lives at school. In chapter 3, "What's Your Bias?: Cuts on Diversity in a Suburban Public School," Kristin Dunderdale, Sara Tourscher, and R.J. Yoo represented their experiences and the experiences of other students they knew or interviewed as short stories or vignettes. They explained at an early meeting of the chapter authors that they wanted to use these forms to convey their experiences but make them more accessible to others. At the suggestion of the researcher/teacher coauthors, the student authors added critical commentary after each set of stories meant to illustrate a particular point they wanted to make about the ways teachers treat students differently based on race, gender, and perceived ability.

Using a form in which the author is more removed from the story than in a first-person narrative, these student authors were no less invested in their texts. Rather, because they felt they couldn't directly address the issues they wanted to, and/or because they felt that fictionalizing their experiences would make them more palatable or accessible to their readers, these students chose to write third-person accounts.

What is striking about some of the authorial choices that students made is that they authorized other students as well. For instance, for "What's Your Bias?: Cuts on Diversity in a Suburban Public School," many of the stories the students incorporated into the chapter were not their own—they were other students' stories that the student authors had gathered. Similarly, in chapter 4, "Cutting Class," Fredo Sanon and Maurice Baxter drew on the stories other students had told them and included them in their discussion. In a sense, then, these student authors were authorizing the stories of other students by including them.

Editing the Chapters

Those of us who write for publication expect to revise and edit many, many times, and yet, as Rebecca Freeman commented about composing the chapters, "A lot of kids think that if you've written a paper, it's done" (discussion among researcher/teacher authors, November 1998). This discrepancy between practices of working with words throws into relief the different worlds within which we as editors, researcher/teacher authors, and student authors worked. As editors, we had to try to bridge this gap as well.

The writing teams each sent us drafts of their chapters. For most of them, we went through at least three revisions, where we would send comments, changes, and suggestions to the writing teams. In this process, we deliberately focused on the framing pieces written by the teachers/researchers. This was a decision we made: the words of the students would not be affected by our editing while we felt comfortable telling the teachers/researchers what we thought they should say and how they should say it. Although we didn't touch their words, the student authors still had concerns about the changes suggested as we edited the chapters.

In response to a question about what the authors felt was awkward or unclear about the process of composing the chapters, Lenelle Moise wrote:

"Sometimes, in the editing process, I felt as if *we* were perceived as being awkward or unclear" (written response to questions, February 2000). And as Jessye Cohen-Dan explained, she felt bothered by "all the stuff about how much the adults should be involved. It was going to be a book that really had student voices but then it had to have all this adult interpretation" (written response to questions, September 1999). Lenelle's critique was directed toward us as editors, and Jessye was clearly disturbed by the extent of adult intervention, both that of her researcher/teacher coauthor and of us as editors. Jessye turned this initial frustration into a productive learning experience—helping her researcher/teacher coauthor "make the introduction and the connecting pieces she was writing, because at first I was saying I didn't like the way she was doing that and then we fixed it" (written response to questions, September 1999).

The researcher/teacher coauthors were caught in the middle of these negotiations. On the one hand they had instructions and guidelines from us about what we wanted the chapters to look like, and on the other they had to invite their student coauthors to write, promise them that their writing would constitute a major part of the chapter, and make decisions about how to frame that writing. As Jody Cohen, a researcher/teacher who was one of Jessye's coauthors, explained:

> One day this summer I showed a draft of the chapter to Jessye. She had read all the girls' writings and we had talked about how to put them all together, but she hadn't read the way that I was actually doing that. When she finished reading she told me she didn't like it. At first I got a little angry—I'd put all this time and effort into it and knew I really respected what the girls were saying. Then I asked if she'd help me work on it. We went to a park and sat at a picnic table and went over the manuscript. Jessye questioned each time that I framed or explained what the girls were saying; she made me translate my academese into clear language. I was astounded at how clearer language illuminated the complexities rather than whiting them out. She was such a patient teacher and critic. (written response to questions, September 1999)

Like Fredo Sanon's comment—"because you guys were always asking us what we want, things like that . . . we have more say now" (written response to questions, June 1999)—Jessye's and Jody's negotiation reflects the kind of communication required to ensure that everyone feels his or her voice is being heard in the coauthoring experience.

Although many of the collaborators successfully engaged in this kind of negotiation, conflicts and frustrations remained. Who had the final authority about the chapter was one issue. As student author Tara Colson explained, "I

felt awkward about not having the last say on all the decisions" (written response to questions, September 1999). Fredo expressed a different form of
frustration: "It did seem ridiculous [to talk about the chapter headings and
subheadings last time] but, I mean, I never did a book chapter before so I
don't know the first thing about what we had to work on" (written response
to questions, June 1999).

These comments from the students reinforce, from their perspective, what
we are calling the difference between worlds and between words. Knowing that
both academic and popular audiences expect texts to conform to certain conventions, we wanted to produce a text that those audiences would take seriously.
At the same time, we worried—and rightly so, given some of the student authors' responses—that by trying to push the students, through the
researcher/teacher mediators, to produce texts that would be acceptable to certain audiences, we were violating the students' voices and thus, in turn, our own
goal for the project. Like all editing projects, this process proved to be a tough
balancing act between trying to preserve the integrity of the writing that was
submitted to us while at the same time trying to produce a coherent product.
But concerns about insuring that the student voices were heard made this
process even more challenging. We hope that we have done justice to the students, that we have created a place within which they could voice their opinions and give their perspectives.

The Rewards of Eliciting and Presenting Student Voices

We have been focusing above on the challenges faced by the various parties involved in producing this book. Lest we leave the impression that this experience
was all challenge with no positive returns, we want to end with what we all found
rewarding.

For the student authors, the rewards came from the opportunity to have
their voices heard, to see their names in print, to think that they might have an
impact on school practices, and to enjoy and learn from the collaboration. Reflecting on her experience of coauthoring a chapter for the book, Jessye Cohen-
Dan wrote that she "liked that people were asking me what I thought about stuff
and that it was going to be real and published and everything" (written response
to questions, September 1999). R.J. Yoo expressed a similar satisfaction: "We
[the student authors] all felt good about seeing the data that we had researched
and put into written form, and knowing that it was going to be published" (written response to questions, July 1999).

Focusing on the possible impact of their contributions, R.J. continued: "It
feels good to know that our student opinions will be read by many teachers

across the nation and hopefully bring about a change in their attitudes" (written response to questions, July 1999). Sara Tourscher echoed this sentiment, saying she thought it was "nice to know that I am possibly helping future school environments" (written response to questions, July 1999).

In a comment that encompasses the exhilaration of being heard and the pleasure of listening to others, student author Sharita Stinson wrote: "I really felt good about expressing my thoughts and sharing thoughts of others who are in the book." Sharita also highlighted how working on this book contributed to her own ongoing education: "This publication was a good experience for my writing talent" (written response to questions, September 1999). Tyeesha Leonard echoed this feeling: "I really enjoyed it because a lot of people that I worked with pushed me to have more of a feel of myself and my work. I learned more about myself from what I wrote. When I got self-centered and really got into it—I didn't know I could write something that good" (written response to questions, September 1999).

The researcher/teacher authors also experienced a variety of rewards from coauthoring chapters with students. We discussed previously the challenges of the researcher/teacher authors trying to find a balance between openly inviting and structuring student participation, but there were benefits to this challenge as well. As Kathy Schultz put it: "It's not easy and, perhaps, not possible to simply step aside, and yet the process, though complicated, has generated new and interesting insights" (AERA symposium, April 23, 1999). Many offered a version of the simple, yet powerful, statement by Holly Kreider: "The collaborative chapter-writing was quite an incredible experience for me" (written responses to follow-up questions, July 1999).

Some of the power of the experience was in reilluminations. As Ondrea Reisinger and Alison Cook-Sather wrote in the conclusion of chapter 3,

> For the last five years, we . . . have been learning from students—constructing dialogues between high school students and preservice teachers, and listening to what they have to say. And yet we are continually amazed and inspired by how much students think about their own education and how their attention demands ours. . . . In working on this chapter, we learned again that students think deeply about educational issues, they have striking insights into them, and they have a great deal to say about them.

Alison and Ondrea expressed the excitement of relearning that students have powerful insights. Other rewards come in the form of experiencing familiar relationships differently. Jody Cohen explained:

> I really enjoyed the opportunity to work with a group of girls that I had such different relationships with—from Quentina, whom I'd known for many years as an "informant" and coresearcher, to Sharita and Tyeasha, whose astute and daring comments had impressed me last year at a large meeting of middle school girls, and Tara, who

emerged midyear as a strong STAR girl, and finally to my own daughter. In each case, working together—talking, reading, and writing, talking some more and (sometimes) adding and revising—changed, deepened the relationship. (written response to follow-up questions, September 1999)

Yet other researcher/teacher authors celebrated their own efforts in naming and healing themselves of what had been disempowering about their school experiences. As Holly Kreider wrote:

I think in retrospect, after hearing about all of our experiences of being silenced and underestimated in school, I felt especially good about trying to create an empowering, respectful and relational process with younger writers; hopefully too, having helped introduce to them the experience of writing for a broader audience, and struggling successfully with the tensions inherent in that. (written responses to follow-up questions, July 1999)

Working with students to compose these chapters took openness and flexibility on the part of the researcher/teacher authors. Coming from worlds in which they lead more than follow, this project required a certain kind of letting go of that authority. Letting themselves be led meant that, as Susan Opotow put it, "Every turn took a different turn" (AERA symposium, April 1999). Learning to listen to and represent the students' perspectives, the researcher/teacher authors felt inspired as well as challenged, reinformed as well as taught anew, and validated in their commitment to listening to student voices.

As editors, we feel fortunate to have been able to work with such expressive and responsive student and researcher/teacher authors. We have learned a great deal from them about the challenges as well as the rewards of creating a forum for students from which to speak, an opportunity to be a part of a conversation from which they are all too often excluded. Through listening to their words and rethinking our own, we have gained insights that enrich our understanding of both our worlds.

Index

achievement, 42, 48, 52, 53, 85; bias of
teachers, 60–64; and grades, 48, 49,
76, 96, 129; support of family, 86, 99,
100, 109, 110, 122, 129. *See also*
motivation; stress
authority: and gender, 70, 71, 150, 151;
and race, 65–67; and writing, 58, 150,
151, 168–72, 174–76. *See also*
relationships; respect; voices

bias, 57–72; gender, 69–71, 151, 155,
156; race, 65–68, 145; and students'
abilities, 60–64; and teachers, 59, 145,
151. *See also* ethnicity; diversity
bilingual education, 10, 20, 23–25, 27,
33–35, 37, 38; and social worlds, 20,
22–24, 28, 34, 35. *See also* ethnicity
boredom, 107; and cutting class, 75, 76,
79
Bruner, Jerome, 2

Cohen, Jody, 7
curriculum: mathematics, 105–25;
reform, 105–7, 111, 112, 115, 116,
119, 122–24
cutting class, 44, 73–91; and boredom,
75, 76, 79; and food, 81, 82; and
learning, 73; and peer pressure, 80;

solutions, 82–88; and stress, 75–77,
79; and substitute teachers, 79, 80

Dahl, Karin, 6
Davidson, Anne Locke, 6
diversity, 41, 42, 58; and teachers'
attitudes, 4, 42. *See also* ethnicity;
gender; race

ethnicity, 34, 35, 99, 149; and teacher
bias, 66. *See also* bilingual education;
race

Fine, Michelle, 7
Flyy Girl, 51–54
freewriting, 149–63; collaboration,
150–53; and gender, 151, 152;
outcomes, 153, 154; process, 153. *See
also* voices; writing
Freud, Sigmund, 151, 152
Friend, Richard, 8

games, 108, 129
Garcia, Florence, 7
gender, 151; girls and math, 107–11,
116, 117, 122, 123; girls in school,
40, 44, 45, 47–49, 151, 156–58; male
and female students, 44, 141, 156–58.

See also bias; freewriting; relationships; teachers

Gibbs, Nancy, 8

Goleman, Daniel, 55

immigration, 22–24, 26–28, 34, 35

Kilgore, John, 7

Kozol, Jonathan, 5, 8

language: bilingualism, 20–29, 33–35, 37, 38; and identity, 24, 25, 28, 33, 35; learning, 23–25, 34, 37, 38; and social worlds, 20, 22–24, 28, 34, 35, 165, 169. See also bilingual education; writing

leadership, 43, 49, 50, 55; and peers, 84, 85; and Sisters Together in Action Research (STAR), 41, 44, 45, 48, 49, 51–54, 56. See also relationships; respect

learning, 77, 83, 84, 98; engagement, 4, 75, 83, 96, 99, 100, 107, 111, 112; styles, 96, 100, 101, 102. See also achievement; cutting class; stress

Lewis, Sidney, 8

mathematics: and anxiety, 107–10, 119, 120–23; curriculum, 104–25; and gender, 107, 108, 110, 116, 117, 122; Interactive Math Program, 105–25

motivation, 47, 48, 88, 100; and cutting class, 75–78, 88; and future aspirations, 87, 88, 97, 98; and testing, 61. See also achievement; stress

Oldfather, Penny, 7, 8

Phelan, Patricia, 6

race, 30, 49, 50, 127–48; and identity, 30, 42, 141, 144, 145; students, 34, 35, 42, 67, 128, 129, 142, 146; teachers, 42, 49, 50, 65–68, 142, 143, 145. See also diversity; ethnicity

reform, 93, 102, 115, 152, 153, 161, 162; mathematics curriculum, 105–25; and students, 106; and teachers, 113–16

relationships, 3; with administration, 52–54; engagement in, 3, 47; family and school, 20, 29, 30, 86, 99, 100, 109, 110, 122, 129; humane, 3, 4, 84, 108; with peers, 34, 35, 42, 48, 67, 97, 98, 115, 116, 128, 129, 141, 142, 146, 153, 154, 156–58; with researcher, 58, 59, 95, 96, 150, 151, 168, 170, 171, 174–76; respect, 48, 86, 87, 98; with teachers, 43, 58, 72, 77, 78, 82, 95, 98, 99, 113, 147, 154–56, 160, 168; and whole selves, 5, 10, 40, 44, 55, 144, 145

researching, 74, 88–91; difficulty, 3, 165–68; students' voices, 6–8, 58, 71, 88–91, 94, 96, 127, 151, 165–70, 172, 174–78. See also voices; writing

respect, 48, 72; for peers, 48, 98; for teachers, 80, 86, 87. See also leadership; relationships

Rodriguez, Richard, 10

schools: condition, 31, 32; and local community, 30–32, 35, 94, 96, 97; security, 80, 81

Shandler, Sara, 9

stress: and cutting class, 75–77, 79, 80; and grades, 61, 64, 79, 108, 119, 120–23. See also achievement; motivation

student-centered education, 77, 83, 84; Interactive Math Program, 105–25; resistance of teachers, 113–16. See also learning; motivation; reform

teachers, 43, 56, 77, 78; biases of, 59–71, 77, 78, 150, 160; expectations of, 107, 115, 116, 118, 145, 160, 168, 169; and favoritism, 61, 63, 65, 66; and gender, 46, 47, 69–71, 116, 117, 150, 151, 160; and race, 42, 49, 50, 65–68,

142, 143, 145; and reform, 105, 106, 113–16, 118; substitute, 79, 80

Thomas, Sally, 7

Tyree, Omar, 51–54

voices, 150, 151; collective, 150, 151; of students in research, 6–8, 58, 71, 88–91, 106, 127, 151, 165, 168–72, 174–78; of students in school policy, 51–54, 73. *See also* research; writing

writing, 40, 41, 51, 55, 142, 152, 158; bilingual collaboration, 21; collaboration, 3, 19–22, 57–59, 74,

75, 94, 101–3, 106, 107, 127, 128, 140, 141, 150–53, 170, 171; drama, 128, 130–41, 172; editing, 165, 166, 168–71, 174–76; freewriting, 13, 149–63; and gender, 40, 41, 149–63; logistics of, 20, 150, 153, 165, 167, 168; negotiation in process of, 166–71, 174–76; on-line, 94–96, 168; and orality, 169, 170; by students, 128, 130–40, 141, 165, 169, 170–74, 176. *See also* researching; voices

Yu, Hanh Cao, 6

About the Authors

Maribelis Alfaro is a ninth-grade student at Edison High School in North Philadelphia. She is a devoted student and a unique writer.

Darreisha Bates attends Dickinson High School in Wilmington, Delaware. She enjoys volleyball, playing the clarinet, reading, shopping, and chillin' with family and friends.

Maurice Baxter, a senior at Dorchester High School in Boston, has worked with the Red Sox at Fenway Park and plays varsity basketball and football. He has met former President Bill Clinton, Massachusetts Governor Paul Cellucci, and has traveled to Ghana on a trip for students and educators. He plans to attend college and study accounting.

Diane Brown has been a Philadelphia School District educator for almost thirty years. She is the director of STAR (Sisters Together in Action Research) and is currently conducting a doctoral study of African American girls at a racially isolated middle school.

Patti Buck is a doctoral candidate in the education, culture, and society program at the University of Pennsylvania. She is currently conducting ethnographic research on the school lives of middle school girls at Summit. After completing her dissertation, she will pursue an interest in experiential education for girls and young women.

Noah Chase is a student at the Charter School of Wilmington, Delaware. He enjoys playing basketball, socializing on the Internet, and playing video games.

Scott Christian was a classroom teacher in rural Alaska for eleven years. He graduated from the Bread Loaf School of English with a master of arts in English in 1993 and is an active member of the Bread Loaf Rural Teacher Network. His book, *Exchanging Lives: Middle School Writers Online*, was published by NCTE in 1997. He is currently the director of the Professional Education Center at the University of Alaska Southeast.

Jody Cohen is a lecturer in the education and college seminar programs at Bryn Mawr College. She collaborates with teachers and students on research aimed at making schools better places to teach and learn.

Jessye Cohen-Dan is a freshman at Cheltenham High School in Philadelphia, Pennsylvania. Her recent play, "Last Week," won an award in the Philadelphia Young Playwrights Festival.

Tara Colston is a young woman growing up in North Philadelphia and a freshman at Simon Gratz High School. She is a very well-rounded and prominent person in her community, loves literature, and hopes to be successful in everything she does.

Alison Cook-Sather is assistant professor and director of the Bryn Mawr/Haverford education program. A former high school English teacher, she now works with college students preparing to teach at the secondary level, high school teachers and students who participate in the preparation, and college faculty interested in pedagogical issues. Recent publications include "Between Student and Teacher: Teacher Education As Transition (in *Teaching Education* 12[2] [2001]) and "Unrolling Roles in Techno-Pedagogy: Toward Collaboration in Traditional College Settings (in *Innovative Higher Education* 26[2] [2001]).

Kristin Dunderdale enrolled in regular education classes and was identified as a learning support student in high school. She currently attends Delaware County Community College in Pennsylvania.

Lydia Fortune, a graduate of the master's program in dispute resolution at the University of Massachusetts, Boston, is a mediation consultant/trainer as well as an accomplished jazz vocalist. She currently holds a short-term position as an interim assistant dean of students for Clark University, Worcester, Massachusetts.

Rebecca Freeman is a language educator and does research in bilingual schools and communities in the United States. She is the author of *Bilingual Education* *and Social Change* (Philadelphia: Multilingual Matters, 1998) and is currently writing another book, titled *Building on Community Bilingualism*.

Emily Gann, a 1997 IMP graduate, is a senior at Harvard University, majoring in social studies. She hopes her future career plans will combine her interests in social issues, activism, and film.

Eva Gold is a founder and principal of Research for Action, a Philadelphia-based nonprofit organization engaged in educational research and reform. She has worked with the Bread Loaf Rural Teacher Network (BLRTN) for seven years and coauthored a report, "Networking Across Boundaries, of Place, Culture and Role," documenting the work of BLRTN. In addition to her work with BLRTN, Eva is also involved in a number of research and evaluation studies investigating dynamics among families, communities, and schools.

Sonia Gordon-Walinsky graduated from Central High School in the spring of 1999. She then lived and worked in Israel and Italy for a year. She is currently beginning her college studies at the joint program of Columbia University and the Jewish Theological Seminary, where her focus is art and Jewish studies. She aspires to be a rabbi.

Dorothy V. Holt of Philadelphia is enrolled in the doctor of pharmacology program at the University of the Sciences in Philadelphia and is entering her second year of school. She is currently working as a pharmacy intern at the Fox Chase Cancer Center in Philadelphia. She is a graduate of the 258th class of Central High School.

Chris Ignasiak is a student at the Charter School in Wilmington, Delaware. He enjoys playing video games, surfing the Web, watching TV, playing sports with friends, and reading.

Yvette Johnson attends A. I. Dupont High School in Wilmington, Delaware, where, as a staff member of the school newspaper, she continues to pursue her interest in writing. She also plays clarinet for the school band and earns high academic marks.

Quentina Judon is majoring in elementary education at La Salle University. She wants to work with young children because that's where it all starts. She plays basketball and does community service work.

Elissa Klinger is a student in the growth and structure of cities department at Bryn Mawr College. She is combining her interest in urban issues with a minor in biology and intends to pursue a career in public health and medicine. At the present time she is an intern with the New York State Department of Health AIDS Institute in New York City.

Holly Kreider is a research associate at the Harvard Family Research Project, where she studies family–school relationships. She received her doctorate at the Harvard Graduate School of Education, specializing in adolescent girls' development.

Tyeasha Leonard is a freshman in the Academy of Travel and Tourism at Simon Gratz High School. She loves to read and write, and she also tutors young children.

Lornaliz Letriz is an eighth-grade student at Julia de Burgos Bilingual Middle Magnet School in North Philadelphia. She is a caring and good person.

Ceci Lewis currently teaches English in Tombstone, Arizona. She is a 1999 graduate of the Bread Loaf School of English. She has also been an active participant in the Bread Loaf Teacher Network, where she has been mentored by Dixie Goswami in teacher research.

Vicki Magee is assistant professor of educational studies and psychology at Illinois Wesleyan University. She recently received her doctorate from the Harvard University human development and psychology program. Her research is focused on the role that adolescent girls' personal writing, such as their diaries and poetry, plays in supporting their psychosocial development.

Steven Marzan graduated from Buena High School in 1999. After a brief stint as the Buena High School print shop assistant, he joined the U.S. Army. He is currently stationed in Germany.

Lenelle N. Moise is a Haitian American poet, playwright, actor, and dancer. She is currently a sophomore at Ithaca College, majoring in women's studies. She aspires to inspire.

Tricia Niesz is a doctoral candidate studying sociocultural foundations of education at the University of Pennsylvania. She is currently conducting an ethnographic study of progressive school reform in an urban middle school.

Susan Opotow, associate professor in the graduate program in dispute resolution at the University of Massachusetts, Boston, was formerly a guidance counselor in the New York City public schools. She is a social psychologist who specializes in justice and conflict.

Amy Peterson graduated from Buena High School in December 1998. She began a yearlong foreign exchange program in Thailand. Amy hopes to continue her education in the Pacific Northwest after returning to the United States.

Ondrea Reisinger teaches English at Central Bucks West High School in Pennsylvania. She has codesigned with Alison Cook-Sather a programmatic approach to including high school students' perspectives in undergraduate, secondary teacher preparation, and she has coauthored articles about that work.

Fredo Sanon, a senior at Dorchester High School in Boston, has worked at the New England Aquarium and Boston City Hall, plays varsity basketball and football, and plans to attend college and study journalism.

Maritzabeth Santos is an eighth-grade student at Julia de Burgos Bilingual Middle Magnet School in North Philadelphia. She is a very respectful young lady.

Katherine Schultz is an assistant professor of education at the University of Pennsylvania in the elementary teacher education program. She began her career as a classroom teacher and elementary school principal. She has written numerous articles on literacy, identity, and urban education, including a forthcoming article in the *American Educational Research Journal* with coauthors Patti Buck and Tricia Niesz, titled "Democratizing Conversations: Racialized Talk in a Post-Desegregated Middle School."

Jeffrey Shultz is professor of education and coordinator of multidisciplinary programs at Arcadia University (formerly Beaver College). He coauthored, with Frederick Erikson, *The Counselor As Gatekeeper: Social Interaction in Interviews* (New York: Academic Press, 1982) and coedited, with Annette Lareau, *Journeys Through Ethnography: Realistic Accounts of Fieldwork* (Boulder, Colo.: Westview Press, 1996). He has worked with middle school students in Philadelphia and London.

Sharita Stinson now attends Bodine High School. She is still writing. She is also a high school leader working with middle school girls at STAR (Sisters Together in Action Research). She suggests to the readers of chapter 2 that they stay strong and forget all the obstacles in their way.

Margo Strucker studies at Harvard University, where she has officially declared her life's passion as "undecided." She is a writer who finds endless inspiration from her sisters, parents, friends, and pets.

Rachel Toliver graduated from Central High School in 1997, having sufficiently recovered from Beat the Clown. She spent the next year working in an inner-city Christian community. She has now completed two years at Barnard College, Columbia University, and is spending her junior year studying abroad at St. Peter's College, Oxford University. She is majoring in English with a concentration in poetry writing.

Sara Tourscher enrolled in both honors- and regular-level courses in high school. She currently attends Bryn Mawr College in Pennsylvania.

Mariela Villanueva is an intelligent young lady. She is an eighth-grade student at Julia de Burgos Bilingual Middle Magnet School in North Philadelphia.

Edward (Ned) Wolff received his bachelor's degree from Dartmouth College in 1968, and Ph.D. in mathematics from the University of Massachusetts, Amherst, in 1977. Ever since, he has taught at Beaver College (now Arcadia University), where he currently serves as chair of the Department of Computer Science and Mathematics. He also codirects the Greater Philadelphia Secondary Mathematics Project, sponsored by the National Science Foundation.

R.J. Yoo is a Korean American student who enrolled in advanced placement courses in high school and currently attends Franklin and Marshall College in Pennsylvania.

Tina Zaza is now a freshman at the Charter School of Wilmington. She still enjoys bowling in tournaments and will be representing Delaware in Las Vegas, Nevada, in the international Coca-Cola Bowling finals. She also likes computing and hanging out with friends.